The Crisis of the State
and Regionalism in West Africa

The Crisis of the State
& Regionalism in West Africa
Identity, Citizenship and Conflict

Edited by
W. Alade Fawole & Charles Ukeje

COUNCIL FOR THE DEVELOPMENT OF
SOCIAL SCIENCE RESEARCH IN AFRICA

© Council for the Development of Social Science Research in Africa 2005
Avenue Cheikh Anta Diop Angle Canal IV, BP 3304 Dakar, 18524 Senegal.
http://www.codesria.org

ISBN: 2-86978-166-0

Page Layout: Djibril Fall

Cover Design: Ibrahima Fofana

Printed by Lightning Source

The Council for the Development of Social Science Research in Africa (CODESRIA) is an independent organisation whose principal objectives are facilitating research, promoting research-based publishing and creating multiple forums geared towards the exchange of views and information among African researchers. It challenges the fragmentation of research through the creation of thematic research networks that cut across linguistic and regional boundaries.

CODESRIA publishes a quarterly journal, *Africa Development*, the longest standing Africa-based social science journal; *Afrika Zamani*, a journal of history; the *African Sociological Review*, *African Journal of International Affairs (AJIA)*, *Africa Review of Books* and *Identity, Culture and Politics: An Afro-Asian Dialogue*. It co-publishes the *Journal of Higher Education in Africa* and *Africa Media Review*. Research results and other activities of the institution are disseminated through 'Working Papers', 'Monograph Series', 'CODESRIA Book Series', and the *CODESRIA Bulletin*.

CODESRIA would like to express its gratitude to African Governments, the Swedish Development Co-operation Agency (SIDA/SAREC), the International Development Research Centre (IDRC), OXFAM GB/I, the MacArthur Foundation, the Carnegie Corporation, the Norwegian Ministry of Foreign Affairs, the Danish Agency for International Development (DANIDA), the French Ministry of Cooperation, the Ford Foundation, the United Nations Development Programme (UNDP), the Rockefeller Foundation, the Prince Claus Fund and the Government of Senegal for support of its research, publication and training activities.

Contents

Part II

The Contradictions of Regionalism in West Africa

Contributors

Said Adejumobi holds a Ph.D. in Political Science from the University of Ibadan, and teaches Political Science at Lagos State University, Lagos. He was editor of the Nigerian Journal of Politics, currently General Secretary of the Nigerian Political Science Association (NPSA), and an active member of the African Association of Political Science (AAPS). He was also recently with the Development Policy Management Forum, Addis Ababa, Ethiopia. He has numerous scholarly articles, book chapters and monographs to his credit, including *Globalization and Africa's Development Agenda: From the WTO to NEPAD* (2003), DPMF.

Abeeku Essuman-Johnson, Ph.D. is a Senior Lecturer in Department of Political Science at the University of Ghana, Legon. His main research focus is on conflict and refugees in West Africa, particularly how the political economy of hosting refugee countries are affected.

W. Alade Fawole is currently a Reader in the Department of International Relations, Obafemi Awolowo University, Ile-Ife, Nigeria. He holds a Ph.D. in Political Science from the George Washington University. He specializes in Nigerian politics and foreign policy, an area in which he has published a number of books, including *Military Power and Third Party Conflict Mediation in West Africa: The Liberia and Sierra Leone Case Studies* (2001); *Beyond the Transition to Civil Rule: Consolidating Democracy in Post-Military Nigeria,* (edited, 2001); *Nigeria's External Relations and Foreign Policy under Military Rule 1966–1999* (2003); *Understanding Nigeria's Foreign Policy under Civilian Rule since 1999: Institutions, Structures, Processes and Performance,* (2004). He was a Visiting Research Fellow at the African Studies Centre, Leiden, The Netherlands, CODESRIA Governance Institute Resource Person (2001), formerly editor-in-chief, *Quarterly Journal of Administration,* and also served on the editorial advisory board of *African Affairs.*

Austine Ovuoronye Ikelegbe obtained a Ph.D. in Political Science from the University of Ibadan, Ibadan in 1988. He teaches Comparative Politics and Public Policy Analysis at the Department of Political Science and Public Administration of the University of Benin, Benin City. He has had Visiting Fellowships in the United Kingdom and Netherlands. His published and accepted papers are in such reputable international journals as the *Journal of Modern African Studies, Canadian Journal of African Studies, Journal of Third World Studies,* African Study Monograph and *Journal of Asian and African Studies.* His edited work on 'Oil, Environment and Resource Conflicts in Nigeria' is being published by the

Lit Verlag Publishers, Berlin/Hamburg. His current research interests are Democratization, Political Violence, Identity and Resource Conflicts, Civil Society, Youth and Gender.

Gbemisola Remi Adeoti obtained a Ph.D. in English from the University of Ibadan, Nigeria. He started his professional life with a career in journalism before joining the staff of the Obafemi Awolowo University, Ile-Ife, Nigeria, as a Lecturer in the Department of English. His areas of specialization include: Dramatic Literature, Poetic Traditions, Literary History and Literary Theory. He has contributed to literary journals both within and outside Nigeria.

Kwame Boafo-Arthur is an Associate Professor and Head of the Department of Political Science University of Ghana, Legon. He holds a Ph.D. in Political Science and is also a Barrister-at-Law and Solicitor of the Supreme Court of Ghana. He has published extensively on Ghana's political economy, international economic relations, foreign policy, civil society, the environment, globalization, NEPAD, African development and democratisation. He has published in several journals including *African Studies Review, Africa Development, Journal of Third World Studies,* and *African and Asian Studies.* His research interests include Africa's developmental issues, Governance and Democratisation, Foreign Policy Analysis, Human Rights issues in Africa, Chieftaincy and Conflict Resolution.

Kiikpoye K. Aaron teaches Political Science at the Rivers State College of Education, Port Harcourt, Nigeria and Co-chair of THEDI-The Health, Environment and Development Initiative, a Non-Governmental Organisation. His research findings on the Niger Delta crises have appeared in leading national and international journals and book chapters. He has also published on Nigeria's enterprise reform, globalisation and the crises of democratisation in Nigeria. His current research interest is on rights abuses in the global South by multinational corporations.

Charles Ukeje, Ph.D. is a Senior Lecturer in the Department of International Relations, Obafemi Awolowo University, Ile-Ife, Nigeria. He is a recipient of several awards: Fulbright Scholarship, CODESRIA Small Grant for Thesis Writing, African Guest Researcher at the Nordic Africa Institute, SSRC Fellowship on Africa Youth in the Global Age, Fellow of the Salzburg Seminar, and recently, the Mary Kingsley Zochonis Distinguished Lecturer 2004 sponsored by the Royal African Society and the African Studies Association both of the United Kingdom. His publications have appeared in major international journals such as *Africa Development, Journal of Terrorism and Political Violence, Scientia Militaria, Issue, International Journal of Politics, Culture and Society, Scandinavian Journal of Development Alternatives and Area Studies,* and *Oxford Development Studies.* He also has several book chapters, monographs and co-edited books to his credit.

Yomi Oruwari is a Professor of Architecture at the Rivers State University of Science and Technology, Port Harcourt, Nigeria, and also a Fellow of the Nigerian Institute of Architects. Her areas of research and professional competence include: Gender and Development; Architectural Education; Urban Studies and Rural/Urban/Regional planning.

Kassim Sikiru Taiwo is a Lecturer at the Department of Sociology, Lagos State University, Nigeria. He is currently (on study leave as) a doctoral student at Cardiff University in the Wales, United Kingdom. He holds a Master's Degree in Sociology with specialization in Demography and Population Studies from the University of Ibadan, Nigeria. His research interest is on Forced Migration, an area that allowed him to spend time at the Forced Migration Centre at the American University in Cairo, Egypt, and participation in programmes on 'Integrating Refugee Newcomer' and 'Refugee Camps and Warehousing', in 2003 and 2005 respectively. His doctoral research is on the Reproductive Health of Refugees in Africa: Implications for HIV Infection and Control among Refugees in Ethiopia and Nigeria.

Amadu Sesay was educated at the London School of Economics and Political Science, LSE, where he obtained his B.Sc. and Ph.D. degrees. He is Professor of International Relations at the Obafemi Awolowo University, Ile-Ife, Nigeria, where he has been based since 1978. He has been the head, Department of International Relations since 2000. His research areas are African politics, security and conflict studies. He is the 2005 Claude Ake Visiting Professor in the Department of Peace and Conflict Studies at Uppsala University, Sweden.

Introduction

W. Alade Fawole and Charles Ukeje

Perhaps more than any other sub-region in Africa, West Africa has acquired the unenviable notoriety as a veritable theatre of violent conflicts, political instability and state implosions. Alongside, critical questions are raised on the survival and continued viability of the Westphalian state model in Africa. The post-colonial state project has suffered so much general misfortunes since the 1960s decade of independence, with several coups d'etat (Senegal remains the only one among the sixteen states that has not experienced a putsch), devastating political upheavals and concomitant authoritarian rule, which progressively alienated the loyalty of most citizens. The euphoria that attended the grant of independence began to disappear not long thereafter as the post-colonial state increasingly became a Frankenstein monster in the hands of the local elite that took over from the departing colonial rulers. Less than three years after the Togolese army violently seized power in 1963, the first of its kind in West Africa, other states also succumbed to military dictatorship. Unable to manage the huge leviathan that they had seized in a bloody putsch, the Nigerian army led the country inexorably into a ghastly 30-month civil war. Other states were overwhelmed by turmoil and instability, with Liberia, Sierra Leone, and Cote d'Ivoire being the most exceptional in that they experienced outright collapse and violent civil wars. In the four decades of military and civilian dictatorships, West Africa has acquired a legendary reputation as the most volatile and unstable sub-region.

With the dividends that independence was expected to bring turning into disillusionment, the people became sadly but progressively marginalised from politics and economy, and severely alienated from the state. This, in turn, gave room for the resurgence and elevation of ethnic and other primordial identities over and above loyalty to the new state. Progressively, the state has become, and is thus being treated by the people as, a mere colonial artefact and a sad reminder of centuries of arbitrary and predatory foreign rule.

Worried by the rate of state failure and its ugly implications for the sub-region, the Council for the Development of Social Science Research in Africa (CODESRIA) in September 2003 hosted a West African sub-regional conference in Cotonou, Benin Republic, on the theme 'West Africa in Search of Democratic Nationhood'. The conference provided an opportunity both to take a sober stock of the achievements of the Council at 30 years, and also that of the sub-region of West Africa in the search for good governance and democratic stability. The conference assembled scholars from across West Africa to engage in dispassionate interrogation and dissection of the origin, nature, context and dynamics of the myriad crises stunting, if not arresting, the nation-building project and democratisation in the sub-region, and the most innovative and viable solutions for tackling them. This volume, which is the outcome of that far-sighted conference, is divided into two: Part One, 'The Crisis of State in West Africa', focuses on the internal dimensions of the identity and citizenship conflicts, while Part Two is on 'The Contradictions of Regionalism in West Africa'.

In 'Identity, Citizenship and Conflict: The African Experience' Said Adejumobi sets the tone for the discourse, by locating the pervasive identity crisis and the resultant conflict plaguing the post-colonial African state within the logic of colonialism, a practice which dichotomised the people into citizen and subject. Employing a slightly amended version of Peter Ekeh's 1975 seminal essay on the two publics, Adejumobi interrogates how the colonial enterprise, through its deliberate creation of two categories of people in the public sphere, i.e., the citizen and the subject, engendered the crisis that has continued to bedevil the post-colonial state. According to him, and relying on Mahmoud Mamdani's thesis on the native and the citizen, the 'native' speaks the language of tradition and custom while the 'citizen' speaks the language of rights, duties and privileges. He contends that this deliberate colonial policy nurtured the type of ethnic particularism that plagues the post-colonial state in Africa. Since colonial rule made subjects rather than citizens out of the 'natives' of the colonies, the ensuing anti-colonial agitations and nationalist struggles were directed towards obtaining the citizenship and those rights that colonialism denied the subjects.

Unfortunately, in pressing for citizenship and those rights complimentary to it, the emerging nationalists carelessly allowed their ranks to be fragmented along ethnic lines, thus rendering them incapable of mobilising broad national consensus to prosecute and consummate the anti-colonial project. Political parties, nationalist movements and liberation groups thus emerged on ethnic platforms, with negative consequences for the post-colonial state. If anything, this made it impossible for the successor elites to reform or refine the character of the colonial state, and to this extent, the 'modern state' that was eventually bequeathed to Africa ran on the old colonial logic of dualism, i.e., the primordial citizenship versus civic citizenship. The only difference was that the executors had an African face.

The inability of the post-colonial state to rise above its colonial provenance led inexorably to its reliance on the same authoritarian measures and instruments of the colonialists—a repressive police, an intelligence apparatus that spies on the people, and security forces for internal pacification—thus further alienating the citizens from the state. Although Rwanda and Nigeria are the empirical referents used by Adejumobi to illustrate this crippling crisis of identity and citizenship, each and every state in post-colonial Africa suffer in varying degrees from this colonial inheritance. Adejumobi concludes by proposing that, since citizenship has become so destructive of the social and political processes of community, perhaps the way to put things back together is by 'reconceptualising citizenship from a group to a national or 'universal' perspective and re-individualising it'. Accomplishing this suggestion will require taking liberal democracy very seriously, as well as the forging of national identities that supersede sub-national sentiments and loyalties.

Abeeku Essuman-Johnson traces how in less than three decades, West Africa transformed from being a sub-region of relative stability into a hotbed of violent conflicts, instability and insecurity. Although his departure point is how the structural contradictions inherent in French and British colonialisms eventually unravelled, the conceptual template of his chapter is around three mutually reinforcing crises: the crisis of production, the crisis of democracy, the crisis of national identity and nationhood. The crisis of production in West Africa, in his view, is akin to the wider one in Africa resulting from the underdevelopment of productive forces, as reflected in huge external indebtedness, food scarcity, and the general weakness of national economies. It shows in the bifurcation of the world into the industrialised and opulent north and the poverty-stricken and under-developed south. The intrusive impacts of globalisation has not only accentuated this festering crisis of production but also gone further by destroying the traditional mechanisms for coping with difficult situations in many countries in the sub-region. He suggests that the trend of marginalisation and exclusion in the continent could only be reversed when countries embrace fully the strategy of cooperation and integration.

The crisis of democracy began almost after independence when the first generation of political elites in different West African countries failed to sustain the unity of purpose that enabled them to triumph over colonial rule. This resulted in a quick succession of one-party civilian and military rules essentially producing the same results: a deepening crisis of governance and the shrinking of the space for popular democratic participation by all and sundry. Essuman-Johnson cautions that the tragic crisis of democracy must not be understood solely in terms of the obvious misgivings of Western liberal democracy in Africa, but also by coming to terms with the subsisting conditions of deepening exploitation, inequality, poverty and discrimination, the denial of human and people's rights, political repression and the militarisation of social life, poor governance, and zero-sum contest among different groups for state power, to mention a few. These struggles for power have accounted for the displacement of millions of Africans. In spite of the extensive labyrinth of decay and outright collapse, however, Essuman-Johnson sees a ray of hope in the gradual emergence of a sub-regional consensus on minimum standards and alternative frameworks for viable political, economic and social systems.

The third crisis of the state in West Africa has to do with the problems and challenges associated with mobilising national identity, and superimposing it on smaller, divisive identities that are emerging at an alarming rate today. A common thread running through most African countries that have gone up in flames from the Great Lakes to the Horn of Africa, is their inability to stem the tide of identities proliferation; instead, allowing the politicisation of various ethnic, racial, religious and minority identities to stall attempts at constructing a unifying national identity. What the crisis of national identity and nationhood has inescapably led to, according to him, is the erosion if not outright breakdown, of the social compact between the state and the citizenry, each behaving in manners uncomplimentary to the other.

How then should the three-pronged crises be addressed? Essuman-Johnson begins by noting that two of the crises [of democracy and of national identity and nationhood] are clearly within the purview and competence of West African states to manage effectively. Since the crisis of production is inextricably linked with global production, distribution and consumption relationships traditionally dominated by the industrialized countries, it is outside the control of West African countries. With regards to the crisis of democracy therefore, the task before countries in West Africa is to accelerate the process of enthroning genuine democracy and good governance, and allowing their unfettered maturity. This will require a conscious de-privatisation of the state such that state power is not appropriated to the benefit of privileged individuals or sections. The crisis of national identity, on the other hand, can best be tackled at the level of the elites since they are the major manipulators of identities for selfish political gains. In most cases, only the emergence of a credible and unifying leadership can blunt the proliferation of multiple identities rampant in West Africa. Without offering much in terms of a way out, however, Essuman-Johnson re-echoes the popular concern that Africa may have no place to hide from the hawkish grips of neo-liberal economic actors in the West who impose all kinds of conditionalities as prerequisites for external support and reprieve. In the final analysis, he claims, it might just be a self-fulfilling prophecy that the mutually reinforcing crises of production, democracy, and national identity/ nationhood would continue to define Africa's future in a profound and far-reaching manner.

In *Colonial History and the Search for Democratic Nationhood*, Alade Fawole plots the trajectory (and travails) of political misadventure in Anglophone West Africa – Nigeria, Ghana, Sierra Leone and the Gambia, after their independence. The four Anglophone countries were consciously selected for the similarity of their colonial provenance, common style of colonial administrations, the existence of inter-territorial institutional linkages between them and their remarkably similar post-independence political experiences. The thrust of his chapter is that such colonial and post-colonial experiences provoked instabilities that made the search for stable and enduring democracy difficult, if not impossible. These are embedded deeply in the defective foundations on which those states were erected. Apart from constructing Pax-Britannica in all its outposts through a 'combination of trickery, lies, and outright use of force', British colonial political tutelage also produced a crop of nationalists who received their training in agitational politics due to their exclusion from the mainstream of colonial politics. By the time these nationalists inherited the mantle of leadership and authority from the departing British, they were saddled with a completely different set of problems for which they had not received any previous training. Apart, they also had to operate with the inherited colonial structures, including a military and civilian bureaucracy accustomed to doing the dictatorial biddings of the colonial masters, and eliminating the will of the people. It was only a matter of time before the political systems constructed were overwhelmed by unresolved contradictions in their provenance.

Although there is a tone of inevitability to the forms of political instability that saddled them, Fawole believes that by drawing critical attention to the shortcomings and pitfalls in their colonial and early post-colonial experimentations, West Africa can still benefit from hindsight in charting the way forward for democracy to take root in the sub-region. Even then, perhaps the biggest misdoing of the so-called first generation political elites was the fact that they made little or no genuine effort to reconstruct the colonial state to suit the exigencies of post-colonial administration and governance. Instead, they pursued business-as-usual using what was bequeathed to them. A concrete example, recalls Fawole, is their lack of foresight in re-defining the original roles of the military and police as 'alien' force in the service of authoritarian regimes to that of protecting and defending the interest of their peoples in a post-colonial dispensation. Another manifests in the continuation of the official policy of ethnic differentiation after delicately gluing together a multiplicity of disparate ethnic and nationality groups under a single colonial umbrella, instead of nurturing and encouraging a sense of common identity and citizenship under a new commonwealth.

But then, it is quite instructive that one of the reasons adduced by Fawole for the oversight on the part of successor elites in Anglophone West Africa was their blind pursuit of independence as the sole object of nationalist agitation and politics. This situation, to an extent, left no room for the resolution of the basic problems of the colonial state that would later haunt them in many different ways. The wisdom from this with regards to taking extreme caution in implementing the on-going agenda of multiparty political reforms in West Africa should not be lost. As he also asks, how real are the prospects of democratic consolidation? His answer is that much would depend on how internal political dynamics (particularly how best the military can be kept in abeyance from politics) and external forces can continue to support the process that has already commenced in those countries.

On a very encouraging note of optimism- perhaps judging by its past legacies- Fawole concludes that having already begun the quest for democratic nationhood, the experiments can mature and bear positive fruits in the sub-region when certain minimum conditions are met. These will include a deliberate reform of critical institutions of the state, especially the armed forces, police, civil service and the judiciary; the delivery of 'democracy dividends' in a manner that helps the people to accept it as the best form of government; playing the game of politics in accordance with established norms and principles of democracy; dismantling existing structures and institutions of oppression, etc. In conclusion, he notes, even though history is a guide to the future, there is no doubt that with desire and conscious efforts, Anglophone West African states can still rise above the limitations of their colonial provenance and become truly democratic.

Austine Ikelegbe narrows the focus of this discourse on identity and citizenship to Nigeria, a major player in the sub-region. He agrees with Adejumobi's submission that colonial rule must be held responsible for deliberately hindering the evolution of a common national identity. For, by consciously promoting divide and rule, colonialism encouraged ethno-religious separateness and consciousness which invariably discouraged identification with and loyalty to the new commonwealth of Nigeria. Perhaps this is not peculiar to Nigeria alone, for as Fawole has argued in this volume, British colonial policy was actually designed to polarise peoples along primordial lines in all its four West African colonies.

Beyond its colonial antecedents however, Ikelegbe tries to locate the problem of identity formation squarely within the context of post-colonial politics and policies which helps in the artificial construction of these separate identities. He holds the post-colonial ruling elites culpable for deliberately resorting to ethnic nationalism in political contestation, as this practice has become a severe obstacle to national unity. According to him, and agreeing with Adejumobi's submission, the nationalist struggle for independence afforded the initial opportunity for the construction and solidification of ethno-religious and regional identities. This has been further compounded by the post-colonial competition for the capture of state and federal power and resources, a contest in which ethnicity is usually deployed to gain advantage. Nigeria's stunted political development, according to him, is traceable to this phenomenon.

Predicating his views on the notion that identity is a deliberate elite construct rather than a given, Ikelegbe argues that the crisis of the Nigerian state can thus be located within the specificities of the identities constructed by Nigeria's political elites in their contest for power and resources. While identity construction is not necessarily inimical or prejudicial to national development, the problem, however, lies with its deployment in the ruthless contest for competitive advantages, especially the mobilisation of ethnicity in the intra-elite struggles for state power and national resources. The concomitant polarisation along ethnic lines engenders tensions and inter-ethnic conflicts and violence. The character of the state, and its neck-deep involvement in the politics of inclusion and exclusion, and its excessive manipulation in elite competition, enhances the hegemony of some over others. The result of this is the amplification of primordial sentiments and loyalties above commitment to national political stability and the Nigerian commonwealth.

It is very tempting to wonder what possible linkages there are between 'Drama and the Quest for Democracy in Post-Military Nigeria', the theme of Gbemisola Adeoti's contribution in this book. On closer and deeper reflection, his account of how dramaturgy captures and explains the changing fortunes of governance and democratisation, in discourse and practise offer very different and refreshing insights from what obtains in popular literature. His chapter takes a cue from the intellectual harvests from the literary works of T.S. Eliot, Ngugi wa Thiong'o, Ken Saro-Wiwa and others who believe, rightly so, that literature – particularly drama- must serve to change the society for the better. Joining issues with them, Adeoti notes that drama as a social form is a product of socio-political and historical realities, and of the condition of human existence. It can be effectively used to construct, stabilise and give credibility to hegemony, or can serve the 'marginalised' by creating a platform for contesting their marginality and deconstructing the dominant culture and power structure. He traces some of the historic interventions by dramatists in politics in Nigeria from their trenchant ventilation of social discontentment against colonial authority during the penultimate days of decolonisation. Indicative of the socio-political potency of drama even at that very early period was the vindictive hostility their authors received from the colonial government that tried in vain to suppress their works by banning them or incarcerating their audacious authors. For a country like Nigeria that is never short of political absurdities, it is understandable why drama continues to thrive, even though its impact is only now being documented with some seriousness in scholarship.

Beginning with playwrights like Wole Soyinka, John Pepper Clark, Wale Ogunyemi, Ola Rotimi and Sony Oti, Adeoti notes the sprout of an engaging discursive tradition in drama which interrogates the political sphere in a very critical manner. Even when the political class started to betray the high ideals for which independence was fought and won, a robust dramaturgy developed to capture popular civic disillusionment in a manner that showed readiness to confront opportunism among politicians than maintain insularity and distance. It is remarkable, for instance, the depth of satirical foresight in Soyinka's *A Dance of the Forests*, released to coincide with Nigeria's independence. The play rightly anticipated the imminent collapse of the democratic experiment after independence and the outlines of authoritarian military rule in its stead. As the enigmatic playwright perceptibly demonstrated, there is nothing in the emergent polity worthy of celebration as the early vital signs at that time pointed clearly to a festering crisis of governance which politicians pretended to ignore. It is amazing how the content of that play continues to caricature Nigeria's unfortunate drift away from the democratic Promised Land. At the generic level, the major themes covered in the Nigerian dramaturgy as they relate to socio-political misgivings are interestingly diverse. They include an unrepentant criticism of the behavioural excesses and negative pathologies among the elite class and the implications of the shrinking of the democratic space, the elevation to national discourse of the language and ethos of authoritarianism; arbitrary rule and military incursion into politics; the marginalisation of women in politics, and other forms of political misadventures facing Nigeria. Adeoti shows how in their theatrical forms, content and convention, dramatists cleverly provoke contempt within the public at the anti-democratic conducts of civilian and military elites.

He notes that one of the problems with drama is that of delivery, that is, how it is able to reach a broad section of the population. This is especially so because theatre patronage has failed to develop fully. In recent times, as Adeoti rightly notes, the phenomenal growth of the home video industry has significantly reversed this situation. The increase in popularity of home video entertainment coincides with the decline in the production and patronage of literary drama for the big screen. Although still largely characterised by mediocrity in their presentation and storylines, Adeoti believes that many Nigerian home videos have become a formidable avenue that dramatists can utilise towards constructively engaging the public vis-à-vis democracy and good governance. Apart from the home videos, he claims that Theatre for Development (TFD), or Community Theatre, is another viable artistic outlet for giving vent to important issues of the day because it draws its subjects, players, costumes, props, stage and audience from within community and its major problems. Usually, its focus group is the subaltern or the underprivileged in rural areas or the sprawling city suburbs–spaces that the elites have given up on. This form of theatre, according to him, can also play a pivotal role in mobilizing popular consciousness and action within the civil society on identity, rights and governance issues.

One of the most crucial issues that countries recovering from prolonged violent conflicts and civil wars, and those that have gone through a brutal and oppressive regime, is usually how to deal with the past, heal the painful wounds on individual and the collective national psyche, reconcile victims with perpetrators of heinous criminality, and incubate national memory as a guide against the repetition of such vindictive situations in the future. In his chapter on the politics of Ghana national reconciliation, Kwame Boafo-Arthur asks whether indeed such a necessary and evidently overdue process of national atonement and rebirth would not inadvertently serve the opposite end of polarising instead of reconciling such deeply divided societies. Naturally, the template for his critique of national reconciliation efforts is set in the context of West Africa; a sub-region which he claims, has turned out to be the most volatile and coup-prone on the continent, and indisputably one with the largest number of military regimes. The chapter captures the fact that the sub-region has since the 1990s, experienced a chain of brutal armed rebellions and civil wars whose unpleasant carnage and brutality are difficult to overlook. Under such an inclement condition, according to Boafo-Arthur, it is difficult to expect that national development would run a smooth course as peoples and groups harbour deep animosities and acrimonies. Although he acknowledges that national reconciliation is increasingly considered a priority in countries that went through bloody civil wars, those that also experienced military rule where opportunities for the expression of personal and civil liberties are severely curtailed are also acknowledging the need to go through this self-purgatory healing process in order to make lighter the burden of history and the difficult task of national development.

Against this background, his chapter outlines the circumstances that occasioned the setting up of the National Reconciliation Commission in Ghana, focusing particularly on the controversies generated within the Parliament of that country. Two questions set the tone of his analysis. One has to do with what different interpretations can be provided to capture the tenor of parliamentary debates on the National Reconciliation Commission Bill. The second is whether there are lessons for the country with regard to the challenges of reconciliation. Whereas the possibilities of either facilitating reconciliation or fuelling the ember of national polarisation are real, he insists that the success of national reconciliation can only be gauged in terms of the eventual ability to prevent the future occurrence of those circumstances that led to the setting up of such a commission in the first place. Even then, whether the anticipated positive outcomes are immediate or come after a while, the process must enjoy popular support from a significant proportion of the population to succeed.

Against the backdrop of Ghana's post-independence political history, Boafo-Arthur warns against believing that the four military regimes in the country were the only culprits, as civilians – including the charismatic Nkrumah government between 1957 and 1966 – also infringed significantly on human and people's rights. This suggests that national reconciliation can only be effective and durable if it is total and holistic instead of selective in terms of investigating regimes. He also shows how it has become manifestly prudent to re-visit the past in its entirety not necessarily for revenge or vengeance, but to draw critical public attention to certain societal wrongs committed in the name of the State, and to face the future with hope, purpose and commitment to national unity. Acknowledgment of past wrongs to some extent can also help reassure victims that their fundamental rights would no longer be violated with indecency and impunity. He demonstrates clearly how time is no longer sufficient to heal wounds since in the case of Ghana (and this is applicable in many other countries), public amnesia is not synonymous with remorse or forgiveness for those directly involved in the bitter experiences of the past.

Even though a robust debate endured throughout the lifespan of the NRC, it must not be assumed that the task of national reconciliation has been effectively consummated. Also, the setting up of the NRC has not in any way closed up the gaps between the diverse socio-political interests in Ghana; rather, it may have further alienated them from one another. Nevertheless, its highly politicised mandate may not have done much in helping the Commission to achieve its mandate within the limited time frame allotted to it. These worries, in part, prompt important caveat that may serve as a lesson to other countries seeking to pursue a similar experiment: whereas national reconciliation provides a useful signpost or guide to national healing and rebirth, the search for comprehensive and conclusive answers to the nagging questions provoked by the process, even with the best of intentions, may be difficult to realise.

The next chapter on 'Truth Without Reconciliation: The Niger Delta and the Continuing Challenge of National Reconciliation' by Kiikpoye Aaron brings another fascinating angle to the debate on reconciliation–how to come to terms with the burden of truth in the search for genuine national reconciliation. Unlike Boafo-Arthur whose analysis relies on a broader national canvas, Ghana, Aaron takes as his departure the deplorable situation in the Niger Delta oil region where decades of unfriendly oil exploration and production activities have despoiled the environment and made the quest for basic subsistence living among ordinary inhabitants difficult, at the same time that government and multinational oil companies drown in riches and sheer opulence. Aaron re-echoes how the facts of colonial history also made by different authors in this book, made Nigeria what Emerson (1960) calls a 'notoriously precarious lumping together of peoples of separate identities', and how this fact is implicated in the festering Niger Delta problem, nay that of Nigeria. He comes from the direction that Nigeria's unstable history stems in large part from the fact that its different peoples never consented to, or had the benefit of, negotiating the terms of their co-existence as one nation. Unfortunately with the steady neglect of agriculture consequent upon the commercial exploitation of crude oil from 1970, virtually all political power and resources were concentrated at the federal centre, thus making competition for access and control a ruthless zero sum, winner-takes-all affair. In the various conflicts that ensued, most especially within the heavily impoverished Niger Delta region, the quest by oil communities to partake in the enjoyment of the benefits of vast oil and gas endowments, have met with persistent brutality and repression by successive military regimes, not without the active connivance of multinational oil companies.

It is against the background of the socio-psychological wound inflicted by the military on the Niger Delta in particular, and on Nigerians in general, that many people expressed the hope that the inauguration of democratic government in 1999 would ensure atonement and perhaps also restitution. This hope was rekindled by the announcement by President Olusegun Obasanjo, two weeks after his inauguration, of a new Human Rights Violation Investigation Commission (HRVIC), popularly called the Oputa Panel, after the Chairman. But as Aaron points out, the HRVIC turned out to be a very bad imitation of the internationally celebrated South Africa's Truth and Reconciliation Commission. His central argument is that under the present civilian dispensation in which Nigerians are believed to be enjoying greater freedoms, it is business as usual on matters relating to the gross violation of the rights to health and a healthy environment by indigenous inhabitants of the Niger Delta – all rights enshrined in the African Charter on Human and People's Rights which Nigeria is a signatory. Emphatically, the chapter claims that to the extent that genuine steps have not been taken to right past and ongoing wrongs against the Niger Delta people from whose region the nation's oil wealth of the nation is generated, the Oputa panel confuses the symbolism of reconciliation with its substance.

Broadly, two tracks exist for pursuing truth and reconciliation: the criminal trial or retributive justice approach and the restorative justice approach. While the former requires bringing criminal charges against perpetrators in the regular court of law or a court specifically set up for that purpose, restorative justice approach focuses attention on the perpetrator genuinely acknowledging his wrongdoings and seeking forgiveness from the victim(s). As Aaron rightly notes, because of the drawbacks inherent in the criminal trial approach, most nations of Africa and Eastern Europe opt for restorative justice. Except for the South African Truth and Reconciliation Commission where amnesty was not blanket but conditional on 'full disclosure', most other countries in the continent provided blanket amnesties for convicted violators of human rights. In the case of Nigeria, the HRVIC had a mandate to investigate cases of human rights abuse from January 1966 through June 1998, and to recommend ways that would bring about healing and national reconciliation. Unlike the South African TRC, however, the HRVIC lacked constitutional and legal backing. Also, it had neither the power to grant amnesty to proven violators of human rights, nor could offer immunity to those on whom investigations were carried out. Besides, it could not compel commensurate penalties on those who contemptuously turned down its invitation, as many principal military actors during the period covered refused. Even those who eventually appeared before the HRVIC, according to Aaron, could not be said to have willingly volunteered the whole truth and nothing but the truth of their roles. In fact, some of them exploited the constitutional inadequacies of the Commission; instead of admission of guilt and pleading for forgiveness, took the path of denial, lack of remorse and sheer arrogance.

Aaron gives two explanations for this turn of event. One, he claims, may well be that President Olusegun Obasanjo, himself one of Nigeria's erstwhile military dictators, allowed the constitutional loopholes to escape accounting for his own regime's atrocious misdeeds. Another possible explanation may be that these constitutional and legal loopholes were deliberately permitted to ensure that some powerful interests, who played less than noble roles in the past, but who also threw their weight behind Obasanjo's presidential bid, were not offended. Whether the loopholes were deliberately created or found their way by default remains conjectural and tentative.

Aaron argues that in the light of persisting injustices inflicted on the Niger Delta, Nigeria's gestures at reconciliation is more about humming the same stale and discordant tune as national reconciliation has not gone beyond slogans and symbolism as far as the Niger Delta is concerned. Till date, for instance, the recommendations of the Oputa panel are yet to be officially made public or implemented, even though a coalition of civil society groups have put the report on the internet. For the Niger Delta, the exclusion and alienation of the people continue to pose a fundamental challenge to national reconciliation. In turn, for as long as marginalised groups in the Niger Delta continue to mobilise against a state seen essentially as serving sectional interests, the project of deepening democracy would remain inconclusive. In the final analysis, Aaron concludes, there cannot be genuine national reconciliation without justice. Just as well, the path to genuine national reconciliation can only begin with addressing substantive national questions, most importantly, whether the units making up Nigeria prefer to continue as bedfellows, and on what terms.

Part Two of the book focuses on the sub-regional manifestations and dimensions of the crisis of state in West Africa. It begins with Charles Ukeje's illuminating analysis of the origins and the dynamics of sub-regional politics that propelled ECOWAS from its original narrow conception as a mere economic integration mechanism into the politico-security terrain. This change is not fortuitous, as Ukeje makes clear, but compelled by the post-Cold War state implosions and the widespread political instabilities that plagued the West Africa sub-region in the 1990s. The civil wars in Liberia and Sierra Leone, two neighbouring countries, provided the requisite impetus, for no meaningful economic integration was possible in the context of sub-regional instability. Such insecurity, as he argues, radically transformed ECOWAS from a mere economic integration scheme into a mechanism for the maintenance of security, political stability, conflict management and resolution.

In arriving at this conclusion, Ukeje carefully traced the trajectory of growth and development of the body from its birth in 1975 to the present, highlighting in the process the significant landmarks and changes the organisation has witnessed, as well as the political, economic, ideological, technical and structural problems it has had to contend with. Although originally configured to function as an institution promoting economic integration, the organisation has to adapt and respond to evolving sub-regional dynamics- instabilities, state collapse, intra-state violence and civil wars – that portend grave threats to peace, security and economic development. No doubt, ECOWAS engagement with conflict management, resolution, peacekeeping and peace-making has recorded mixed blessings. While it has responded appropriately to evolving regional dynamics, its success has sometimes exposed and brought to the fore lingering problems- linguistic and cultural differences, personality incompatibilities, economic weakness and inadequacy of funds for its operations. While the ECOMOG operations can be seen as a great learning experience, they also highlight the inherent capacity of the sub-region to respond to complex situations in a new world order that gives African issues very little attention. Arising from the numerous political, economic and institutional problems of ECOWAS, the sub-region took bold steps to reposition the organisation to cope with contemporary challenges and to perform more effectively in a highly globalised world. The Charter was revised; new institutions such as the ECOWAS Parliament, Court, etc were created, while other far-reaching measures have also been adopted to reposition ECOWAS for more efficient performance.

Operating from a different platform, Yomi Oruwari believes that it is time the West Africa sub-region took regionalism a step further by transcending the state-centric approach to integration and involving the households and the informal sector in the development process. In spite of all the efforts made thus far, integration has remained more of a mirage because of the reliance on 'received wisdom' from the developed world rather than on home-grown concepts and theories. Integration and development may remain elusive so long as Africans depend on the global capitalist economic networks. To escape from this stranglehold therefore requires that integration be redefined to include the households and their informal economic activities with the objective of redeeming them from poverty. Whilst formal intra-ECOWAS trade is very low, informal trade across borders contribute significantly to the sub-regional economy, hence the justification for its inclusion in the integration process. In any case, due to political, economic and technical reasons, which both Ukeje and Sesay have also highlighted, ECOWAS has been unable to achieve most of the objectives set out for it. It has thus become more preoccupied with grappling with intra-regional security in response to emerging sub-regional dynamics. Oruwari submits that ECOWAS can overcome its current limitations by, amongst others, developing regional transportation and communication infrastructure, and by concentrating on creating an enabling environment for the emergence of indigenous multinational corporations that would look inwards for financing to tap and harness the available natural resources, especially in mining and agriculture, for the general well being of the people of West Africa.

One of the new and provocative threats to the nation-building project in West Africa comes from the growing intensity of violent conflicts and civil wars, and the chain of events they provoke for the countries involved and those across national borders. Kassim Sikiru Taiwo takes a critical look at the refugee crisis provoked by incessant civil wars in West Africa, with specific focus on the social status of Liberian refugees in Nigeria, whom he aptly describes as 'citizens without a home', in apparent reference to the fact that under the relevant protocols of the Economic Community of West African States (ECOWAS), they are expected to enjoy right of residence in the host member countries. He notes the steady increase in the number of refugees across the world, but most especially in West Africa where Liberian and Sierra Leonean refugees in neighbouring countries run into thousands. Against this broad canvas, the chapter specifically highlights some of the major plights of Liberian refugees in Nigeria based on empirical study of the refugee camp at Oru, near Ijebu Ode in Ogun State, southwest Nigeria.

The chapter begins by enumerating some of the root causes of the refugee problem in Africa followed by an investigation of the genesis of the refugee outflow from the first Liberian civil war in December 1989, and the second round of hostilities prompted by the Liberians United for Reconstruction and Development (LURD) from 2000. Taiwo also examines Nigeria's profile as a refugee-hosting country against the background of the specific method the country eventually adopted to address the problem of settlement of refugees in, and the actual condition at, the Oru refugee camp. Afterwards, Kassim Taiwo critically x-rays the pattern and dimensions of relationship that developed between the refugees on the one hand and their host community on the other, and also the different limitations of the resettlement procedures adopted for the refugees in the camp. As he rightly points out, even though the causes of refugee production may have changed significantly over the years, they are now caused more by civil wars than by other political, economic or natural complications. According to him, prior to the 1990s, the influx of aliens into Nigeria was dominated by indigenes of West Africa attracted by the fabled oil boom of the 1970s and the early 1980s. By the 1990s, however, many refugees fleeing civil wars in Liberia and Sierra Leone were forced to choose Nigeria as a safe haven. Quoting an earlier study, Kassim claims that by 1999, the number of refugees in Oru based on their nationality were as follows: 355 from Sierra Leone, 369 from Liberia, 11 from Congo, I Somalian, 3 Sudanese, 1 Ghanaian, 3 Rwandans and 1 Chadian. By August 2003, the figure rose to over 5,500 African refugees in the camp out of which 3,500 came from Liberia.

Several options were identified for the resettlement of refugees. In the case of Nigeria, long-term settlement seemed to have become the preferred option. Sometimes, this can be spontaneous as the refugees themselves choose to live in existing villages among local residents or form their own villages, encouraged or welcomed by existing inhabitants and authorities. Sometimes these refugees have kinship or friendship relations with local people and rely on their initial hospitality to find food and work. Another option is where the government acquires a large piece of land, usually with the permission of local authorities, to provide refugees will smallholding agricultural settlement project. But then as Kassim rightly notes, these various options have far reaching implications; firstly, for the refugees themselves and secondly, in terms of the relationship between refugees and host communities. In the later case, problem may arise when host communities believe that refugees are competing with local residents for scarce food stocks, medical supplies, arable land and wage labour opportunities. Since refugees also tend to settle closer to national borders or in places where the writ of government is either minimal or non-existent, it can be particularly treacherous as they are exposed to all kinds of insecurity problems, including cross-border raids. Although Nigeria's hosting of refugees is generally in line with its perceived big-brother role in Africa, Kassim highlights the heavy burdens their presence continues to cause on the refugees, the host communities and the government. He calls on the government to make concerted effort to improve the facilities in the camp so that the 'visitors' can live a more decent life.

The final chapter wraps up the future challenges facing ECOWAS member countries, individually or collectively, in terms of reinventing the nationalist dream in the sub-region. Amadu Sesay wonders if indeed today's African leaders are as convinced (and committed) as their predecessors that the continent's future lies in collective self-reliance efforts, and that economic integration is the sure panacea to the myriad of problems of nation building and prosperity. West Africa, with its plethora of mini-states is perhaps more convinced of this, hence the establishment of ECOWAS and other sub-regional integrative mechanisms and other efforts since the decade of independence. Noting that efforts at sub-regional integration actually pre-dated the independence of the states, he traces the trajectory of this development from colonial times when the principal colonialists established certain inter-territorial institutions – WACB, WAAC, WAEC, and CFA – for effective exploitation and administration of their respective colonial possessions. These institutions, with the exception of WAEC and CFA, were dissolved almost immediately upon independence.

Since the felt-need for integration was already ingrained in the psyche of post-independence leaders, they also saw it as an effective means of protecting newly won independence, ensuring prosperity of their peoples and fulfilling the original dream of the early nationalists who gallantly fought for independence. To them, economic integration was a much more attractive option than Nkrumah's radical idea of a continental political union. The conception of regional economic integration as critical to nation building and development resulted in the establishment of several smaller, issue-specific organisations that eventually coalesced into ECOWAS in 1975. While ECOWAS has lagged behind in the fulfilment of its fundamental objectives of economic integration and development, it has nonetheless recorded commendable success in the maintenance of peace, security and stability. Realising the impossibility of economic integration in the face of state implosions, insecurity and instabilities that rocked many states in the 1990s, the organisation rose creditably to the occasion. This was necessary especially against the backdrop of super power retreat from the global peripheries like Africa after the Cold War. It is thus in the spheres of conflict management, peacekeeping and peace-enforcement, which are not even in its original list of objectives, that ECOWAS has recorded most of its major successes thus far.

Sesay dissects the ECOWAS Protocol on Democracy and Good Governance, which he led a Committee of Eminent Persons to draft, as a vehicle for achieving the laudable dream of the early nationalists and founding fathers. He however calls for cautious optimism by raising the question of the organisation's capability to fearlessly implement the provisions of the protocol, especially against such sub-regional giants like Nigeria, Ghana and Senegal. Identifiable political, institutional and practical difficulties notwithstanding, the adoption of the Protocol is a step in the right direction, a useful starting point for the eventual realisation of the dream of the nationalists for a developed and prosperous West Africa sub-region.

Part I

The Crisis of the State in West Africa

1

Identity, Citizenship and Conflict: The African Experience

Said Adejumobi

Introduction

More than ever before, there has been an unprecedented denationalisation of the state, with sub-national identities challenging, and in many cases unravelling, the nation-state project. From the Balkans to the Caucasus, Asia to Africa and the Middle East, the state is under an unprecedented siege. As Ali Mazrui (1999:5) observed, 'the state is challenged at the macro-level by new levels of continental race consciousness and by old sacred solidarity and religion. The state is being challenged at the micro-level by ethnicity and by new gender revolution in the world. That the state may be "withering away", but in a sense which is dramatically different from what either Marx, Engels or Lenin envisaged'. Samuel Huntington (1996) views the development as a clash of civilisations. That is, these ascendant identities represent cultural forms and expressions which are to define the political landscape in the 21st century. According to him, political ideology and the state are to play decelerating and less important roles in social conflicts in the world; identities and culture will do so in a post-modern world of the 21st century.

The explosion in identities and identity-based conflicts in the world ordinarily contradicts the logic of globalisation. The social dynamics of globalisation should impel social integration through transculturalism or multiculturalism and engineer inter-group harmony on a global scale as the world comes to share the same capitalist social values and norms. This however is not the case. The content and character of globalisation promote social fragmentation, disintegration and disaggregation; splits groups and identities into warring factions; undermines the state by emptying it of its social content and relevance; and sacrifices the 'human soul' for the fundamentalism of the market. The deepening of poverty, social inequalities and declining social welfare under globalisation, especially in the developing countries, has pushed many individuals into sectarian identities, reinforced their potency in society and made them alternative sites of political expression and struggles fuelling tension and conflict in many countries. As the United Nations Institute for Social Development puts it in its 2000 report, 'globalisation is splintering many societies' (UNRISD 2000:2).

Both Africa and Asia are major sites of conflicts in the world, although of a greater dimension and proportion in Africa. From 1970, no less than 30 wars have been fought in Africa, most of them intra-state in nature (Annan 1998: 2). In 1994, out of a total of 48 countries in sub-Saharan Africa, no less than twelve countries were at war, while two were in the post-war phase, and 14 had a recent or current experience of significantly high levels of political violence. In all, in 1994, a total of 28 countries, more than half of the countries in sub-Saharan Africa, were or had been recently afflicted by serious violent conflicts (Sandberg and Smith 1994: 5). In 1996, 14 countries were engaged in armed conflicts, while by 1999 the number increased to 18, with no less than 11 countries suffering severe political crises (Adedeji 1999: 5). Evidently, most countries in Africa are vulnerable to conflicts, civil wars and state collapse.[1]

This chapter considers the African experience with regard to identity-based conflicts by arguing that underlying the litany of identity-based conflicts in Africa is the issue of citizenship and rights, a phenomenon that has been exacerbated by globalisation. The genealogy to this is the history of African society dating to colonialism in which primordial identities were the foci of individual rights, and not the state. State citizenship was constructed on and above primordial logic. Currently, group identities have assumed not only the primary means of social expression, but also of rights and privileges in the polity. The concept of national citizenship of equal rights, benefits and duties for all citizens has been attenuated or bifurcated, with the state sunk in a cesspool of inter-group struggles and conflicts over the distribution of public goods. The claims of marginalisation, domination, and social injustice by groups and individuals often derive from this reality. Otherwise, inter-group or identity-based conflicts and civil wars are manifestations of a deep-seated problem of citizenship in different national contexts.

The chapter is organised into four parts. Part one is a theoretical analysis of the interface between citizenship and the nation-state. What, for instance, is the nexus between the state and citizenship, and how does the latter seek to create a common national identity for the members of a political community (i.e. state)? Part two focuses on the historical trajectory that paved the way for the development of citizenship and the state in Africa from the colonial era. Part three dwells on the construction of identity and citizenship in the post-colonial period in Africa. Part four is an empirical illustration of how such a construction manifests itself and translates into political conflicts in Africa with a focus on two countries: Rwanda and Nigeria.

Citizenship and the nation-state: The theoretical interface

The relationship between the state and citizenship has been the subject of an age-long theoretical discourse dating back to the classical political theorists. In the view of Aristotle for example, a state is nothing but 'a compound made up of citizens; and this compels us to consider who should be properly called a citizen and what a citizen really is' (Aristotle 1958). For social contract theorists like Rousseau, Hobbes and Locke, the very basis of the 'social contract' through which the state evolved as a form of human organisation, is the conferment and recognition of citizenship on those in the political community. In other words, the notion of citizenship is tied up with the evolution of the state.

Although the concepts of state and citizenship have changed in time and space, the idea of modern citizenship is still closely connected with the notion of the state. Conceptually, a state is an entity endowed with political sovereignty over a clearly defined territory; that has a monopoly of the use of legitimate force; and that consists of citizens whose terminal loyalty is to the state (Oomen 1997: 23). In other words, a modern state is conceived as a collectivity of citizens.

The idea of a state or nation-state cannot therefore be meaningful without citizenship. Although empires and colonies are comprised predominantly of subjects and not citizens, those forms of political entities have become anathema in contemporary times. Every nation-state identifies a particular set of persons as its citizens and defines others as non-citizens, or as aliens (Brubakar 1992: ix). Citizenship therefore is an instrument of social closure through which the state lays claim to and defines its sovereignty, authority, legitimacy and identity. The identity of the citizen in a global context is, in turn, defined by the state. The institution of citizenship is that political artefact through which the state constitutes and perpetually reproduces itself as a form of social organisation. It is the means through which the modern nation-state made of various nationalities seeks to forge a common identity and collective experience for its people. Indeed, without the concept of citizenship, the idea of a modern nation-state cannot be translated into practice.

But how is citizenship to be conceptualised, how did it evolve and what are its elements? The word 'citizenship' as Anh Nga Longva noted (as French *'citoyennetté'*) derives from the root word 'city'. As a historical concept, it arose in the context of the town and reflects the relationship between the individual and the city. Indeed, the word originally referred to the freeman of the city. Thus citizenship may be conceived as an urban phenomenon (Longva 1995: 201). Perhaps the notion of citizenship being viewed in a city or urban context may be partly related to the fact that most of the states in the medieval and ancient periods were conceived as city-states, small in territory and largely urban in nature. Also, the struggle for citizenship probably was at inception basically urban-centred, the struggles of the working class. However, what is important is that citizenship in this context is viewed as a form of relationship between the political sovereign, state or city, and the individual.

Although consensus exists that citizenship is a form of state-individual relationship, there are variations among scholars, both modern and early political theorists, on what citizenship means and its content. Aristotle and Rousseau viewed citizenship as a form of political activity, citizenship is the right to rule and be ruled (Aristotle 1958). The citizen must be an active figure if the state is to be virile and able to provide for the common good of everybody. Civil society is seen as being destructive of citizenship as it obstructs the relationship between the state and the citizen. But both Aristotle and Rousseau admitted that their notion of citizenship is limited to the small city-states. In a broader conception, citizenship is viewed as the right of the individual to the protection of life, liberty, property and welfare (Bodin 1945). In this wise, a citizen may choose to be passive, so long as his activities are not subversive of the state.

In modern times, citizenship is conceived in a symbiotic manner between the state and the individual. It is defined as a regime of rights, privileges and duties. T.H. Marshall breaks those rights into three categories – civil, political and social rights (Marshall 1964). These include the right to free speech, association, due process, and equality before the law, franchise, and social welfare. The obligations of the citizens include tax payment, military conscription if necessary to defend the state, loyalty and allegiance to the state. From a different perspective, Charles Tilly argues that citizenship can be interpreted from four main angles, namely as a category, role, tie, and identity. As a category, citizenship designates a set of actors- citizens – distinguished by their shared privileged position vis-à-vis a particular state. As a tie, citizenship identifies an enforceable mutual relation between an actor and state agents. As a role, citizenship includes all of an actor's relations to others that depend on the actor's relations to a particular state. And as an identity, citizenship can refer to the experience and public representation of category, tie or role (Tilly 1996: 7-11).

This multi-dimensional conception of citizenship by Tilly does not vitiate but only complements that of Marshall. Indeed, Tilly eventually opted for citizenship as a tie, and defines it as 'a continuing series of transactions between persons and agents of a given state in which each has enforceable rights and obligations uniquely by virtue of (1) the person's membership in an exclusive category, the native-born plus the naturalised and (2) the agent's relation to the state rather than any other natural authority the agent may enjoy' (Tilly 1996: 8).

From the foregoing, therefore, citizenship in my view is a form of social pact, constituted by the dual elements of reciprocity and exchange between the individual (citizen) and the state. The individual enjoys those rights and privileges which no other social or political organisation offers, while in turn, he gives his obligations, loyalty and commitment to the state. While citizenship sounds like an egalitarian and equalising concept, it does not presuppose class but civic equality: equality before the law, equality of access and opportunities in state institutions and structures, and fairness and justice in the interactions between the state and individuals and amongst individuals in a political community.

The criteria for citizenship differ from country to country. Three different criteria can be identified. The first is citizenship by birth (*jus soli*). The second is citizenship by descent or ancestral claims (*jus sanguinis*). The third is citizenship acquired through naturalisation. In most cases, countries adopt a combination of two or all of these criteria. The first criterion is more inclusive and liberal in nature. This is adopted more capaciously in a country like the United States. Countries like Germany deny citizenship on the basis of birth, permanent or prolonged residency. In a country like France, children born in the country cannot lay claim to citizenship except under certain conditions. That is when they reach the age of eighteen, have lived in France for five years and have committed no crime (Kerber 1997: 834). What is important is that every state stipulates rules through which it defines those who are its citizens and those who are not.

There have been attempts to classify or create typologies of citizenship based on the level of the social engagement of the individual with the state. These range from the passive to the active citizens, the thick or the thin, and the oppressed, alienated and pluralist citizen. These categories are good heuristic devices that embody a subtle undertone for citizens' mobilisation and participation in the state, except for the oppressed citizen, who in the practical sense of it cannot be called a citizen, but rather a subject. Subjects are objects of domination and cannot really lay claim to the benefits of citizenship. Citizenship, when properly constituted, should provide 'common' or 'equal' rights and benefits to those considered as such (i.e. citizens) in the state.

However, two factors in the global arena are rapidly redefining the notion of citizenship within national contexts. First is the trend of regional integration with the creative, still emerging, experience of the European Union (EU). By this initiative, citizenship is being gradually recontextualised away from national frontiers to the supra-national level. The EU is gradually creating 'regional citizens' who enjoy wide range of rights and benefits not as citizens of their respective countries, but as citizens of the Union. This experiment continues to generate intense debate among academics, politicians and civil society groups in most countries of the EU. Even in non-member states like Norway, it remains a central issue of public discourse.

The second factor is the increasing political globalisation of the world, particularly with the hegemony of the liberal capitalist ideology. International codes of rights and privileges of individuals are being designed, institutionalised, and gradually enforced by supra-national organisations. Legal norms and conventions for minimum standards, especially on the issue of civil rights, are evolving which nations are being encouraged and sometimes coerced to acquiesce to. In other words, the rights of citizens are no longer the sole prerogative of states. Extra-state actors mediate these. To be sure, the state remains a major actor in global interactions and the institution of citizenship.

It is essential to touch on the relationship between social pluralism or multiculturalism and citizenship. Some argue that the former has negative effects on the latter. That is, multiculturalism creates multiple and competing identities for the individual which attenuate his loyalty and allegiance, as a citizen, to the state. Sectarian identities like nationality, ethnicity and religion, are believed to be exclusive identities, which generate inequalities, while citizenship is basically inclusive and equality oriented (Oomen 1996: 20). The goals of equality embodied in citizenship and multiple identities can co-exist and complement each other, provided the constitutive rules in the socio-political space are well defined. In other words, multiculturalism or pluralism should not necessarily conflict with or be subversive of national citizenship or the state. Indeed, the idea of a nation-state is a plurality of nationalities bound together by a common state identity. Pluralism offers multiple layers of organisational participation or interaction for the individual in the state, which should enhance his citizenship qualities. As Michael Walzer (1970: 218) rightly noted, 'the citizen stands to the state not only as an individual, but also as a member of a variety of other organisations (class, professional, racial, ethnic etc), with which the state must relate, in relating to him (i.e. citizen)'. Multiple identities of the individual should not detract from his/her allegiance as citizen, to the state, but should complement and enrich it. Indeed, human beings are gregarious and thereby essentially identity seeking.

However, it is when citizenship is more nominal than substantive, that is, when citizenship rights and benefits are largely denied and the state seems out of reach, that pluralism may be subversive of the state. Those sub-national identities then form the basic source of support to the individual and may constitute a platform of resistance against the state. As Morton Grodzin (1966: 213) puts it, 'all patriots are potential traitors'. In this context, those groups may take precedence over the state as the primary object of identity and allegiance and may seek to contest political space with the state. It is the consciousness of the denial of citizenship rights by a people which usually facilitates the transformation of sectarian groups, like racial and ethnic groups, from being 'groups in themselves' into 'groups for themselves'. The idea of elite mobilisation of ethnic or racial ideology, which most analysts emphasise in explaining politics and conflicts in Africa, is only possible in the context of a fertile ground of citizenship exclusion of the group or people concerned. We shall demonstrate this shortly in the narrative of the African experience.

Between the two publics: Colonialism, identity and the citizenship question

The concept of the two publics was first used by Peter Ekeh to describe how colonialism created a split in the personality of the average African elite under colonial rule (Ekeh 1975). This personality split is typified by a set of dual identities, which Ekeh referred to as the amoral or civic public and the moral or primordial public. I have used the concept of the two publics here slightly differently. In my usage, it refers to how colonialism created two categories of people in the public sphere in the colonies; citizens and subjects or as Mahmood Mamdani (1996) puts it, the native and the citizen. The former speaks the language of tradition, and customs; the latter, the language of rights, duties and privileges. How did this evolve and what are its implications for the post-colonial state, identities and politics in Africa?

Colonialism, though primarily an economic project meant to facilitate the brutal exploitation of labour and natural resources in the colonies, evolved a political infrastructure that fostered relations of domination and control, which were a prerequisite for the colonial enterprise. Although methods of colonial governance differed slightly among the colonial powers, for example, between the British 'indirect rule' policy and the French policy of 'assimilation', the logic and dynamics of these regimes, and the institutional structure and process of state formation which they set in motion, were basically the same.

Colonial political structure was predicated on the logic of dualism, of spatial institutional and territorial segregation and laws, which Mahmood Mamdani (1996) aptly characterised as a bifurcated state or the logic of decentralised despotism. On the one hand, there was the central state governed by civil laws which was the domain of the colonisers, largely urban-based, and on the other hand, there was the local state or the native authorities, which enforced customary laws. The former was the domain of rights and privileges associated with citizenship; the latter was a terrain of 'culture' and 'custom'. The natives or the colonised were subjects and therefore not entitled to citizenship rights or benefits. The seat of customary power in the rural areas was the local state: the district in the British, the *cercle* in French, and the *Indigenato* in the Portuguese colonies (Mamdani 1996; O'Laughlin 2000). The agent for the local state and native authority rule was the chief who was vested with administrative, executive, legislative, extractive and judicial powers. He was the law. In essence, while civil law was racialised, customary law was ethnicised.

However, the import of native authority rule was not only with the denial of citizenship and its bundle of rights to the natives. It had two other important aspects. First colonialism through the native authority system radically transformed social structures in Africa, including the chieftaincy institution (Ekeh 1980). The sphere of control, sources and the nature of power, and those who exercised it at the local level changed dramatically. Native authority rule and customary law under the colonial regime meant the reinvention and bastardisation of what were traditional political institutions and what may be called customary laws in most pre-colonial societies in Africa.

Although modes of political governance differed in many pre-colonial African societies from the acephalous and highly democratic age-grade system in Iboland, the dispersed and regulated monarchical system of the Yoruba kingdoms, to the fairly centralised Fulani empire and the Zulu kingdom, hardly was there a society in which all powers were absolutely fused in a single authority (Ikime 1980; Asiwaju 1976). On the contrary, the colonial state ensured that there was no local regulatory check on the chief, who invented and reinvented what constituted 'customary law' in line with the wishes of the colonial authorities. Also, the selection of chiefs under colonial rule was not based on any tradition or customs of the local people, but on the whims and caprices of the colonial regime. As Michael Crowder and Obaro Ikime (1970: ix) observed, 'in a very real sense, none of the chiefs who "ruled" under the French and British were legitimate'. In other words, there was nothing traditional or customary about 'customary laws' and the native authority system in the colonial era. Second and perhaps more important, is that the colonial regime, by fragmenting the local people into 'native authorities', with different sets of 'customary or tribal laws', constructed and fomented ethnic identities which were later to plague the state and polity in most African states during the nationalist struggle and in the post-colonial era.

Anti-colonial political struggle in Africa was couched in the language of citizenship: that is, the right of the natives to become citizens. As Pixley Kazaka Seme, a founder of the African National Congress (ANC) in South Africa noted at one of the functions of the organisation: 'the white people of this country have formed what is known as the Union of South Africa - a union in which we have no voice... We have called you therefore to this conference for the purpose of creating national unity and defending our rights and privileges' (Walshe 1971: 34).

Everywhere in the colonial territories the political slogans of the nationalist movements were 'power to the people'; 'equal rights for all'. Colonial rule suffered from severe contradictions that were to later stand the system on its head. The provision of limited educational opportunities to the natives, which was designed to better facilitate the process of colonial exploitation and domination, served other contradictory purposes. It created a new class of natives, who were to use acquired western political pedagogy on citizenship and rights to make claims and contest political space with the colonial state. The social base of nationalism in Africa, as Mamdani points out, was the educated native or the small, but emergent native middle class who had crossed the boundary between the rural, which incorporated the subject ethnically, and the urban that excluded the subject racially. Though beyond the lash of customary law, this native was denied access to civil and political rights on racial grounds (Mamdani 2000: 45). He was the agency of political nationalism and the decolonisation project in Africa.

However, the entrenched institutional structures of colonialism engendered contradictions and tension-ridden tendencies in the anti-colonial struggles, and influenced the nature and pattern of the political movements. The sharp division between the rural and the urban, the native and the settler, and the horizontal fragmentation of the natives into ethnic entities and identities through the Native Authority system placed severe limitations on the ability of the emergent indigenous political elite to muster a broad national base. In most countries in Africa, most of the nationalist movements and resultant political parties were ethnically defined, drawing their support base from the fragmented ethnic social structures of the colonial era. For example in Nigeria, the three major political parties in the decolonisation era namely the Northern People's Congress (NPC), the Action Group (AG), and the National Council for Nigerian Citizens (NCNC) reflected ethnic configurations in their origin and character. In the case of South Africa, the semi-industrialisation of the country facilitated a high level of urbanisation and a labour force which made possible the formation of largely urban-based political movements against apartheid. However, as those movements sought to mobilise the rural population in the liberation struggle ethnic expressions gained currency. The liberation movements were confronted with the power of the chiefs, whom they had to incorporate into the nationalist struggle. The fragmentation that ethnic expressions unleashed defines the status of a party like the Inkatha Freedom Party (IFP) in South Africa.

The points being emphasised are basically three. One is that the bifurcated nature of the colonial state produced and encouraged ethnic-based political identities in the decolonisation period and beyond. As Mamdani (1996: 24) aptly puts it 'every movement of resistance was shaped by the very structure of power against which it rebelled'. Second, the logic of dualism germane to the institutional structure of colonialism created divisions between the rural and the urban, the native and settler; the subject and the citizen. This was to produce profound problems in the post-colonial era in the discourse and politics on citizenship in most Southern and Eastern African countries where 'settler colonialism' was the norm. Up till now, a raging debate exists in most of those countries as to who is a citizen and who is not, between the 'settler' and the 'native'. Third, colonial structures affected the nature of anti-colonial politics and the character of the post-colonial state.

Post-colonial state, identity and citizenship

Two factors coalesced to shape the nature of the post-colonial state in Africa. These are the colonial antecedent and the direction of state policy in the post-colonial era. Although redesigned in form and content, the colonial political structure and state formation witnessed no radical or qualitative transformation in the post-colonial era in most African states, beyond the change of personnel. The reasons for this are quite numerous and have been the subject of discourse elsewhere (Ake 1980; Onimode 1988). But suffice to note that factors like the politics of power transfer, the configuration among local social forces, the perceptions and interests of the emergent ruling elite, and external political influences were some of the variables which stultified a radical transformation process. In some countries where transformative policies were initiated, those policies sometimes reproduced the logic and contradictions of the colonial state with little meaningful results achieved.[2]

There are several areas in which the colonial heritage was palpable. Although the nature of the political arrangements adopted by African countries in the post-colonial era differs, ranging from the unitary to the federal system, there are similar discernible features in their state structure. The post-colonial state was not reorganised to attenuate difference, either institutionally, ethnically, identity wise, or symbolically. With regard to the institutional dimension, the logic of dualism in the state structure was not obliterated, but reproduced and assumed a new dimension. The nature of the dichotomy between the central and local states, though reformed, still had implications for the issues of identity and citizenship in the post-colonial era. While national citizenship was liberalised with civil laws applicable to all, the local state remains largely ethnicised.

This situation reinforces the bifurcation of citizenship as local and state governments remain exclusionary in their norms and practices, and the rights and privileges they confer on the people. In the localities, there is usually a clear distinction between the 'natives' or 'indigenes' of those areas, who are considered as the 'local citizens', and the 'immigrants' or 'settlers' who are considered as 'non-citizens' (in spite of the fact that they are all nationals of the same country). In countries like Uganda and the Democratic Republic of Congo where the ownership and control of land (the main means of livelihood) is still vested in native authorities, 'non-natives' are largely denied access to land and also denied the right to have their own native authorities, as doing so will imply recognising them as 'indigenes' and require allowing access to land. In other words, residency is not the criterion for inclusion as 'local citizens', but 'indigeneity'. In most cases, the local or state laws sanction this arrangement. In Nigeria for example, not until recently, 'indigeneity' was a criterion for qualification to contest in local elections and not residency. Consequently, it is possible for someone to live all his life in a locality without having a right to stand for office there. The point is that while political reforms and decentralisation occurred in most African states in the post-colonial era, there was little real democratisation of decentralised institutions. Thus the state system that subsists reinforces local ethnic and political identities, fragments the political process and undermines the concept of common citizenship for the people in the country.

Also, at the national level the logic of difference of an ethnic nature is factored into the rules and norms of political interactions and the state system, especially with regard to social rights. Ethnic identity as opposed to citizenship identity determines who gets what, when, how, and how much in the state. Issues of employment, public appointments, education grants, scholarships, etc, are subjected to ethnic arithmetic by the central state. In some countries, this practice enjoys a constitutional basis, while in others it is one of state norms and conventions. In Nigeria, there is a key constitutional provision known as the 'federal character principle'.[3] It is an ethnic formula for the allocation of public goods. Although this constitutional provision was designed as a political technique for managing Nigeria's federal system, of giving equal opportunities to all ethnic groups; in practice however it is a policy that has proved to be largely counter-productive. It places ethnic identity as the primary identity for state entitlements and social rights. It de-individualises citizenship and makes it more of a group phenomenon. As such, in gaining access to state institutions, the individual does not relate with the state directly as citizen, but relates with it as a member/representative of an ethnic group. The result is that the central state becomes an arena of ethnic contest with the more powerful ethnic groups excluding and submerging the lesser ones and denying their people the benefits of citizenship. This tendency undermines the integrity and cohesion of the fragile African state and supplements the principle of territorial loyalty and citizenship with that of ethnic and community loyalty.

Furthermore the logic of dualism remains palpable in public images, meanings and social expressions. This assumes racial, ethnic or spatial dimensions. This tendency is reinforced by deep social and economic inequalities in the society. In countries with the experience of 'settler colonialism' like South Africa and Zimbabwe, the public image of difference is racial; between the 'white settlers', who are considered by the 'local population' as 'oppressive aliens' not desirous of 'citizenship', even in a juridical sense; and the 'natives' who regard themselves as the real citizens. Unfortunately economic leverage tilts in favour of the former. This phenomenon often provokes tension in the discourse on citizenship and sometimes facilitates inter-group conflicts in those countries. This is the crux of the current land question in Zimbabwe and was at the heart of the constitutional crisis in Mozambique in 1990. With regard to the latter, the most controversial issue in the constitutional review of that year was the question of citizenship. The issue centred on whether citizenship in Mozambique should be limited to the original natives (*originarios*), or extended to the Asian and Portuguese settler population (O'Laughlin 2000: 5). The inability of the post-colonial state to engineer economic redistribution and bridge social inequalities based on race, institutionalised in the colonial era, continues to thwart the process of social integration with negative political effects on the issue of citizenship. The question, as Mahmood Mamdani (1998) posed in his inaugural presentation, is: 'when does a settler become a native?'

Finally, with regard to the entrenched state structures, the post-colonial rulers tapped the authoritarian culture and possibilities inherent in the coercive machinery of the state, which included the police force, military, intelligence corps and so on. Those state institutions under colonial rule were basically instruments of oppression and domination of the society. Adapted to the exigency of post-colonial politics, those structures served as the bedrock of dictatorial and authoritarian political regimes in Africa. Authoritarian rule further weakened the capacity of the state and exacerbated the gulf between the state and the citizens. Civil and political rights were gradually withdrawn or foreclosed under authoritarian states. With the already shrinking space for social rights, citizenship became nominal or formalistic, rather than substantive. This development generated hidden spaces of solidarity and resistance by groups – ethnic, religious, civic etc, whose identity formation, mobilisation and activities became contradictory and conflictual to the state in the political process.

In summation, the post-colonial state could neither provide a strong trans-ethnic or secular national identity for its citizens, nor safeguard the values of citizenship. In most cases, the state is submerged in a cesspool of sectarian struggles-ethnic, racial, religious, as its internal processes and constitutive rules are largely influenced or defined by those social elements. Scholars like Archie Mafeje have noted that it is arguable to contend that states exist in Africa. According to Mafeje, a state in order to have firm roots must develop organically out of society and must construct hegemony and legitimacy for itself in society (Mafeje 1999: 67-82). The post-colonial state in Africa has not been able to do this. As such lacking in the basic prerequisites of a state, it is not able to entrench itself as the terminal and major reference point of citizens' identity.

Identity, citizenship and political explosion: Empirical illustrations

The struggle for social inclusion and citizenship rights has been waged in different ways in different African countries. In some countries, it has assumed an armed expression in which ethnic groups take up weapons against each other or the state in the quest to claim their 'rights' as citizens, as occurred in Rwanda and

Burundi. Or there may be a sort of 'low intensity war' amongst groups and communities as in the case of Nigeria. In other cases, the struggle has taken a more inclusive dimension with the clamour and popular agitation for democratisation. Democratisation in Africa is a struggle by the people for civil, political and social rights, which are the substantive social values embodied in citizenship. I narrate below the experience of two countries - Rwanda and Nigeria. The first has just undergone a gruesome period of civil war and genocide, the latter is in a post-military phase in which serious identity-based conflicts hold the potential to undermine the new democratic experiment and the nation-state project.

Rwanda

The Rwandan experience serves as an empirical illustration of this problem. There are two reasons why the case of Rwanda is altogether apposite and lends itself to a serious enquiry on the problem of citizenship. First, Rwanda is a relatively compact country in terms of social composition, which ordinarily should make the evolution of a nation-state less arduous, and inter-group relations, less conflictual. Second, the level of human tragedy that occurred in Rwanda from the inception of that country as an independent state in 1962, peaking with the genocide of 1994, has been alarming. The Rwanda narrative depicts how the colonial construction of group identity was factored into the structures and processes of the state system, a phenomenon that thwarted the logic of a common national identity and equal citizenship for the people of Rwanda. This virus continues to plague the country up to the present.

In social composition and identity, Rwanda is a fairly homogenous country. Its three ethnic categories of the Tutsi, the Hutu and the Twa share the same language, type of social organisation, often the same lifestyles, and have lived together with each other peacefully for centuries while sharing the same collective commitment to monarchical symbols (Adekanye 1996: 38). Colonialism radically transformed the social structures and identity formation of this society. It created rigid identity differentiation and sharp social distinctions among these groups. The background to this development was the colonial cultural mythology and historiography of the Rwandese people, which sought to reconstruct the country's social reality and identity. Colonial historians and anthropologists were the precursors of this historical reconstruction. Using differences in physical traits they claimed that the groups in Rwanda were of different historical origins. The Tutsi were classified as of 'Hamitic' origin, the Hutu as Bantu, and the Twa as pygmies. A curious logic of racial superiority was injected into these scholars' analyses with the claim that the Tutsi were superior human beings than the others. This dubious historical reconstruction as Gerald Prunier (1995: 9) noted became a kind of 'unquestioned "scientific canon", which actually governed the decisions made by the Germans and even more so later by the Belgian colonial authorities'.

In the eyes of the colonial regimes (both German and Belgian), the Tutsi were considered to be white men in black skins in Rwanda. As such, they were formally designated as the first class natives to whom decentralised local power and resources were to be devolved. The Hutu though a majority of the population were conferred with the identity of second-class natives, with the Twa completely relegated to the background.[4] This identity reconstruction by the colonial state underwent the three processes of social influence, which Hebert Kelman (1998) identifies as being central to identity formation and consolidation. These were compliance, identification, and internalisation. All the social groups complied with the new identities conferred upon them (with an initial threat of force) and internalised them through a socialisation and generational cycle. In addition, those identities were codified with the colonial policy of separate identity cards for the groups.

The colonial ideology of racial or group superiority among the native population had both normative and social consequences. In the former regard, the Tutsi identity became the standard or optimal identity by which other forms of social identities were to be measured. Its signs, symbols and meanings became the cultural base for the society. In the latter regard, Tutsi identity came to be synonymous with power, wealth and influence. The Tutsi controlled the native authorities, were in charge of land in the localities, and were the major recipients of colonial education policy. For example by 1959, forty-three out of the forty-five local chiefs and 549 out of 559 sub-chiefs were Tutsi (Prunier 1995: 27).

The colonial state transformed what were flexible and complementary social categories into rigid ethnicities, engineered group identity competition through an inverse process of the domination of one group by another, and gradually undermined the basis of a common national identity and equal citizenship among the Rwandese.

However, as the politics of decolonisation unfolded contradictions began to manifest themselves in the colonial state policy on ethnicities. The Tutsi elite armed with the weapon of western education positioned themselves strategically as the vanguard for self-rule. The Belgian colonial authorities were apparently dissatisfied with the position of their ethnic clientele- the Tutsi- and therefore decided to shift support to the Hutu. This is not a new politics of power control by the colonial authorities. The tendency by colonial powers is to give political support to groups that are least susceptible to nationalist agitation. The same thing happened in Nigeria.[5] This saw the gradual displacement of the Tutsi from the control of the state machinery. Hutus swiftly replaced most of the Tutsi chiefs. Also overt support was given to the Hutu political party.

The decolonisation era saw the emergence of ethnic-based political parties in Rwanda. The major parties were the PARMEHUTU (Rwandan Democratic Party/ party for the movement and of Hutu emancipation) and the UNAR (Rwandese

National Union), which represented the Tutsi. By 1960 when local elections were organised the Hutu emerged as the new local power elite in Rwanda. They won about 80 percent of the seats and took control of the local state; 210 communes came under Hutu control, while the Tutsi had only 19 (Prunier 1995: 52). As the transfer of power gradually proceeded, the sphere of political control by the Hutu also expanded progressively. In September 1961, the legislative elections were held, with the Hutu party winning about 78 percent of the vote and obtaining 35 seats out of a total of forty-four. The process of constructing Hutu hegemony in the political process was capped with the ascendance to power of Gregoire Kayibanda, a Hutu, as president in 1962. Rwanda became independent in July 1962. While the Belgian colonial authorities considered their drastic shift regarding their preferred ethnic clientele in Rwanda as a 'grand revolution', the process generated intense inter-group conflicts. The minority identity group in the political process fought back but commanding only a weak capacity, while the ascending power, the Hutu, unleashed their pent-up aggression and their psychological demeaning of the colonial period on the Tutsis. Between 1959 and 1962, no less than 130,000 Tutsis were driven into exile in the neighbouring countries of Tanzania, Uganda, Zaire and Burundi. Right from independence, the stage appeared set for inter-group conflagration in Rwanda.

From 1962 to 1994, when the pogrom occurred, an ethnic republic in all ramifications, except in name, was instituted in Rwanda. Hutu nationalism took the centre stage in which the Hutu elite sought to make-up for the historical backlog of inadequate social identity and recognition of their ethnic group. The process involved the ethnic appropriation of the state and the establishment of a regime of social exclusion regarding citizenship rights. During this period, to be Hutu was to be a recognised Rwandan citizen, *de facto* and *de jure*, by the state. This qualified the individual to enjoy access to state employment, military service, right of association, participation in state affairs, and security. A uni-ethnic military formation was established in Rwanda, which was a Hutu preserve. A uni-ethnic military formation is a system of institutionalised inequality based on group domination and control of the military (Adekanye 1996: 37-71). It has the potential to destabilise the state, as the excluded groups often have valid fears of insecurity that usually prompts them to recruit, train and organise their own 'unofficial armies'. However, the idea of a uni-ethnic army in Rwanda was not because of what Cynthia Enloe (1980) regarded as the penchant of authoritarian regimes to construct an 'ethnic security map', but fundamentally because a logic of state ethnicisation had been set in motion and institutionalised in Rwanda from the colonial era. The structure of power in post-colonial Rwanda is a Janus-face of its colonial background.

Also, in the post-colonial era, the Hutu elite turned the colonial cultural mythology of Rwandan society on its head, with the argument that if the Tutsi were of a superior race, then they could not have been part of the original local population or the natives. Thus they were at best 'foreigners', and not to be regarded as bona fide citizens of Rwanda. This is the intellectual platform on which the institutional discrimination against the Tutsi was justified. Gerald Prunier puts it quite poignantly:

> Tutsi were still 'foreign invaders' who had come from afar, but now this meant that they could not really be considered as citizens. Their government had been grandiose and powerful: In the new version of the Rwandese ideology, it had been a cruel and homogenously oppressive tyranny. The Hutu had been the 'native peasants', enslaved by the aristocratic invaders: they were now the only legitimate inhabitants of the country. Hutu were the silent demographic majority, which meant that a Hutu controlled government was now not only automatically legitimate but also ontologically democratic (Prunier 1995: 80).

The Rwandan state under both the Kayibanda (1962–1973) and Habyarimana regimes (1973–1994) mirrored its colonial ancestry. The state was the enforcer of exclusive group rights and privileges and provided the institutional context and legitimacy for the discrimination and domination of one group by another. Citizenship was not defined on an individual or common national basis, but from a group dimension. The ethnic identity card policy, which the colonial state instituted, was retained. (It was later to serve as the basis of easy identification of the target group during the human pogrom of 1994). A perverse policy of 'quota democracy' or 'majoritarian rule' was enforced by the state, which reserved 80 percent of all public goods to the Hutus. This policy was the flip side of the colonial one which emphasised the rule or governance by the 'superior species' or 'qualitative rule'. Group identity and social stratification were fused in the state system.

The phenomenon of group exceptionalism or exclusivity became bizarre when Hutu extremists took control of the state. The Hutu irredentists insisted that the Tutsi were not Rwandese and must be forced out of the country. In 1992, a journalist, Hassan Ngeze, published a political catechism known as the Ten Commandments, which was to serve as the Manifesto of the Hutu nationality. Those commandments included:

(i) Every Hutu should know that a Tutsi woman, wherever she is, works for the interest of her ethnic group. As a result, we shall consider a traitor any Hutu who: marries a Tutsi woman, befriends a Tutsi woman or employ a Tutsi woman as a secretary or concubine.

(ii) Every Hutu should know that our Hutu daughters are more suitable and conscientious in their role as women, wife and mother of the family.

(iii) Hutu women be vigilant and try to bring your husbands, brothers and sons back to reason.

(iv) Every Hutu should know that every Tutsi is dishonest in business. His only aim is the supremacy of his ethnic group. As such, any Hutu who does the following is a traitor: makes partnership with a Tutsi in business, invests his money or Government's money in Tutsi enterprise, lends or borrows money from a Tutsi or give favours to a Tutsi in business.

(v)   All strategic positions, political, administrative, economic, military, and security should be entrusted to Hutu.

(vi)   The education sector (school, pupils, students, teachers) must be majority Hutu.

(vii)   The Rwanda armed forces should be exclusively Hutu. No member of the military should marry a Tutsi.

(viii) The Hutu should stop having mercy on the Tutsi.

(ix)   The Hutu, wherever they are must have unity and solidarity and be concerned with the fate of their Hutu brothers.

(x)   The social revolution of 1959, the referendum of 1961, and the Hutu ideology must be taught to every Hutu. Every Hutu must spread this ideology widely. Any Hutu who persecutes his brother Hutu for having read, spread, or taught this ideology is a traitor. (Omar and Waal, cited in Kukah 1998: 17-18).

Group exclusion from citizenship rights, as Anthony Marx (1996: 162) rightly observed, tends to define subordinate identity and usually provokes a struggle for inclusion by the dominated groups. In other words, citizenship thus creates the 'social construct' of relevant identities, with 'oppositional consciousness' forged in reaction to the frame of domination. The Tutsi who have largely become immigrants in neighbouring countries, persecuted at home and vilified abroad by their hosts, were compelled to counter-mobilise for political action. They realised that a 'stateless' individual or group has few rights or claims in a state-driven international system. Between 1980 and 1990, the Tutsi immigrants formed various movements and links abroad, with a view to sharpening their focus and organisation for effecting political change in Rwanda. The result was the birth of the Rwandan Patriotic Front (RPF) in 1990, which waged a ceaseless war against the Habyarimana regime and seized political power in 1994. In the context of the war, no less than 800,000 hapless civilian Tutsis were murdered in what is today referred to as the Rwandan genocide.

How best, then, can the Rwandan tragedy be problematised? My persuasion is that what happened in Rwanda transcends the issue of elite manipulation of ethnicity. It is also not simply a case of shared material deprivation. It is a destructive phenomenon of social identity competition grounded in the historical trappings of the construction of citizenship and rights in Rwanda. Rights and citizenship had been largely defined and institutionalised as a group affair, which were synthesised in the cultural and historical processes of the Rwandan society as reconstructed and legitimised by the colonial state. Citizenship in its normative and instrumentalist dimensions, both in the colonial and post-colonial era, as I have shown in the above narrative, was not a 'universal' and common public good. It was exclusionary and bifurcated. This is the basis of the intractable political conflicts and the civil war which enveloped Rwanda.

Nigeria

Nigeria is a multi-ethnic and multi-religious society and perhaps a classic case of an artificial nation state. Apart from the fact that the nation underwent a civil war between 1967 and 1970; in the last two decades there has been the resurgence of identity-based conflicts mostly of ethno-religious dimensions. These conflicts have seen communities and clans take up arms against each other, with religious groups adopting extreme positions insisting on a particular religious code as the basis for civil law and judicial matters. The secular nature of the Nigerian state as enshrined in the 1999 constitution is in retreat, subjected to various legal interpretations and redefinitions. The communal conflicts that have unravelled the nation are threatening the nation's nascent democratic rule, which was established in May 1999.

An intriguing phenomenon about these conflicts is that they span the entire breadth of the country, embracing the different geo-political zones. They also assume both rural and urban dimensions. In the Southern part of the country, there is the Ife-Modakeke, Ijaw-Ilaje, Umuleri-Aguleri conflicts, in the northern part there is the Tiv-Junkun, Zangon-Kataf, and the Chamba and Kuteb conflicts - amongst others. Added to this, are the religious-based crises spurred by the introduction of the Sharia penal code in some northern parts of the country. This has ignited serious infernos in places like Kaduna, Kano and Jos. This crisis has led to forms of spatial relocation among religious groups. Muslims have now moved to concentrate in one area and Christians in another. This is what Momoh (2001: 5) refers to as the creation of Mecca for the Muslims in Kaduna North and Jerusalem for the Christians in Kaduna South, and in Kano, the creation of America for the Christians and Afghanistan for the Muslims. This crisis becomes more acute as the boundaries between ethnic and religious identities tend to overlap.

Major urban cities like Lagos and Kano that are mostly cosmopolitan in composition have also witnessed a new dimension of ethnic-based urban violence. There has been the rise of ethnic militias, whose interest is to protect their ethnic interests in those localities, and they insist on the ideology of 'home rule' or 'indigeneity', which comes down to exclusive claims of territorial control of the social space in those areas. The logic of inclusion and exclusion is based on ethnic identity. The ranks of the ethnic militias include the Oodua People's Congress (OPC), Arewa People's Congress (APC), Egbesu Boys, and Ijaw Youths. Claims over social goods of land, control of markets, local government authorities, etc. have led to serious violence and conflicts among the ethnic militias.

The scales of human tragedy that often accompany identity-based violence in Nigeria are monumental. In the last four years no less than ten thousand people have lost their lives in communal, ethnic and religious violence. An unprecedented loss of property and social displacement also occurred. For instance in the Kaduna religious crisis of February 2000, no less than 1,400 people were reportedly killed, over 1,944 buildings comprising of hotels, business centres and residential accommodation were destroyed, and about 70,000 people displaced (Abdu 2002: 127-128). In the Tiv-Jukun communal conflict of November 2001, it is estimated that no less than 2,000 people were killed and property worth over N50 million destroyed, with over 50,000 people displaced as internal refugees.

Closely linked to these conflicts is the social construction of citizenship in Nigeria, which either confers or excludes rights depending on the categorisation of inhabitants. Although in a juridical sense, the Nigerian constitution talks about a common national citizenship, the same constitution sanctions local rights and citizenship through the notion of 'indigeneity'. By and large, the constitution places more emphasis on the ethnic entry point to citizenship claims. There are four levels of citizenship in Nigeria, which mostly correspond with the levels of political power in the country. There is the communal citizenship that incorporates the indigenous people of the locality, followed by the citizens of a local government, which is an aggregate of indigenous people of a particular local government area. The next layer is that of state citizenship, and the final level is the national or federal citizenship. These layers of citizenship are in an ascending order, and the baseline of inclusion is one's ethnic or communal identity, and not residence. At virtually all these levels discriminatory practices occur and are sanctioned by the state. Access to public goods like employment, land, school enrolment and fees for children, and business transactions are determined by this ethnic identity. Thus, the logic of separateness is not only emphasised but also reinforced by this social construction of citizenship in Nigeria.

The consequences are threefold. First is that the spirit of 'otherness', or 'we' and 'them' is tangible in many communities. In other words, it becomes expedient to identify and label the 'settlers' or 'foreigners' as opposed to the 'indigenes' or 'natives'. The 'indigenes' are the 'sons of the soil', and no matter where they may live they can at any time make claims in their communal territory. In the same vein, no matter how long a 'settler' has resided in a particular locality he/she remains a 'stranger'. Second is that in the urge to claim 'indigeneity', social histories are being reconstructed and reinterpreted by different groups with the sole aim of appropriating 'ownership' of the community. This by itself generates conflict. Third, is that groups are usually set in contestation with one another based on the divisive social dichotomy of 'indigenes' and 'settlers'. In a situation of shrinking social resources, excruciating economic crisis, retreat of the welfare state and its consequences on contracting social services, and a market ideology of 'fend for yourself', sharp divisions are wrought in social relationships, in which the citizenship issue becomes a major weapon of economic and social competition. Conflict becomes inevitable in this context. The Citizens Forum for Constitutional Reform (CFCR), a coalition of NGOs brought together on a single issue of constitutional reform in Nigeria, notes:

> This multi-layered system of citizenship breeds confusion and controversy. It inhibits the development of national unity and the evolution of harmonious political community. One obvious consequence is that it inevitably engenders discrimination in jobs, land purchase, housing, admission into educational institutions, marriages, business transactions and the distribution of social welfare services. Many Nigerians are therefore forced to limit their social and political horizons, as the only level of realising the essence of citizenship is the lowest level of identity (Citizens Forum for Constitutional Reform 2002: 12).

The scale and intensity of the conflicts engendered by the crisis of identity based on the politics of citizenship undermines the new democratic regime of President Olusegun Obasanjo. Deeply concerned by the situation, the federal government in 2002 set up a Presidential Committee on Provisions for and Practice of Citizenship in Nigeria. The committee is yet to submit its report. A major current of public opinion in Nigeria considers that in order to attenuate the 'low intensity war' that characterises the relationship between many communal, ethnic and religious groups, the concept of citizenship has to be clearly redefined in a sharp and concise manner.

Conclusion: Putting things back together

The current civil war in Côte d'Ivoire is another example underlining the fact that the question of citizenship is yet to be resolved in Africa. One of the major demands of the rebels in the country is for an inclusive conception of citizenship in which 'settlers' and 'foreigners'[7] will be incorporated with equal rights and benefits. The country is dangerously polarised into two camps: those who support the rebels – mostly the 'foreigners', and those who support the government – mostly the 'indigenes'. This dimension to the conflict makes peace negotiations very tenuous, with fanatical supporters and deeply conflicting views on both sides.

However, engendering peace, security and stability in Africa is a task which must be accomplished by Africans if the quest for development is ever to take firm root on the continent. Clearly, war and debilitating conflicts are antithetical to development. Negotiating peace and stability will require reconceptualising citizenship from a group to a national or 'universal' perspective and re-individualising it. Citizenship is destructive of the social and political processes of a political community when conceived in group terms. It undermines national identity and attenuates the loyalty and commitment of the citizen to the state.

Putting things back together in Africa will require policy changes in two major areas. First, it is necessary to begin to take liberal democracy very seriously. It is a means through which some of the values embodied in citizenship can be realised. Liberal democratic norms like elections, political participation, the rule of law, and the right of association and expression, could provide the basis for the expression of citizenship in its substantive form. However, for this to be the case, political development should be an all-inclusive process in which all state structures and institutions are to be democratised. This process should transcend and obliterate the rural-urban, and the central-local state dichotomies. In other words, there should be the evolution of what Elizabeth Jelin (1996: 101) described as a new culture of citizenship 'from below', intertwined with formal institutional changes and the expansion of democratic practices and norms.

A second priority is to tackle the normative dimension of citizenship, which the liberal democratic project cannot guarantee. Who qualifies to be a citizen, and who does not, even in the juridical sense? How is national identity to be forged over and above sub-national or group identities and how is the state to be the primary and terminal point of citizens' loyalty and commitment are issues which relate to, but transcend, the liberal democratic project. These questions have a bearing on how the state is constituted and how the direction of state policy ensures that the state affects the life-chances of the citizens in a just and equitable manner, such that subordinate identities do not contest the legitimacy of the state in society.

Notes

1. The nature of Africa's political history, its diverse social and ethnic composition, the character of the state, the problem of poverty and acute material shortages and other endemic socio-political problems, make many African countries susceptible to conflicts.

2. In countries like Tanzania and Mozambique where centralist socialist policies were adopted in the immediate post-independence era, traditional authorities were abolished and replaced with state agents. However, this did not promote the democratisation of the local structures, but only substituted a decentralised with a centralised form of despotism.

3. The federal character principle is a provision in the Nigerian constitution that seeks to provide for state, ethnic and regional balancing in public appointment opportunities at the federal level. It is meant to give equal access to all groups in the country through equal representation of states in

federal public appointments. The objective is to prevent the marginalisation and domination of one group over another.

4. The Twa constitute about 3 percent of the population in Rwanda. They do not feature prominently in identity group politics in the country.

5. In Nigeria the preference of the British colonial regime with regard to the transfer of power in the decolonisation era was the Hausa-Fulani aristocracy, who have a conservative political outlook, with little or no agitation for the political independence of Nigeria. Indeed, when Anthony Enahoro raised the motion of self-government at the Federal House of Representatives in 1953, the Hausa-Fulani political elite opposed this. They argued that they were unprepared for independence. Also, the same thing occurred in the Sudan, where the preference of the British colonial authorities was for the Northern political elite, with a conservative bent.

6. Nigeria has over 250 ethnic groups with numerous religious beliefs, however, Islam and Christianity are the two dominant forms of religions.

7. Those regarded as 'settlers' and 'foreigners' are either people whose second generation has lived in the country or were born in the country. They by no yardstick qualify as foreigners, yet they are so regarded.

References

Abdul, H., 2002, 'Ethno-Religious Crisis in Kaduna: Impact on Women and Children', in E. Alamika and F. Okoye (eds.), *Ethno-Religious Conflicts and Democracy in Nigeria: Challenges*, Kaduna: Human Rights Monitor.

Adejumobi, S., 2001, 'Citizenship, Rights and the Problem of Conflicts and Civil Wars in Africa', *Human Rights Quarterly*, Vol. 23, No.1.

Adejumobi, S., 1999, 'Reconstructing the Future: Africa and the Challenge of Democracy and Good Governance in the 21st Century', *Development and Socio-Economic Progress*, No.75. January/June.

Adedeji, A., 1999, ed., *Comprehending and Mastering African Conflicts: The Search for Sustainable Peace and Good Governance*, London: Zed Books.

Adekanye, B., 1996, 'Rwanda/Burundi: Uni-ethnic Dominance and The Cycle of Armed Ethnic Formations', *Social Identities*, 2 (1).

Adekanye, B., 1995, 'Structural Adjustment, Democratisation and Rising Ethnic Tensions in Africa', *Development and Change*, 26 (2).

Ake, C., 1980, *A Political Economy of Africa*, London: Longman.

Ali, T. and Mathews, R., eds., 1999, *Civil Wars in Africa: Roots and Resolution*, Montreal: McGill-Queen's University Press.

Annan, K., 1998, 'The Causes of Conflict and the Promotion of Durable Peace and Sustainable Development in Africa', Report of the Secretary General on Africa to the Security Council. Mimeograph, April.

Aristotle, 1958, *The Politics*, Edited and Translated by Ernest Baker, London: Oxford University Press.

Asiwaju, A., 1976, *Western Yorubaland Under European Rule (1889–1945)*, London: Longman.

Brubakar, R., 1992, *Citizenship and Nationhood in France and Germany*, Cambridge: Harvard University Press.

Boudin, J., 1945, *Method for Easy Comprehension of History*, Translated by Beatrice Reynolds, New York.

Citizens Forum for Constitutional Reform, 2002, *Memoranda Submitted to the Presidential Committee on the Provisions for and Practice of Citizenship and Rights in Nigeria and the Presidential Committee on National Security in Nigeria*, Lagos: CFCR.

Copson, R., 1994, *Africa's Wars and Prospects for Peace*, New York: M.E. Sharpe.

Crowder, M. and Ikime, O., 1970, 'Introduction', in Michael Crowder and Obaro Ikime (eds.) *West African Chiefs: Their Changing Status Under Colonial Rule and Independence*, New York and Ile-Ife: African Publishing Corporation and University of Ife Press.

Egwu, S., 2001, *Ethnic and Religious Violence in Nigeria*, Abuja: AFRIGOV.

Ekeh, P., 1975, 'Colonialism and the Two Publics in Africa: A Theoretical Statement', *Comparative Studies in Society and History*, (17) 1.

Ekeh, P., 1972, 'Citizenship and Political Conflict: A Sociological Interpretation of the Nigerian Crisis', in J. Okpaku (ed.) *Nigeria: Dilemma of Nationhood*, New York: The Third World Press.

Ekeh, P., 1980, 'Colonialism and Social Structure', Inaugural Lecture, University of Ibadan, Nigeria.

Enloe, C., 1980, *Ethnic Soldiers*, Athens, GA: University of Georgia Press.

Grodzin, M., 1966, *The Loyal and the Disloyal: Social Boundaries of Patriotism and Treason*, Cleveland.

Gurr, T., 1994, *Minority at Risk: A Global View of Ethno-Political Conflicts*, Washington: United States Institute for Peace.

Huntington, S., 1996, *The Clash of Civilizations and the Remaking of the World Order*, New York: Touchstone.

Ikime, O., ed., 1980, *Groundwork on Nigerian History*, Ibadan: Heinemann.

Jelin, E., 1996, 'Citizenship Revisited: Solidarity, Responsibility and Rights', in Elizabeth Jelin and Eric Herhberg (eds.) *Constructing Democracy: Human Rights, Citizenship, and Society in Latin America*, Boulder: Westview.

Kelman, C., 1998, 'The Place of Ethnic Identity in the Development of Personal Identity: A Challenge for the Jewish Family', in Peter Meddling (ed.) *Coping with Life and Death: Jewish Families in the 20th Century*, Oxford: Oxford University Press.

Kerber, L., 1997, 'The Meaning of Citizenship', *The Journal of American History*, December.

Kukah, M., 1998, 'The Fractured Microcosm: The African Condition and the Search for Moral Balance in the New World Order', Lagos State University, Faculty of Social Sciences Guest Lecture Series 1, June.

Lake, D. and Rothchild, D., 1996, 'Ethnic Fears and Global Engagement: The International Spread and Management of Global Conflict', Report of the International Global Conflict and Cooperation Working Group on the Spread and Management of Ethnic Conflict, Mimeograph.

Longva, A., 1995, 'Citizenship, Identity and the Question of Supreme Loyalty: The Case of Kuwait', *Forum for Development Studies*, No.2.

Nabudere, D., 1999, 'African States and Conflict in Africa', in Henrich Boll Foundation (ed.) *Networking With a View To Promoting Peace: Conflicts in the Horn of Africa*, Addis Ababa: Henrich Boll.

Mafeje, A., 1999, 'State and Civil Society in Independent Africa', in Henrich Boll Foundation (ed.) *Networking With a View To Promoting Peace: Conflicts in the Horn of Africa*, Addis Ababa: Henrich Boll.

Mamdani, M., 2001, *When Victims Become Killers: Colonialism, Nativism and Genocide in Rwanda*, Princeton: Princeton University Press.

Mamdani, M., 2000, 'Indirect Rule and the Struggle for Democracy: A response to Bridget O'Laughlin', *African Affairs*, 99.

Mamdani, M., 1998, 'When Does a Settler Become a Native? Reflections on the Colonial Roots of Citizenship in Equatorial and South Africa', Inaugural Lecture, May 13, University of Cape Town, South Africa.

Mamdani, M., 1996, *Citizen and Subject: Contemporary Africa and the Legacy of Late Colonialism*, Princeton: Princeton University Press.

Marshall, T., 1964, *Class, Citizenship and Social Development*, New York: Doubleday and Company Inc.

Marx, A., 1996, 'Contested Citizenship: The Dynamics of Racial Identity and Social movements', in Charles Tilly (ed.) 'Citizenship, Identity and Social History', *International Review of Social History*, Supplement 3, Cambridge: Cambridge University Press.

Mazrui, A., 1999, 'Identity Politics and the Nation-State Under Siege: Towards a Theory of Reverse Evolution', *Social Dynamics*, Vol. 25, No.2.

Momoh, A., 2001, 'Even Birds Have a Home: Explaining the Pathologies of the Citizenship Question in Nigeria', Empowerment and Action Research Centre (EMPARC) Annual Lecture Series, No. 7.

O'Laughlin, B., 2000, 'Class and the Customary: The Ambiguous Legacy of the Indigenato in Mozambique', *African Affairs*, 99.

Onimode, B., 1988, *A Political Economy of the African Crisis*, London: Zed Books.

Oomen, T., 1997, *Citizenship, Nationality and Ethnicity: Reconciling Competing Identities*, Cambridge: Polity Press.

Osaghae, E., 1990, 'The Problems of Citizenship in Nigeria', *AFRICA: Revista Trimestrale di Studi e documentazione* (Roma), Vol. XLV, No. 4, December.

Prunier, G., 1995, *The Rwandan Crisis, 1959-1994: History of a Genocide*, London: Hurst.

Sanberg, K. and Smith, D., 1994, 'Conflicts in Africa', *Afrika Mellon Konfleter Og Utrkling*, Inormasjonshefte, No.2.

Tilly, C., 1996, 'Citizenship, Identity and Social History', in Charles Tilly (ed.) 'Citizenship, Identity and Social History', *International Review of Social History*, Supplement 3, Cambridge: Cambridge University Press.

United Nations Institute for Social Development (UNRISD), 2001, *Invisible Hands: Taking Responsibility for Social Development*, Geneva: UNRISD.

Wallerstein, P., and Sollenberg, M., 1999, 'Armed Conflict', *Journal of Peace Research*, 39 (5).

Walshe, P., 1971, *The Rise of African Nationalism in South Africa*, Berkeley: University of California Press.

Walzer, M., 1970, *Obligations: Essays on Disobedience, War and Citizenship*, Cambridge: MIT Press.

World Bank, 1999, *African Development Indicators: 1999/2000*, Washington: World Bank.

2

The State in West Africa: The Crisis of Production, Democracy and National Identity

Abeeku Essuman-Johnson

Introduction

In the 1960s, West Africa was the haven of African refugees fleeing the conflicts resulting from the racist and apartheid regimes in Southern Africa. Refugees from South Africa, Mozambique, Namibia, Zimbabwe and Angola found refuge in relatively peaceful West African countries. There were no conflicts that generated refugees as with the situation in Eastern and Southern Africa. In its contemporary setting the sub-region however is a far cry from the peace and stability it knew in the 1960s. West Africa now rivals the Great Lakes region of Central Africa as the hotbed of conflict, as has been demonstrated by the conflicts in Sierra Leone, Liberia, Casamance in Senegal, Guinea Bissau, Côte d'Ivoire, Togo and Nigeria. Some of the conflicts, namely those that raged in Sierra Leone, Liberia, Côte d'Ivoire and Nigeria, have been particularly horrific. The conflict in Sierra Leone was particularly infamous for the hacking-off of the limbs of non-combatants by the ferocious Revolutionary United Front (RUF) rebels. The conflicts in Liberia and Côte d'Ivoire witnessed the unpleasant use of children as combatants and saw the indiscriminate killing of innocent civilians. The conflicts in Nigeria have been between ethnic groups, religious groups and in some cases between the state, as represented by the army, and other ethnic groups. All these events combined have earned West Africa the image of a region in protracted turmoil. Even though one might argue that the West African conflicts come nowhere near the genocide in the Great Lakes, these conflicts have attracted global attention for their banality and ferocity as warring groups engaged themselves in an orgy of violence. Guinea Bissau has experienced series of low intensity conflicts for some time, which came to a head in the military intervention to oust the government of President Kumba Yala. A similar low intensity conflict has been raging in the Casamance region of Senegal. The Sierra Leone and Liberia conflicts required the intervention of UN and ECOWAS peacekeeping forces.

Nations and states in West Africa

Most West African countries attained independence in the 1960s, following Ghana which attained independence in 1957. The nationalist leaders who led the struggle for independence looked to the future with hope that they would lead their countries to nationhood and democracy. Ali Mazrui has argued that Francophone African countries did better at nation building due to the French policy of assimilation. This absorption of the educated Francophone elite into the French colonial administrative system meant that nationalism was late in developing in Francophone Africa. The Francophone elite ended up sitting as deputies in the French chamber of deputies. Anglophone Africa on the other hand did better at state building due to the British policy of developing human and economic resources within its vast outposts. The British policy of Indirect Rule sought to use indigenous political institutions for local government and the selection of indigenes to sit on the advisory law making body - the legislative councils. This had the effect of excluding the educated elite who, in turn, engaged in proto-nationalistic activity to make a case for their inclusion in the subsisting colonial system. The early nationalists were opposed to the colonial system in so far as it excluded them. In their struggle for inclusion, they stirred and touched off nationalist sentiments among the population, putting them at the vanguard of political nationalism and the movement towards independence in British West Africa. It also explains to a certain extent why nationalism was both slow and late in maturing in French compared to British West Africa. Whereas the territoriality of French West Africa tended to weld Francophone West Africa more into nation builders, the individual state-building process taking place in Anglophone West Africa encouraged the emergence of states rather than nations. This chapter conceptualises the crises of the state in West Africa along three mutually reinforcing levels: the crisis of production, the crisis of democracy, and the crisis of national identity and nationhood.

The crisis of production

The crisis of production in West Africa, like the wider crisis in sub-Saharan Africa, is the result of the underdevelopment of productive forces, reflected in external indebtedness, weak national economies, dwindling levels of food production, all culminating in economic crisis and overall national poverty which many West African countries have been experiencing for some time now

(Rugumamu 2001). This crisis is related to the growing division of the world into the industrialised north and the under-developed south. The north maintains a near monopoly over the centres of industrial research, technology and production. The under-developed south relies on the importation of know-how, technology and finance - all under the control of the north. The net effect of this lopsided development of the world is that the organic balance between people in the underdeveloped south and the natural environment is broken. The imposition of the world market, now globalisation, on the system of production in most under-developed countries is such that it has adversely altered the traditional system of production and the management of the environment. It has tended to undermine the confidence of people in these countries to harness their resources creatively to meet pressing needs and interests. The impact of this character of production relations in the underdeveloped countries of Africa is that most of the countries have become extremely vulnerable to drought, desert encroachment and floods. The slightest negative ecological condition results in massive famine and refugees, as has been the case in Ethiopia and the Sahelian zone of West Africa. The point to note is that rarely do these harsh ecological conditions represent novel events. However the processes that generated the underdevelopment of the continent have destroyed the traditional strategies for coping with these natural conditions, and no viable alternatives have developed, as the Karamoja famines have shown.

Considering the situation of Africa and globalisation, Rugumamu (2001) points out that the African continent remains marginal to almost all the major global trends. Particularly during the last three decades, the share of African countries in the global distribution of wealth and power has witnessed a steady reversal. Whatever aspect one considers- security, foreign investment, aid, trade, the information revolution, and skilled labour force- the African outlook gives little or no cause for jubilation. While the dynamics of intense economic competition, technological advancement and economic integration were underway in much of the world in the past two decades, African countries were engrossed in a succession of crises. While the short- and medium-term prospects for most African countries and peoples are depressing and bleak, the challenges required to surmount existing problems are also daunting. It has become increasingly clear to most analysts and policy makers across the continent that in order to arrest the scourge of marginalisation and exclusion, Africans have to embrace fully the strategy of cooperation and integration before sustainable national growth and development can become a reality. The Abuja Treaty on African Economic Cooperation and Integration as well as the Sirte Declaration on African Political Union speak eloquently to the urgency of this development strategy.

The on-going processes of globalisation, regionalisation and liberalisation are posing entirely new sets of complex challenges to the unstable, debt-ridden, aid-dependent, and technologically backward African economies. The capacity of individual countries to function effectively and in a sustainable manner is becoming increasingly compromised. As far back as the late 1970s, the social and economic conditions on the continent have been widely rated as the worst in the world. This was unambiguously reflected in the weak growth in productive sectors, a poor export performance, mounting debt, deterioration in social conditions, environmental degradation, and the collapse of the politico-institutional order. Of the forty-seven countries classified by the United Nations as the least developed, no less than thirty-two are found in sub-Saharan Africa. In 1992, the UN General Assembly added Zambia, former Zaire, and Madagascar to the list of the least developed countries. Botswana and Mauritius were the first two African countries to graduate from this club of the destitute (Harsh 1992: 11). Even more telling, the incidence and depth of poverty have been on the rise since the 1970s. It was estimated that about fifty percent of the sub-Saharan African population live in abject poverty. The World Bank (1993) predicted in the early 1990s that given the continent's exceptionally high population growth rates - over 3 percent a year - and low economic development, as many as 100 million more Africans could be living in poverty at the turn of the twenty-first century. Reflecting on this gloomy scenario, the 1997 Human Development Report concluded, '... in a global economy of $25 trillion, this is a scandal - reflecting shameful inequalities and inexcusable failure of national and international policies' (UNDP 1997: 2).

Thus, with the end of the Cold War, and the inauguration of the 'New World Order' in 1991 by the then US President George Bush, Africa entered the twenty-first century marginalised from the world economy, yet highly dependent on it. Looking further ahead, Africa may expect to face a diplomatic and political deflation potentially as great as its economic marginalisation. Now that the Russian strategic and ideological interests in Africa have declined, the West can also afford to reduce its interests. Evidently, this is already occurring on a daily basis. The European Union (EU), which includes Africa's former colonial masters and close Cold War allies, has markedly shifted its development cooperation priorities away from the continent. This is reflected largely in the recently concluded ACP-EU Partnership Agreement in which the EU is seeking to replace non-reciprocity trade with reciprocal trade arrangements. The apparent failure of sub-Saharan African economies in the 1980s and 1990s led to a climate of doubt and 'Afro-pessimism' regarding the prospects of Euro-African relations. In recent years, the EU has come to demonstrate increasing interest in the neighbouring countries of the Mediterranean region as well as in growth areas of South America, notably the Southern Cone Common Market (MERCONSUR). Compared to African countries, the Mediterranean region seems to have greater economic potential and greater political significance, not least because of EU fears of immigration from the region and the spread of religious fundamentalism. In all these political and economic configurations, Africa has fallen to the bottom of the global development agenda.

With the end of the Cold War and the collapse of the Soviet Union, Africa has lost key advocates for its cause in major international organisations, particularly within the UN. The former Soviet Union and other East European socialist countries were often allies of Africa in world affairs. On most issues of concern to Africa, members of the old Warsaw Pact could be relied on to vote with those forces in Africa that were eager for change. The collapse of communism in Eastern Europe, the disintegration of the Soviet Union and the dismantling of the Warsaw Pact, have produced an Eastern Europe far more likely to be attentive to the wishes of Washington than the yearnings of Third World countries in general, and Africa in particular. As will be argued in subsequent pages, with the conclusion of the Cold War and the end of ideological conflicts, Africa is becoming geo-politically and economically irrelevant to the major Western powers and other important global actors. It is little wonder then that the West's gradual loss of any real interest in the continent in the coming years and decades seems almost inevitable.

Against this larger issue of a crisis of production raises some thought-provoking implications of the New World Order for Africa. For instance, does the end of the Cold War imply that there will be a peace dividend for the world at large, let alone Africa? How can the reality of the continent's appalling circumstances and the growing sense of despair be turned into hope and opportunity? How can African economies, singly and collectively, position themselves strategically to minimise the imminent costs of globalisation? If African unity is the continent's sole salvation, what kinds of cooperation and integration arrangements are likely to secure her economic and political emancipation in the emerging global economy? What sorts of internal restructuring are needed to empower the region to take advantage of the current and future changes in the global order? What framework of rules and institutions should be put in place to preserve the advantages of global markets and competition while ensuring that globalisation works for people and not just for profits?

Once again, the current crisis of production in Africa demonstrates the illusion, and indeed, the impossibility, of independent national development strategies. It is argued that a collective structural transformation is central to Africa's survival. The issue is whether Africa survives this globalised system of production. The signs are not too good for Africa. West African countries as members of the World Trade Organization (WTO) are obliged to participate in liberalised world trade arrangements, which for all intents and purposes will take a long time to earn them any benefits. It does not look like there will be much in the new globalised market for West African countries that would change their position as the hewers of wood and drawers of water in the global system.

The crisis of democracy

The political stability that the new countries of West Africa needed to enable them fashion nation-states out of their diverse ethnic groups was soon shattered by the military in the first interventions in Togo, Benin and Nigeria. Like a contagion, coups became the order of the day in West Africa, with Ghana, Sierra Leone, and Burkina Faso also falling victim to military takeovers. By the end of the 1960s coups had occurred in other countries in the sub-region, demonstrating a growing crisis of governance, and of democracy in Africa.

At independence nationalist leaders in the sub-region looked forward to developing nations whose platforms can then be used to perform better than the departing colonialists. Ostensibly, the nationalists had learned the system of 'democratic' procedures of the colonial powers, namely the parliamentary system of the British and the strong presidential system of the French. But the new states soon set about tinkering with the system of governance that they inherited. They argued that the system was not in tune with the traditional system of governance of the country concerned. Leopold Senghor for example argued:

> Europeans, from the West and from the East, often speak to us of democracy, each in his own way. Yet we have our own conception of democracy, the African conception, in no way inferior to that of Europe. We would do well to go back to it. It is founded, at least among the Negroes and the Berbers, on the palaver. Palaver is a dialogue, or rather a discussion, where everyone speaks taking his turn, expressing his opinion... But when everyone had expressed his opinion, the minority followed the majority so that there was unanimity (Cited in Riley, n.d: 3).

Such notions underpinned the views of first generation nationalist leaders like Julius Nyerere of Tanzania, Leopold Senghor of Senegal, Kenneth Kaunda of Zambia and Kwame Nkrumah of Ghana. The early African leaders saw traditional African life as egalitarian and democratic in doctrine and practice. This view gave an historical justification for single party rule and a post-independence socialist strategy. Soon opposition parties became endangered species and the organic ossification of political parties began. Most countries progressed from a multi-party system at independence to a two-party system, then a one-party system and finally to a no-party system. The one-party system developed into authoritarian form of governance across Africa. The problem here is captured in the popular saying of those in favour of multi-party politics in Tanzania: 'Even God has allowed opposition by allowing Satan to live among His people' (Riley, n.d: 1).

The evidence is that Africans were quietly opposed to the one-party system that was paraded across Africa as the system of governance of choice. Before standing down, former President Julius Nyerere recanted his earlier advocacy and institutionalisation of a one-party system in Tanzania. In April 1991, Nyerere's successor, President Ali Hassan Mwinyi, established a commission on the possibility of introducing multi-party democracy. Following that, growing domestic pressure for change, coupled with a new insistence by external aid donors and creditors on 'good governance', democracy and human rights, was to herald the introduction of multi-party politics in Tanzania.

In West Africa, the crisis of democracy manifested itself in the twin issues of one-party civilian President-for-life systems and military regimes that existed in the 1960s and 1970s as well as the general issue of poor governance. The only country in the sub-region that did not fall victim to either of the two non-democratic systems was Senegal. It took the intervention of external donors and creditors in the 1990s to get African countries back on the path of democratic governance. The crisis of democracy with its one party and military regimes was to lead to the creation of refugees across Africa and West Africa. The problem of refugees and displaced persons in the sub-region and Africa generally since independence in the 1960s has been the direct result of the lack of democracy and the subsequent struggle for control of national political space. In West Africa the major conflict areas have been Sierra Leone, Liberia, Côte d'Ivoire and Togo. The conflicts in all these countries led to the flight of refugees to neighbouring countries.

The crisis of democracy is not simply to be understood in terms of the failure of Western liberal democracy in Africa, whose death knell was sounded in the early days of independence with the spate of military coups. The crisis of democracy in Africa is much more far-reaching: the conditions of increasing exploitation, inequality, poverty and discrimination under which most African people live, the denial of human rights, growing political repression and the militarisation of social life were some of the deepest manifestations of the democratic crisis. However, the most blatant expression of the crisis of democracy in Africa, which is germane to the growing number of refugees and displaced persons, is the untrammelled competition for state power, which has become a hallmark of the African political landscape. These struggles for power, in which the control of the state is reduced to a zero-sum game, have accounted for the displacement of millions of Africans. Uganda, Liberia, Sierra Leone and Somalia have been classic cases of this condition.

Civilian-style politics, with regular elections and peaceful change of government, have not been the norm in post-colonial Africa. Military-led coups d'état represent the typical way in which regimes were changed and rule by the military was as widespread as that by civilians. According to McGowan and Johnson (1986: 539-546), between 1956 when the Sudan became the first country to achieve independence from colonial rule and 1985, 126 plots to overthrow African governments were reported; 71 were attempted and 60 coups were carried out in 40 out of the 45 independent African countries. The worst example was the situation in South Africa, where the Apartheid regime's policy of racial segregation, injustice, prejudice and political repression combined to displace millions of South Africans while thousands were forced into exile.

The other aspect of the crisis of democracy relates to poor governance by both civilian and military rulers. The exercise of power, in the broad sense of the word, extends the notion of governance to include the management of people, their livelihood and their relationships. It includes the activities that condition the existence of people: the economy (corporate governance) and the political sphere (the state, institutions, public goods, standards, 'rules of the game' etc.). It also embraces culture, society, management of differences, and competition for access to state resources, cultural differences, religious differences and so on. Although occurring at a slow pace, the framework for viable political, economic and social systems are beginning to emerge and take hold, despite having been significantly weakened by festering social instability and violent conflicts. The governments of West Africa largely endorse this assessment. In the current politics of democratisation, once the governments have met the requirements of the funding agencies, there is an erroneous assumption that the 'universal laws of democracy' as perceived by the West, is being respected. If this thesis were borne out by the facts, then African countries should be able, using their own resources and support from their donor friends, to overcome conflict, eradicate poverty and endemic diseases, undertake activities that generate wealth and well-being, and find acceptable responses to most of the vital needs of their citizenry.

This, however, is not the case presently. There is no illusion about African countries being able to eradicate poverty under the Highly Indebted Poor Countries (HIPC) status- especially if one recalls that years of neo-liberal structural adjustment programmes (SAP) could not preclude or prevent a country like Ghana from being classified as a HIPC, thereby qualifying for World Bank-assisted poverty reduction intervention. Another manifestation of the crisis of democracy is the emergence and growth of violent crises that generate structural instability in which at the same time that old modes of production are collapsing, new ones emerge to put affected countries on the path to national development. Clearly all attempts to find salvation in viable political and economic systems were either lost along the way or failed outright. Despite the serious problems facing the continent, the overwhelming trend is towards reform programmes inspired by local experiences with governance, and comparative experiences from other countries instead of externally-driven initiatives advocated or imposed from outside.

The crisis of national identity and nationhood

The crisis of national identity is illustrated by the intensive politicisation of ethnicity, ethnic conflicts and wars in modern Africa. Generally, the spate of ethnic, racial and religious conflicts in Africa is symptomatic of an unending crisis of national identity. Nigeria, DR Congo, Burundi, Rwanda, Sudan, Ethiopia, Somalia, Sierra Leone and Côte d'Ivoire are only a few of the countries where this has led to open armed conflicts between groups and against the state, leaving in their wake, an unprecedented displacement of people as refugees. For example, most of Ethiopia's over one million refugees are products of the struggles between the Amhara-controlled Ethiopian state and other national groupings like the Eritreans, Oromo, Sidama, Somali and Tigray (Bulcha 1988). This struggle culminated in the collapse of the government of Mengistu Haile Mariam in 1991 and the acknowledgement of Eritrea by the new government in Addis Ababa as sovereign and independent entity. In Burundi in 1992, massive Tutsi reprisals against the Hutu led to the flight of 40,000 Hutu into Zaire, 40,000 into Tanzania and another 20,000 into Rwanda (US Committee for Refugees 1991). The 1994 genocide in Rwanda was largely the work of extremists in the entourage of President Habyarimana who were not prepared to tolerate any power-sharing agreement with the Rwanda Patriotic Front (RPF) and moderate Hutus as provided for by the Arusha Peace Agreement of 4 August 1993; believing that by implementing this agreement to the letter would eventually erode or undermine their control over the country and its vast resources. Rather, they rallied around the exclusionist ideology of 'Hutu Power', according to which killing a Tutsi was considered an epic civic duty (Mamdani 1982). Following the defeat of the Hutu extremist by the RPF, thousands of their compatriots fled to Goma in Eastern Democratic Republic of Congo, DRC (Nzongola-Ntalaja 2001: 13). In Nigeria, the civil war of 1967–1970 over the attempted secession of the predominantly Igbo Eastern region led to the displacement of over a million people. The Katangese secession in Zaire, the war between northern and southern Sudan, the crisis in Somalia, are all well known manifestations of the crisis of national identity in Africa (Farah 2005: 14-23). The most recent evidence of this crisis in West Africa is the policy of Ivoirité in which the loyalty of Ivorians of Malian and Burkinabe descents were questioned, and a leading opposition candidate reportedly of Burkinabe descent, Allassane Ouattara, was barred from contesting the presidency. This was to lead to an attempted coup d'état by a section of the army dominated by soldiers of Burkinabe descent. Although the coup failed, it touched off a bloody civil war, with the rebels controlling the northern sections of the country, while the south remains under the government. A crisis of similar proportions is simmering in Togo where the opposition leader Gilchrist Olympio of the Ewe ethnic group in the South has been battling President Eyadema, a Northerner who has been in power since

1967. (Editor's Note: President Eyadema died suddenly in February 2005 after 38 years of rule, leaving a festering succession crisis).

The crisis of national identity and nationhood in West Africa can be further summed up by the manner in which the social compact between the state and the citizenry is fast eroding, as shown increasingly by non-compliance with the institutional authorities of the state. If we look at the extent to which the state in the developed and the newly industrialised world elicits compliance from its citizens, it readily becomes obvious that many West African states are far behind. In most of them, the popular trend is for citizens to show very little or no regard for law and order. At a level, this non-compliance with order and authority can be blamed on the privatisation of the state in many African countries over the last two decades or more. The citizens are simply behaving in a manner that recognises that the state is the private property of the President and his cohorts, and since they do not belong to that elite grouping they see no reason to obey those regulations that form part of the embodiment of the state.

This raises the larger issue of the recognition of the states in West Africa by the international community. If we consider states like Sierra Leone, Liberia, Guinea Bissau and Côte d'Ivoire as weak states because the central governments, to the extent that they exist, are the result of external props and not of popular support, then Somalia is a clear testimony of failed statehood in Africa. Yet, what happened in that country is virtually happening in notoriously unstable countries in West Africa. The authority of the state was challenged in Côte d'Ivoire, as was the case also in Sierra Leone. There are genuine doubts today that the government in Freetown will be able to effectively and single-handedly manage its affairs once the United Nations withdraws its elaborate peace building and maintenance infrastructure. Liberia has teetered on the brink of collapse and the state may as well break up and split among the three groups: the Liberian government, Liberians United for Reconstruction and Development (LURD) backed by Guinea, US and UK, and the Movement for Democracy in Liberia (MODEL) backed by the Ivorian government. Guinea Bissau is a sad case of a state that continues to exist by miracle since popular will has been effectively usurped by the government. There is a danger that some of the people who would not comply with the authority of the state might spark a civil war. Such are the realities in many West African countries where the state is forced to maintain an elaborate armed force; the type privatised by those in power.

Dealing with the crises

The issue now is how the sub-region can come to terms with the crisis of production, democracy and of national identity and nationhood. Out of the three variants, two are particularly obvious within the capability of West African countries to address. These are the crisis of national identity and the crisis of democracy. The third, crisis of production, is outside the capability of West African states to surmount as it is linked with global production, distribution and consumption relationships traditionally dominated by the industrialized countries.

The major task for the sub-region with regard to the crisis of democracy is in ensuring that genuine democracy and good governance are allowed to nurture and mature. To achieve this, the sub-region urgently must come to terms, not just with conducting free and fair elections but also more importantly, deepening the norms and culture of democracy. This also relates to the larger issue of the willingness of incumbents to surrender power. The privatisation of the state – the situation where state power is appropriated for the benefit of one individual and his cronies – must change in order to create the atmosphere for meaningful pluralist politics. The problem often is that even where pluralist politics prevail, there is either an uneven playing field, or a field where the players, the political parties and especially the opposition, are at best like seasonal streams that flow only in the rainy season – during election years. In many African countries, political parties are not viable and credible players in the democracy game. Most of the parties themselves show very little evidence of internal democracy and are often hostage to the leadership. Where rulers have not refused to leave power they have in effect remained in control by manipulating the rules of the game, by buying off the weaker elements of the opposition and by rigging elections. Despite the rhetoric of democracy many countries in West Africa are yet to cultivate the salient ethos of democratic governance. Of course, what would make democracy percolate and flourish would go well beyond the intermittent holding of elections, to also include access to economic and social rights. It is obviously no use trying to incubate and inculcate democracy when people are hungry or have no roof over their heads, have no jobs, cannot send their children to school and have no access to primary health care.

The crisis of national identity goes to the issue of the elite manipulation of popular identities – be it ethnic, class, religious identities. Politicians have always tended to take refuge in the support of their co-ethnics by mobilising them for electoral purposes. West Africa requires modernising leaders of the Kwame Nkrumah type whose appeal and base cut across ethnic lines. During his lifetime, Nkrumah was able to use his political party, the Convention Peoples Party (CPP), as a unifying organisation. Indeed, Ghana owes a good deal to his unifying politics in saving the country from the crisis of national identity that presently bedevils many other West African countries. The issue of ethnic identity is a very sore and emotive one in Nigerian politics for various reasons. Nigeria obviously needs a unifying leader cast in the mould of Nkrumah or Mandela to stem and blunt the rather sharp edges of the crisis of national identity in that country. Most countries in the sub-region would also need such unifying and modernising leaders rather than those with domineering but self-centred personalities.

Managing the various fallouts of globalisation is perhaps the most daunting challenge for Africa in general, and the sub-region of West Africa in particular. If the reckless unilateralism of Washington, and its close ally, Britain, is a benchmark for gauging globalisation, then there is limited hope for Africa at this time, or in the near future. Given the fact that Africa has no alternative economic development path to tread, the prospect that the US will continue to use major International Financial Institutions such as the IMF and the World Bank to impose harsh neo-liberal economic agenda in Africa is high. The continent would therefore go from one macroeconomic policy option prescribed by the World Bank and IMF to another. The prospects that a vicious cycle of crises: of production, democracy, and national identity would remain present in Africa in the near future is incontrovertible.

References

Bulcha, M., 1988, *Flight and Integration*, Uppsala: Scandinavian Institute of African Studies.

Harsh, E., 1992, 'More African States as Lest Developed' *Africa Recovery*, 6 April, p. 11.

Mamdani, M., 1982, 'Karamoja: Colonial Roots of Famine in North-East Uganda', *Review of African Political Economy*, No. 25.

McGowan, P. and Johnson, J.H., 1986, 'Sixty Coups in Thirty years: Further Evidence Regarding African Coups d'état', *The Journal of Modern African Studies*, Vol. 24, No. 3: 539-546.

Nzongola-Ntalaja, G., 2001, 'Political Reforms and Conflict Management in the African Democratic Transition', in Raymond Suttner (ed.) *Africa in the New Millennium*, Nordiska Afrikainstitutet, Uppsala, p.13.

Farah, N., 2005, 'Peace and Disarmament in the New Somalia' *Taflastse* Vol. 1, No. 1 p. 2 February 14-23.

Riley, S. P., 'Democratic Transition in Africa', *Conflict Studies*, No. 245.

Rugumamu, S.M., 2001, Globalization and Africa's Future: Towards Structural Stability, Integration and Sustainable Development, *AAPS Occasional Paper* No. 5.

UNDP, 1997, *Human Development Report*, New York: Oxford Univ. Press, p.2.

US Committee for Refugees, 1991, 'Exile From Rwanda: Background to an Invasion', *Issue paper USCR*, February.

World Bank, 1993, *World Development Report*, New York: Oxford University Press.

3

Colonial History and the Search for Democratic Nationhood: The Case of Anglophone West Africa

W. Alade Fawole

Introduction

Nigeria in January 1966 was the first of the four former British colonies in West Africa to fall under the barrel of the gun when the military overthrew its first post-independence civilian government in a bloody putsch that claimed the lives of the Prime Minister, two regional premiers, a federal minister and some of the most senior army officers (Luckham 1971; Ademoyega 1981). Ghana and Sierra Leone succumbed to military rule in quick succession in February 1966 and March 1967 respectively. Gambia was the last two decades later, in 1994. Significantly, the entry of the military forces of the various states into politics and governance effectively terminated the nascent British democratic experiment of the Westminster model in West Africa. As it turned out, the centralising tendencies of decades of authoritarian military rule subsequently produced strong presidential systems in all the four countries after the retreat of the military from the centre stage. Nigeria adopted the presidential system, first under the 1979 constitution and successively thereafter, while Ghana and Sierra had done away with the Westminster model much earlier. The 'exit' of the Gambian military from politics with the election of its former ruler, Yahya Jammeh as civilian president, equally produced a presidential system which gives the leader much greater political powers. In a number of cases, the immediate post-military administrations in Nigeria, Ghana and Sierra Leone were themselves later subverted by serial military interventions. These three states remained under one form of authoritarian rule or the other until the 'second wave of democracy', which began in the 1990s, brought back civilian rule.

But in spite of the apparent democratic ferment in the continent, these four Anglophone states have been engaged in what seems a futile search for enduring democracy. It seems that no matter how hard they tried, their democratic experiments are confronted by what has been termed the 'inevitability of [their] instability' (O'Connell 1967: 181-191). The contention here is that the post-colonial instabilities that made democracy impossible in these states are deeply embedded in their very foundations. The defective foundations on which the colonial states were erected have now come to haunt their post-colonial successors, thereby making sustained and enduring democratic rule a Herculean task.

The basic argument of this chapter is that the British colonial political tutelage in these countries produced a core of nationalist elites who, severely excluded from the colonial political mainstream, received their training instead in anti-colonial and agitational politics. These same elites, later as the inheritors of the mantle of authority from the departed British authorities, were inevitably saddled with having to operate democratic systems of rule for which they had not received any previous training. Unfortunately they also had to operate with inherited civilian bureaucracies that were already accustomed to the dictatorial and overbearing style of the British overlords, and national armies that had been created originally for the subjugation of the peoples to the will of the colonial authorities. It was no wonder that the new post-colonial 'democracies' wobbled along for only a few years before they became overwhelmed by the inherent and unresolved contradictions in their provenance.

The chapter examines critically the colonial origins of Anglophone West African states with a view to determining the very fundamental factors and foundational imperatives that have made sustainable and enduring democratic rule very difficult. It examines especially the contributions of the inherited state structures, civilian bureaucracies and the armed forces, to the instabilities that have made democratic rule seem difficult. No doubt, a deeper understanding of these problems may help chart the way forward for enduring democracy in the sub-region. The four Anglophone states have been selected because of the similarity in their colonial provenance, common style of colonial administrations, the existence of inter-territorial institutions linking the four of them, their remarkably similar post-independence political trajectories, and the kind of early post-colonial governments that were bequeathed to them.

Colonial background: History as guide

It is a fact of history that the colonial enterprise in Africa was carried out by a combination of trickery, lies, and outright use of force. These diverse stratagems involved tricking the rulers of the various kingdoms and city-states to sign treaties of protection and cession of their territories to the British monarchy, cultural infiltration through of religion, language, and Western 'civilisation', and a remarkably consistent policy of *Pax-Britannica*. The powerful Yoruba and Bini kingdoms and the Sokoto caliphate in present-day Nigeria were subdued by brutal armed force. Other parts of the territory were added incrementally as the colonialists extended and deepened their tentacles into the hinterland.

In a manner similar to the conquest of Nigeria, the Gold Coast, as Ghana was called before its independence in 1957, was also put together by armed subjugation when an alliance of the British forces and Fantes totally crushed the Asante, the largest kingdom in the area and brought it under British control. By 1874, Britain had annexed the coastal Fante and Ga kingdoms, fully occupied the Asante kingdom, and deposed the Asantehene in 1896. But throughout the period of colonial rule in the Gold Coast, the colonialists did little to weld together and unite the disparate kingdoms into a new commonwealth. The acquisition of the other territories that made up British West Africa was also accomplished through a combination of subterfuge, force and later by diplomatic concession at the Berlin Congress of 1884.

Having fully secured each of the colonies firmly under its control, British colonial rule then turned into an authoritarian enterprise to forcibly deny the 'natives' their freedom and plundered their resources to for the benefit of the mother country. As aptly described by Nkrumah, atop the administration of each colony was a colonial Governor who was only answerable to the British Crown. He had no corresponding responsibility to the natives or the local 'electorate'. Colonial authority, as pointed out by O'Connell, 'combined executive, legislative and judicial powers in the hands of a single foreign caste and permitted only a minimum separation of those powers' (O'Connell 1967: 183). And here, according to Nkrumah, 'the truly authoritarian nature of the regime becomes apparent' (Nkrumah 1963: 16). Even though Africans were later on appointed or elected into the Executive and Legislative Councils of the colonial administrations, the Governor's authority was nonetheless supreme. The authority also allowed him to enjoy such 'reserved powers' to invalidate legislations, suspend the constitution and even assume emergency powers in times of trouble. It is thus no wonder that the new African ruling elites in the post-colonial states, when also faced with political opposition, found it convenient to behave like their colonial predecessors. This practice, in particular, was responsible for putting post-colonial democratic rule in jeopardy, and made single-party rule rather irresistible.

The infrastructure of governance that the colonialists left behind was actually constructed on authoritarian and anti-democratic foundations for which the emergent African nationalists could not be held responsible. As Basil Davidson has so aptly observed, even though government in the mother country, Britain, was democratic, in the sense that the expressed will of the people was reflected in the policies and actions of government, the absolute contrary obtained in the colonies. In the colonies, government was nothing but 'rigid dictatorship' and colonial governments simply governed by decrees without any input from the local people. These decrees, he noted further, were 'administered by an authoritarian bureaucracy to which any thought of the people's participation was damnable subversion' (1992: 208). The reality which Africans had to confront much later is that 'the new nation-states inherited the dictatorship and not the democracy'. The political system that the nationalists inherited presupposed that the actual work of government, and all the crucial decisions depending on it and from it, would be exercised by a bureaucracy trained and tested in authoritarian habits and practices' (1992: 208). The outcome of the operation of the inherited political system 'had to be authoritarian even when the nationalists wished it to be democratic' (1992: 209). This position tallies with O'Connell's assertion that 'there is a certain inevitability about the political instability in contemporary independent African countries' because the conditions of instability were actually built into the structural foundation of the states (O'Connell 1967: 181). The experiences of Nigeria under Prime Minister Sir Abubakar Tafawa Balewa were not different from those of Nkrumah and the others (Nkrumah 1963). The new states that they had to govern had only the appearance rather that the substance of democracy, and thus they had to operate political systems and constitutions that were actually imposed on them by the departing colonialists.

Apart from the authoritarian bureaucracy that was essentially put in place to do the bidding of the colonial rulers, the military and security services were also established for the sole purpose of maintaining foreign law and order against the will of the peoples of the colonies. This had to be so, again as O'Connell has argued, because 'colonial power rested on the overt or latent threat of force' (1967: 183). What later became the national armies of the countries were detachments from the general colonial constabulary force, particularly the Royal West African Frontier Force (RWAFF). This Force was initially assembled to help the foreign colonisers impose their will upon the subjugated local peoples (Miner 1971; Fawole 2001). As time went by, military detachments were regularly deployed for internal pacification duties throughout the territories. For instance, the Nigerian wing of the RWAFF was deployed to suppress rebellion in the Gold Coast in 1948 and in Southern Cameroons in 1959 (Miner 1971: 12). The police forces were not any different. They were, in the words of erstwhile Nigeria's Minister for Police Affairs, David Jemibewon, maintained as a 'repressive weapon employed by the colonialists for subjugating the recalcitrant natives' (Jemibewon 2001: preface, xx). Even after independence, the generally negative perception of the police as an anti-people force persisted. As the minister states further, 'the negative impact of colonial heritage continues to manifest in the conduct, operations, orientation and overall life of the police personnel in Nigeria' (2001: preface, xx).

As if to demonstrate that there was little difference between the colonies, the British colonial authorities established a series of inter-territorial institutions that linked them. With Freetown serving as the headquarters of British colonial enterprise, it was quite common for civil servants to be deployed anywhere their services were required across the sub-region. But above all were such institutions as the West African Currency Board (WACB), the West African Airways Corporation (WAAC), and the still existing West African Examinations Council (WAEC). All except the WAEC were dismantled upon the independence of the countries.

Even while the British were preparing the colonies for eventual independence, they did very little to Africanise and change the orientations of the armed and police forces to face the challenges of defending the rights of their peoples. Instead, the colonialists held on tightly their control of the security forces for the sole maintenance of their power over the colonies. Unlike the civil service in Nigeria, the armed forces were the least Nigerianised, so much so that even after independence the army was largely officered by Britons and commanded by a Briton, Major-General Sir Christopher Welby-Everard, until 1965 (*West Africa*, 20 March 1965: 309). At that time also, British officers occupied the topmost hierarchy of the police force. Indeed, not less than 55 percent of all police officers after independence were Britons who resented service under Africans, a situation that did not allow Nigeria to have an indigenous Inspector General until Louis Edet was appointed in 1964 (Jemibewon 2001: preface, xx). Significantly enough, this did not allow for a proper re-definition of their roles as alien forces to those that should protect and defend the interest of their peoples under a democratic system. Instead, they have continued with their original role in the service of authoritarian regimes.

Colonial rule in practice opportunistically promoted and encouraged ethnic differentiation as a matter of official policy. Even after having brought together a multiplicity of disparate ethnic and nationality groups under a single colonial umbrella, nothing was done to nurture and encourage a sense of common identity and citizenship under a new commonwealth. Instead, ethnic differentiations were allowed to fester and to ensure divide and rule among the population. In the Gold Coast, for example, the Asantes, Fantes and the other groups were prevented from forging a united platform against colonial authorities. In Nigeria, Governor Sir Hugh Clifford openly emphasised that his policy rather than unite the various peoples was actually 'to secure to each separate people the right to maintain its identity, its individuality and its nationality, its chosen form of government; and the peculiar political and social institutions which have been evolved for it by the wisdom and accumulated experiences of generations of its forebears' (Nnoli

1978: 112). Admirable this may look on the surface, but deep down the intention was to encourage disunity among the various ethnic formations that made up each of the colonies in such a way that they would not be able to act in concert to challenge the colonial authority. In Sierra Leone, the schism created between the coastal Creoles and the indigenous peoples survive up to the present. Initially the Creoles had pre-eminence in the colonial civil service and in professions such as law, medicine, teaching and the Church (Sesay 1999: 287-288). Unfortunately, the British sowed the schism by establishing special schools - the Bo schools - for the children of chiefs of the Protectorate, such that as independence approached political mobilization and political parties developed along ethnic divides. In fact, the Sierra Leone Peoples Party (SLPP), which was the most popular party at independence was overly aristocratic in composition. These practices were later carried into the politics and governance of the newly independent states in a way that was not significantly different from their colonial predecessors.

Nationalist politics and the struggle for independence

Prior to the Second World War, political agitation by the peoples of the colonies were mostly in the form of demands for social reforms and improvements, revolts against exploitation, unjust legislation, regressive taxation, rather than as demands for outright political independence. Consequently, real nationalist political organisations that championed the cause of independence came into existence and prominence only in the aftermath of the Second World War. The formation of the National Council of Nigeria and the Cameroons (NCNC) in 1944 and the United Gold Coast Convention in 1947 heralded a new era of anti-colonial agitation that would eventually result in the independence of the colonies in the late 1950s and early 1960s.

But the emergence of political parties whose activities paved the way for independence was also a product of the socio-political fault-lines that colonial rule had deliberated created. Apart from a few, most political organisations that emerged in the various colonies revolved around strong personalities that established them, while drawing the bulk of their supporters from the ethnic catchments areas of such leaders. In Nigeria for example, the Northern People's Congress (NPC), Northern Elements Progressive Union (NEPU) had their bases among the Hausa/Fulani, while the National Council of Nigerian Citizens (NCNC), and the Action Group (AG) drew their support from among the Ibo and Yoruba respectively. The reality was that the quest for independence for the new nation-states was actually carried out within the contexts articulated, by and the platforms of, these ethno-regional political parties. The United Gold Coast Convention (UGCC) and Convention Peoples Party (CPP) in Ghana, and the

SLPP and All Peoples Congress (APC) in Sierra Leone, were not significantly different from their Nigerian counterparts. And as part of the continuation of the policy of divide and rule, the British did virtually nothing to ensure that they would hand over power to a united political elite. Instead, they left behind disunited entities that would unravel with time, having been nourished by the seeds of instability deliberately implanted into the foundations of the successor nation-states by the departing colonial authorities.

The rise of a new crop of nationalist-politicians, with their principal focus directed towards securing independence, succeeded in unravelling the worst in the character of colonial rule. Made uncomfortable by the new agitation for political reforms, colonial authorities persistently employed drastic and draconian measures to deal with the situation as independence approached; including the arrest and incarceration of frontline politicians and local leaders. Nkrumah and Enahoro suffered this fate a few times before independence finally came. Unfortunately, rather than integrate the new nationalists into the political system and create democrats out of them, their exclusion from the political mainstream succeeded in driving them towards agitational and confrontational politics. Their exclusion made it inevitable that they would see themselves as the natural vanguards of the struggle for the independence of their peoples.

Unfortunately, again, the feverish quest for political independence after the Second World War left the nascent nationalist elites little time to study and understand the problems of the colonies in all their ramifications. Instead, the pervasive notion among them was that political freedom was the inescapable and irreducible starting point from which other socio-economic problems would be tackled. This was the cardinal belief and expectation, although it was only Nkrumah's Convention Peoples Party (CPP) that adopted the slogan, 'Seek ye first the political kingdom' as its battle cry for independence (Nkrumah 1963: 50). Other political associations articulated the same position in slightly different ways.

The blind pursuit of independence as the sole object of nationalist agitation and politics also left no room for the resolution of the basic problems of the colonial state- problems that would later turn round to haunt different post-colonial states themselves in many different ways. Since it was reckoned that the sustenance of the colonial empire in West Africa was no longer possible, the colonialists merely repackaged the colonial states in their crudest formats and bequeathed them as new independent nation-states. Unfortunately, the new contraptions were neither a 'state' in the proper Westphalian sense nor a 'nation'. As 'nation-states', in the view of Basil Davidson, the new contraptions represented Africa's curse (Davidson 1992). Perhaps with the exception of Nkrumah who came to power on a more radical platform, all the other new leaders in Anglophone West African were of the conservative mould who were also rewarded with British knighthoods: Sir Abubakar Tafawa Balewa and Sir Ahmadu Bello in

Nigeria; Sir Milton Margai, and his brother, Albert, in Sierra Leone, and Sir Dauda Jawara in the Gambia. The more radical ones like Kwame Nkrumah, Siaka Stevens, Nnamdi Azikiwe, Aminu Kano and Obafemi Awolowo were not considered fit for such honours.

Post-colonial politics and military rule

One common attribute of the newly independent states was the fragility of the political systems they inherited. With power handed over to ethnically dominated political parties, the emergent post-colonial states merely continued with the exclusionary political system that was perfected by the departed colonialists. The difference this time is not the exclusion of the natives by foreigners but by one major ethnic group against several others. Ultimately, the majoritarian type of democracy inherited was unsuitable for maintaining peace and harmony among the conglomerate societies that the new states represented. Right from the start, for instance, politics frequently degenerated into a zero-sum affair. The ugly consequence was also that the new governments, impatient with the antics of the opposition that would wish to wrest power from them, had to resort to the same authoritarian and anti-democratic policies and practices of the colonial rulers. Even when the new rulers wished to operate democratic politics, they were incapable of doing so because the foundations of their new states were profoundly authoritarian and violent. As Nkrumah explained the situation from his own personal experience, the new post-colonial states had to endure the frustration of how to break down extant tribal loyalties and barriers to unity. His experience with dealing with the opposition was altogether unpalatable, especially for a leader who had a vision and ambition to transform his new society into a developed one for the demands of the 20th century (1963: 66-78).

Apart from the authoritarian nature and character of the colonial state which were not redefined at independence, even the politicians who were in charge of the new states were themselves ill-equipped and ill-prepared to operate the inherited democratic systems. They had learned and achieved mastery of agitational politics under a colonial system where all the executive, legislative and judicial powers of the government were concentrated in the hands of the Governor who ignored and excluded them from all consideration. They also learnt in the course of agitational politics during the colonial era, that when faced with organised and militant opposition in favour of social and political reforms, the typical response of the colonial authorities was to wield the big stick in a repressive manner. After independence, the proverbial chickens would come home to roost, as those who had been tutored in this model of politics could not be expected to do less than their predecessors had done. O'Connell has put the case well:

> Given this exercise of power and the manner of its concentration, the successor authorities to the colonial regimes were not only ill-schooled in the politics of representation, participation and conciliation, but they were quick

to resent the imposition of constitutional and other restraints by the departing metropolitan state which left them with apparently less power than the colonial officials enjoyed (1967: 183).

Unable to tolerate their reduced powers under the post-independence arrangements, the successor rulers resort to draconian measures to control opposition not only encouraged authoritarianism but also ensured that one-party rule became increasingly attractive, if not irresistible. Nkrumah callously incarcerated his political mentor, Dr. J. B. Danquah; Tafawa Balewa jailed Obafemi Awolowo and opportunistically sought to remove the carpet from under his feet by carving out the Midwest from the Western Region. Politics transformed increasingly into a merciless zero-sum competition as rulers sought to retain power by all means while those outside the corridors of power schemed to remove them. Violence, thuggery and hooliganism became the singular distinguishing hallmark of political competition, with abductions, assassinations, incarceration of political opponents on trumped-up charges, enfeeblement of the opposition parties through legislation, being the veritable manifestations of democratic rule gone berserk.

The unresolved contradictions internal to the new states began to manifest themselves immediately after independence. Without doubt, the inherited state structure and the institutions of the state were not readily adaptable to the new political situations. When the British departed from the colonies, they paradoxically bequeathed to the people modern institutions of governing nation-states that also rested precariously on authoritarian foundations. The new governments were then expected to run their affairs according to popular democratic principles. Thus, even if the new inheritors of power had intended to run democratic governments, the reality that confronted them made nonsense of such intentions. In the first instance, the civil service that they inherited was neither configured nor intended to function as a reliable democratic infrastructure. At independence, for instance, the most senior and experienced administrative officers were Britons, not Africans, and were already used to carrying out the orders and wishes of the omnipotent colonial governments. The new governments had no choice but to retain them since there was no way to discard them without serious disruption to the smooth and peaceful administration of the newly independent states. Nkrumah's observation from experience is apt here:

> In the case of our civil service, we were reliant not upon our own nationals but almost entirely upon nationals of a power which had been ruling us and who had been trained to conduct the policy of that power. Bound to the interests of their own country for so long, it could hardly be expected, apart

from a few exceptional cases, that they would change their attitude towards us overnight (1963: 90).

If this was the civil service which the newly independent states had to rely on, the armed forces were not much different. The armies of the new states, originally territorial units of the Royal West African Frontier Force, were largely officered by Britons until a few years after independence. The Nigerian example, which was replicated in the other colonies, is quite instructive for understanding the instability of post-colonial states. The army was the least Nigerianised or indigenised of all the national institutions, with only 18 percent of the officers at independence in 1960 being Nigerians (Luckman 1971: 163). It is no wonder that the army top brass refused to co-operate with Dr. Nnamdi Azikiwe against Alhaji Sir Abubakar Tafawa Balewa after the massively rigged 1964 General Elections. In Ghana, Nkrumah's attempt at rapidly changing the structure of the armed forces and officers inherited from the British inevitably pitted him against many army generals who resented his policies (Afrifa 1966). In Sierra Leone, the same inherited army simply took over the reins of power rather than allow a smooth and peaceful democratic transition from the SLPP to the opposition APC that had won the 1967 general elections (Sesay 1992: 288).

The reality is that military institutions that had originally been established to help foreigners subjugate and rob the people of their sovereignty could not readily adapt to a different, more responsible role under a democratic atmosphere. Having been used to enforce the will of the creators, they had difficulty adjusting to democratic control and subordination to civilian authority after independence. The spate of coups that subverted the democratic aspirations of the people was therefore in consonance with the historic missions of these anti-people armed forces (Fawole 2001: 59-64). The propensity to subvert democracy and popular will is innate in all the armies of British West Africa.

By the middle of the independence decade of the 1960s, only Gambia of the four former British colonies in West Africa had not yet succumbed to military rule. The collapse of the Westminster form of government heralded the eclipse of democratic rule in those countries for many years to come. Nigeria experienced three decades of military dictatorship from 1966 to 1999, interspersed only by a brief democratic interregnum between 1979 and 1983. Soldiers also held sway in Ghana from 1966 until the early 1990s. Military rule in Sierra Leone lasted only one year, from 1967 to 1968, but the resultant civilian rule of the APC was perhaps the most repressive, corrupt and anti-democratic. As Amadu Sesay has made clear, the APC under Siaka Stevens employed diverse stratagems such as repression, co-optation, clientelism, political assassination, prebendalism, and manipulation of ethnicity, to destroy democracy (1992: 291). The military struck in 1992 to impose their own brand of authoritarian rule. Gambia, whose experience with military dictatorship was relatively brief in the 1990s, has yet to taste real democratic rule since its former military ruler, Captain Yahya Jammeh, orchestrated his transmutation into a civilian president.

The quest for enduring democracy: A futile search?

The global democratic ferment occasioned by the collapse of Communism in Eastern Europe and the disintegration of the Soviet Union brought a renewed agitation for a return from dictatorship to democracy in Africa, and the four Anglophone West African states were not left behind in the movement. Ghana's Jerry Rawlings transformed himself into a civilian president in 1992 and served two elected terms before handing over to John Kuffor after a successful transition election. Immense pressures forced the ruling military oligarchs in Nigeria to beat a retreat to the barracks in mid-1999. Sierra Leone's civilian government was overthrown in May 1997, only for it to be forcibly restored by Nigeria's military intervention in March 1998. The security of the restored civilian government in Freetown is currently guaranteed by a large UN military presence. Gambia's military ruler transformed himself into a civilian president.

It is now no longer news that the erstwhile British colonies have embraced liberal democracy as the new form of government, and that they are at different stages of its consolidation or institutionalisation. In varying forms, the various administrations are currently grappling with the challenges of democratic rule after decades of civilian and military dictatorships. Perhaps the pertinent questions to ponder are: how well has liberal democracy been entrenched in these states? How real are the prospects of democratic consolidation, that is, when will democracy eventually become part and parcel of the popular political and governance consciousness, and the spectre of military rule will recede permanently? In attempting to answer these posers, it is perhaps necessary to bear in mind the internal political dynamics and external forces that compelled a return to liberal democracy. In the case of Nigeria, a totally discredited military had run out of the wherewithal to govern effectively after the unresolved political crisis created by the annulment of the June 1993 presidential elections. So it was not fortuitous that the Abdulsalami Abubakar regime that succeeded the Abacha dictatorship in mid-1998 unmistakably understood the handwriting on the wall: the game was up for the military (Williams 1999). To have done otherwise and continue to rule a reluctant nation by sheer coercion would have put the future of both the nation and the armed forces itself in mortal danger.

In Ghana, the political trajectory that brought an end to military rule was quite different. Even though Jerry Rawlings had, earlier in his two-decade dictatorship, shown disdain for multi-party rule, the return to liberal democracy was conditioned, as Konings (2000) has noted, by three main factors, namely: the fact that Ghana's structural adjustment programme depended on external aid, to which the Western donors had added liberal democracy as a conditionality; the growing opposition that confronted Rawlings and the unrelenting agitation for democratisation which also received encouragement from the wind of change blowing on the continent; and Rawlings's own realisation that a controlled democratisation process would enhance his capacity to retain power under a democratic system. The case of Sierra Leone is peculiar in the sense that the sustenance of democratic rule is guaranteed only by the presence of a UN multinational peacekeeping force. One can only speculate that the ghost of military rule may be permanently exorcised by the creation of a new and transformed national army than the one implicated in the last civil war. The smallest Anglophone West African state, the Gambia, is continuing with a political experiment that looks more like a 'democratic caricature' (Williams 1999) than a real democracy. President Jammeh remains a 'strongman' even though he is an 'elected' leader. No one can predict the fate of the Gambia after his exit.

It is difficult to predict how far the process of democratic consolidation will be allowed to flourish and deepen in Anglophone West Africa, or indeed, throughout the continent of Africa. This is essentially because democratisation was partly imposed from outside, attached as a political conditionality to the grant of aid and fresh loans, foreign direct investment, and debt relief in the post-Cold War era (Hoogvelt 2002: 23-24). The question that remains to be answered then is: can a foreign imposition function properly and endure beyond the limits of the interests of the sponsors?

Another clear and present danger to the fledgling democratic experiments in the four countries is the unresolved role of the armed forces in national politics. Most post-military civilian governments are always too impatient for power that they tend to assume that soldiers would be obedient to authority once they have returned to the barracks. Unless serious attempts are made to de-politicise and re-professionalise the military institutions that had enjoyed decades of unrivalled political power and national prominence, the dangers of democratic reversal and return to full-blown military rule will remain ever-present in the sub-region. This is a problem common to virtually all the countries in the sub-region because their armies had tasted political power at one time or the other in the past. In any case, in such deeply fractured polities, these armies remain the most cohesive national corporate groups whose propensity to subvert the popular will must not be underestimated. Only Nigeria under President Obasanjo seems to apprehend the dangers of a highly politicised military institution. Immediately he assumed power in 1999, President Obasanjo summarily cashiered all armed forces officers who had held political appointments under all previous regimes. This 'cleaning out of the barracks' was done to sanitise the nation's security apparatus. In effect, the onus will be on the current crop of political leaders in other countries to summon the will to govern well and avoid creating conditions that soldiers can exploit to disrupt governance and to take over power again.

Conclusion

The general configuration of the post-colonial state as a successor to the colonial state leaves little room for accountability, even when they pretended to be democratic. Built on a largely defective, anti-democratic foundation, the post-colonial state remains fatally hobbled by its colonial provenance. It is incapable of functioning properly as a Westphalian state ought. In Anglophone West Africa, as in other parts of the continent of Africa, the state remains a pathetic imitation of its Westphalian progenitor, an atavistic residue of colonial rule, and a sad reminder of the evils of foreign rule. Consequently, since the inherent contradictions in its history cannot be ignored, the post-colonial state cannot be expected to 'mirror the Western democratic trajectory or even the west's idea of democratisation' (Williams 1999: 16). But it is important to look beyond this pessimism and assume that democracy still has a chance to thrive and deepen if the people collectively make conscious efforts.

Having already begun the quest for democratic nationhood, the experiments can only begin to produce positive fruits in the sub-region when certain irreducible minimum conditions are met. These will include a deliberate reform of critical institutions of the state, especially the armed forces, police, civil service and the judiciary, in line with the demands and challenges of democratic rule; the delivery of 'democracy dividends' which will help the people to accept that democracy is the best form of government; playing the game of politics in accordance with agreed democratic norms and principles; dismantling existing structures and institutions of oppression, such as paramilitary forces that are only loyal to and serve the personal interests of leaders, etc. In conclusion, the intention in this chapter is certainly not to paint a gloomy or pessimistic forecast. Even though history is a guide to the future, there is no doubt that with desire and conscious efforts, Anglophone West African states can still rise above the limitations of their colonial provenance and become truly democratic over time.

References

Ademoyega, W., 1981, *Why We Struck: The Story of the First Nigerian Coup*, Ibadan: Evans Brothers Nigeria Ltd.

Afrifa, A. A., 1966, *The Ghana Coup, February 1966*, London: Frank Cass.

Davidson, B., 1992, *The Black Man's Burden: Africa and the Curse of the Nation-State*, New York: Times Books, p. 208.

Fawole, A. W., 2001, 'The Nigeria Military and Prospects for Democratic Rule', in W. Alade Fawole (ed.), *Beyond the Transition to Civil Rule: Consolidating Democracy in Post-Military Nigeria*, Lagos: Amkra Books, pp. 57-76.

Hoogvelt, A., 2002, 'Globalisation, Imperialism and Exclusion: The Case of Sub-Saharan Africa', in Tunde Zack-Williams, Diane Frost and Alex Thomson (eds.) *Africa in Crisis: New Challenges and Possibilities*, London: Pluto Press, pp. 23-24.

Jemibewon, D. M., 2001, *The Nigeria Police in Transition: Issues, Problems and Prospects*, Ibadan: Spectrum Books, (preface), p. xx.

Konings, P., 2000, 'Institutionalising Democracy in Ghana', Text of seminar paper delivered at the African Studies Centre, Leiden, The Netherlands, 16 November.

Luckman, R., 1971, *The Nigerian Military: A Sociological Analysis of Authority and Revolt, 1966-67*, London: Cambridge University Press.

Miners, N. J., 1971, *The Nigerian Army, 1956-1966*, London: Methuen and Co.

Nkrumah, K., 1963, *Africa Must Unite*, London: Panaf Books, p. 16.

Nnoli, O., 1978, *Ethnic Politics in Nigeria*, Enugu: Fourth Dimension Publishers, p. 112.

O'Connell, J., 1967, 'The Inevitability of Instability', *Journal of Modern African Studies*, Vol. 5, No. 2, , pp. 181-191.

Sesay, A., 1999, 'Paradise Lost and Regained? The Travails of Democracy in Sierra Leone', in Dele Olowu, Adebayo Williams and Kayode Soremekun (eds.) *Governance and Democratisation in West Africa*, Dakar: CODESRIA, pp. 287-288.

Williams, A., 1999, 'Nigeria: A Restoration Drama', *African Affairs*, Vol. 98, No. 391, July.

Williams, A., 1999, 'Democracy in Nigeria: Retrospect and Prospect', Text of seminar paper delivered at the African Studies Centre, Leiden, The Netherlands, 11 February.

4

The Construction of a Leviathan: State Building, Identity Formation and Political Stability in Nigeria

Austine Ikelegbe

Introduction

The Nigerian state is failing. Its post-independence hope of greatness and of 'giant-hood' in Africa is faltering. The Nigerian project has remained at best problematic. A major manifestation of this failure is evident by the resurgence of identity politics and conflicts, and their violent suppression by the state in a ruthless and uncompromising manner. Given the convoluted nature of identities and the crises they provoke in Nigeria, violent ethnic, communal, religious and regional conflagration have led to concerns about the weakening notions of citizenship, attachment and loyalty. This is precisely because ethnic, communal, religious, regional and sectional identities are providing a safe haven for an increasing number of people given the circumstances of an incompetent, weak, and insensitive state. In the same manner, the festering of identity-related issues and problems continue to impact in several negative ways on state and governance crises and/ or failures.

The state and the competing ruling elites from its constituent parts have been identified as culpable in the resurgence and heightening of identity politics and conflicts in Nigeria. Being the main base of class formation and accumulation, and central to the determination of individual and group welfare, the state has turned into a space for fierce competition and conflict steadily degenerating into political lawlessness. With the state at different times as principal actor, the locus of conflict and an instrument of the inter-group struggles, politics in Nigeria has become characteristically that of exclusion, marginalisation, disadvantages that, in turn, intensifies social cleavages and powerlessness.

The initial wave of identity mobilization and formation was a colonial creation. Colonialism hindered the emergence of a common national identity and consciousness by promoting ethno-religious separatism, consciousness as well as parochial loyalty. But beyond this historical colonial genealogy, identity construction has been predominantly indigenous, promoted especially by post-independence nationalist leaders who desired to score cheap political and electoral mandates. The nationalist struggle against colonial rule was the initial opportunity for mobilization and construction of ethno-religious and regional identities. Since then, the ruling class and elite have merely built on the different forms of identities inherited from colonial rule in their unending factional struggles for access to regional/state and federal power, resources and other advantages. The manifestations of these struggles have, among others, turned the state into an unruly leviathan, apart from damaging and undermining socio-economic and political development in the country.

The above scenarios and situations raise numerous issues and questions that require critical historical and theoretical insights and analyses to explain. This is especially so in order to understand how elites and state officials construct and mobilise different types of identity to provoke different types of citizenship crisis, push the citizenry inexorably into or towards primordial conclaves, and create a popular base for inter-elite struggles. What were and are the patterns, processes and outcomes of multiple identity construction during the formative era of Nigeria's nationhood? What different instrumentalities were deployed to construct and mobilise different identities in postcolonial Nigeria? What different arenas provided the contextual template for the proliferation of identities in the country? What factors facilitated and accounted for the transmission and transformation of identities over time and space within Nigeria, and for their politicisation? The thrust of argument in this chapter is that identity formation and mobilisation, and their eventual politicisation, results from the peculiar character and process of state building and consolidation in Nigeria. By extension, the chapter argues that the festering and diffusion of identities have provoked unprecedented and seemingly unsolvable political conflicts and instability that have grave potentials of complicating the Nigerian project at least in the long run.

Theoretical exposition: Identity, instability and the state

There is a resurgence of identity politics and related conflicts in contemporary Nigeria. Since the 1990s, the negative effects of the mobilisation of identity politics have become one of the most immediate and potent sources of violent riots in the country. At the same time that interdependence and globalisation are shaping the world in fundamental ways, so also are new forms of assertive sub-nationalisms expressing themselves from below in manners that also significantly hurt and erode the authority of the nation-state, especially in Africa. In this chapter, 'identity' refers to a subsisting sense of belonging and attachment to a group or institution, or such other social, cultural and political entities. The group or institution could be a nation state, an ethnic group, a religious sect, a community, an age group, gender or even a work group. Identity acquires salience in socio-political relations when it becomes one of, or the only platform for the articulation of common interests, the mobilisation of cooperative efforts, the pursuits of shared beliefs and culture, the organisation of structures, and the conduct of socio-political actions. Identity raises awareness, knowledge, consciousness and interests. It also shapes and guides behaviour and actions, and constitutes an important platform for concerted actions towards achieving certain predetermined or desired ends.

As products of definition and identification, ethnicity, religion and region are accepted and acknowledged differently by insiders and outsiders. In terms of dynamics, this process of definition and identification is situational and ever evolving; thereby also subjective or objective depending on the social context. For example, the definition of the ethnic group in common usage tends to be very subjective. Thus northerners are regarded as Hausas; a classification which blurs the Hausa-Fulani dichotomy in that region. In the same way, most south-easterners are regarded as Ibos or *Kobo*-kobo thereby submerging numerous other minority ethnic groups such as the Ibibios, Efiks, Ijaws and others.

Thus identity is dynamic, continuously being reproduced, re-discovered, and 'socially and politically constructed' (Maiz 2003:197). From the standpoint of constructivism, different types of identities undergo considerable re-construction and transformation by virtue of their interactions with colonialism and with the post-colonial states. Even today, the face of identity based-nationalism and struggles, as well as the politics and problems they provoke, have been shaped and are still being shaped by the same forces (Atkinson 1999; Ottaway 1999; Osaghae 2001). The production and reproduction of identities tend to be overly political and/or politicised to the extent that their *avant garde* are nationalists and political elites who are stimulated by state policies and practices, and by their own experiences and the exigencies of strategic political competition (Warren 1993; Maiz 2003:199).

One claim is that the construct of identity in Nigeria is a recent, post-colonial phenomenon. Ekeh (1975:105), for instance, asserted that no ethnic group existed before Nigeria with a distinct corporate identity in terms of the contemporary corporate character, boundaries and loyalty. To Nnoli (1978), ethnic identity in Nigeria is a colonial and post-colonial construction. Prior to their construction, ethnic groups were merely amorphous groups that existed within and were organised in different empires, kingdoms, city and village states in contiguous territories. Hodgkin (1957:42) and Abernethy (1969) confirm the recent construction thesis in relation to the Yoruba and Igbo. Hodgkin asserts that the identity of "Yorubaness" is not very much older than the notion of Nigeria. While arguing that the Yoruba corporate identity is recent, Abernethy (1969) asserts that the Ibo corporate identity is a 20th century phenomenon, whose inclusiveness was still being resisted or even rejected by the Onitshas and Arochukwus in the 1930s.

We have to note first that the mere existence of identity and even its mobilisation is not necessarily inimical to national development. Indeed, identity mobilisation was and has been a major platform for the mobilisation of support towards development and democratisation; and by so doing, provided the ordinary citizens with some sense of representation, freedom, welfare and security. Thomson (2000:65) has noted ethnic loyalties have not necessarily been 'counter-productive to state political systems'. Thus, identity is ordinarily a good social, cultural and psychological attribute. However, it can become a social problem when it is politicised and deployed to gain competitive advantage in the recurrent inter-elite struggle for power and resources. This negative mobilisation of identities is obviously at the roots of inter-group tensions and conflicts, as well as those between different groups and the state. Second, identity mobilisation is not unique to less developing countries or Afro-Asian nations. Identity-based movements and mobilisation pervade the developed democracies of Britain, Canada, Spain and less developed countries in eastern and western Europe. Gurr and Harf (1994: 4-7) note that politicised ethnicity and protracted communal conflicts pervade Africa, Asia, Latin America, Middle East, Eastern Europe, and the Western democracies. Third, historical experiences of inter-group relations such as long standing beliefs and attitudes, no matter how negative they may be, may only provide a supportive climate for identity mobilisation and conflict (Richardson & Sen 1997:88).

The factors and processes that stimulate identity consciousness as a basis for political mobilisation have been acknowledged and documented in the literature. These include economic conditions and variables, state character, behaviour and politics, elite behaviour and democratisation. The economic variables are often related to uneven development across different regions of the country in a manner that glaringly favour some groups over others. The social deprivation model of identity consciousness, mobilisation and politicisation is situated in the differential modernisation and development of groups and the ensuing inequalities and stratification (Beck 1980; Horowitz 1985; Siobhian 2001; Wilson 2001). These, in turn, generate violence and insecurity. Second, economic variables relate to the inter-group competition for scarce resources (the resource competition model) particularly if group dis/advantage becomes visible during the struggle, and if such issues at stake have higher ascribed values for different groups (Melson & Wolpe 1971;Olzak 1983; Rothchild 1998). The third economic variable central to identity formation and mobilisation has to do with the strain, stress, upheaval and tension that arise or are associated with economic development. They include unplanned urbanisation, industrialisation, unemployment and job insecurity, all of which in different ways exacerbates social alienation and group concerns, and make subscription into and membership of identity-based associations attractive (Richardson & Sen 1997). The last one has to do with economic decline accentuating scarcity, heightening group sensitivity towards distributional patterns, raising the stakes among groups within the existing resource configuration ending up by intensifying rivalry, competition and the salience of identity. Compounded by identity-based polarisation, economic decline and attempts to address them undermine living standards and cause social immiseration and dislocations (Osaghae 1994; Ogachi 1999). Such widening inequalities that emanate provoke group and inter-group grievances and raise the need for identity roles and identity-based shelters. The huge class of the poor, unemployed, largely uneducated youth and school dropouts that economic crisis has created constitute the social baseline for the proliferation of violent militia or rebel groups in some African countries (Sundberg 1999). It is appropriate to tender the caveat that even though economic factors may explain the varying potency of identity conflicts, they are usually more of a catalyst than the main cause. Their salience may therefore vary depending on the situation and circumstance. For example, a pervasive inequity in state resource distribution intensifies the value of economic factors in identity conflicts (Esman 1994: 233-239).

The elite construction model also explains identity formation. Here, the elite groups in multiethnic countries are known to be at the forefront of generating or heightening in-group identity by using the identity card as the ace in mobilizing political support and sustaining acceptance. In this regard, they constantly appeal to sentiments, ties, differences, animosities and other in-group cohesive but out-group divisive strategies. Identity consciousness and mobilisation from this perspective, then are tools created and deployed by elites locked against their kinds in inter-elite group struggles for power and control (Sundberg 1999; Ogachi 1999). This is particularly effective where certain general apprehensions, threats or potential threats to group welfare and survival instincts already exist (Horowitz 1985; Esman 1994; Osaghae 2001).

The character of the state and the nature of politics it plays is also a potent explanatory model (Egwu 2001). There are several dimensions of such behaviours and practices that can trigger the kind of identity consciousness whereby the state becomes the locus for mobilisation. One has to do with the large stakes surrounding access to and control of the state, coupled with the far-reaching consequences of been in and out of this locus of state power for the constituent units. After all, it is this involvement in or exclusion from the broader political terrain that confers group worthiness, status, and entitlements in plural societies. Eventually, politics can easily become a basis for struggles among competing groups for inclusion and/or dominance. Such a political configuration is susceptible to inter-group antagonism, fear, tension and insecurity that raises the spectre of identity consciousness, mobilisation and violence (Otite 1990; Timbiah 1990; Newman 1991; Esman 1994; Ikelegbe 2003).

In most cases, the manner in which post-colonial African states have been abused also accentuates identity consciousness and mobilisation. By its very nature, the post-colonial African state is an instrument for promoting and protecting personal and parochial interests; a hegemonic apparatus that can function at different times and in different capacities as agency for exclusion, subordination and deprivation (William & Turner 1980; Osaghae 1994; Esman 1994; Ihonvbere 2000). The state is employed both by the dominant forces within it, and by state officials to suppress weaker, subordinate classes and to cater for and enrich the privileged (Ihonvbere 1988). It is also used, especially its officials, to construct and reconstruct identities and to mobilise them to conceal regime illegitimacy and weaknesses, and to fragment nascent resistances as, when and where they develop (Ake 1983; Kieh 2001). In short, state power is employed to generate and strengthen group inequality and insecurity. It is important to acknowledge the fact that these concrete attributes of the post-colonial state in Africa have had significant alienating effects and outcomes. At different times, past and present, the state is repressive and abusive, corrupt and arrogant; personalised and insensitive to the aspirations and problems of the citizenry. In other instances, it is weak and irrelevant in terms of recognizing and addressing vital social issues promptly and adequately; usually resulting into growing insecurity, violence and criminality. In these circumstances, alienation, frustration and violence becomes a vicious and self-fulfilling process that allows different identities to make recourse to identity-constructed shelters for solace and support (Ihonvbere1988; Ekeh 1998; Ndikumana 1998; Ignatief 1999; Baker 1999; Wilson 2001).

The final point to be made relates to the peculiar circumstances facing countries treading those difficult paths towards transition and regime change. In different countries, especially those that have experienced prolonged authoritarian rule, transition to civil rule projects tends to raise hopes for greater rights, participation and reforms. But paradoxically in Africa, such high hopes have been accompanied by a continuous spell of authoritarianism, repression and limited popular participation. Many transitions have thus been characterised by the foreclosure of dialogue and peaceful resolutions of group grievances in manners that further heightens existing social frustrations or precipitates new ones (Osaghae 2001: 7-8). Transitions have also compounded identity problems not least because they increase awareness of group disadvantages and point to different avenues for their redress (Osaghae 1994: 22).

The Leviathan state: Identity politics, instability and the state in Nigeria

Nigeria is presently bedevilled with a chronic identity-based crisis. There are intense identity-based fears, suspicions and anxieties. Politics is suffused with competing identity assertions and contestations. The mobilisation of identity has reached an all-time high to the extent of suffocating political life. It is true that ethnic, regional, religious and sectional identities and consciousness have been obvious since the colonial period. But then, they have become more pervasive and chronic within the last decade and half. Group animosity; sometimes outright hostility, has served to undermine inter-group relations, further intensifying the spiral of competition and opposition (Nnoli.1989: 10). More significantly, inter group relations have provoked countless and catastrophic intra- and inter-communal conflicts (Diamond 1988: 3,15). Osaghae (1994: 4-5) identifies two phases of identity-based conflicts. The first, which followed independence, was largely orchestrated by the intense inter-elite competition for state power. This competition was not limited to politics, but permeated labour, state institutions and the universities (Nnoli 1978: 215-255). Ethnic violence pervaded the public domain during the period. Incidences included the Jos unrest (Hausa/Igbo) (1945), conflict at Kano (Hausa/Igbo) (1953, 1960–1964, 1966), the Tiv riots (1962–1964), the pogroms of 1966–1967 (Hausa/Igbo) and the botched Biafran secession that led to the Nigerian civil war from 1967 to 1970 (Nnoli 1978: 215–255). The second phase, according to Osaghae, commenced in the 1980s as witnessed by the resurgence of the old conflicts and the emergence of new ones. This phase coincided with the deepening of Nigeria's economic crisis, and later, the unravelling of the contradictions inherent in prolonged military rule which led to pressures in favour of democratisation. Inter-ethnic conflicts have since become more persistent, more intense and more devastating as shown by very bloody and highly destructive inter-communal and inter-ethnic clashes between the Ife and Modakeke, Aguleri and Umuleri, Ijaw and Yoruba, Itsekiri and Ijaws, Itsekiri and Urhobo, Bassa and Egbura, Hausa/Fulani and Sawaya, Zango-Kataf and Hausa/Fulani, Tiv and Jukun/Kuteb, and Hausa/Fulani and indigenous groups in Plateau and Benue states, to mention a few.

Perhaps a third phase, marked by the rise and proliferation of militant movements, otherwise known as ethnic militias, and their involvement in bloody confrontations, can be added. This phase, which began from the late 1990s, has been associated with an unprecedented politicisation of identity-based conflicts. It also coincided with festering injustice, neglect, marginalisation, exclusion and domination, as in the case of the Niger Delta and South East. The later phase blossomed during decades of military rule which rewarded the elites in certain segments of the country, especially the North, to the neglect of those in other parts. In order to regain lost grounds and to meet up with the favoured segments of the country, these groups have been at the forefront of the struggle for a constitutional conference of ethnic nationalities, resource control, regional autonomy and decentralisation of power from the overbearing central government (Ijediogor 2000). One other dimension of this phase has been the violent engagements of the state as the instrument and mastermind of group neglect, marginalisation and domination. Militia confrontations with the state have become common in the Niger Delta where they are accompanied by attacks on crude oil installations, disruptions of oil production, and in the South West, by bloody clashes between the Oodua People's Congress (OPC) and state security agencies.

In whatever format they are presented and/or mobilised, the identity basis of politics has created a convoluted form of citizenship distinguished by the absence of a genuine sense of national belonging and cohesion. It is this curious sense of double citizenship; first and principally that of a particular ethnic group before the diluted citizenship of Nigeria, that is responsible for the spate of violent conflicts between indigenes and settlers (Ife and Modakeke, Itsekiris, Urhobos and Ijaws, the Hausa/Fulani and the ethnic groups in Benue and Plateau, the Tivs, Jukuns and Kutebs, the Hausa Fulani and the Zango Katafs and numerous others). The crisis is further complicated by the alienation that has resulted group marginalisation, domination and exclusion. These conditions have shifted individual and group loyalties progressively towards sub-nationalism and increasing agitation for self-determination; the kinds that creates not just a problem of dual citizenship but the heightening of ethnic nationalism (Ekeh 1992: 77; Taiwo 1996: 19; Idowu 1999: 31-55; Ifidon 1996: 101). Primordial institutions such as the local community, clan, and ethnic and religions groups now compete favourably with or better than national authorities in commanding and retaining the allegiance of individuals and/or groups (Post & Vickers 1973:11-16). Furthermore, the above trends have accentuated a major crisis of national unity and stability to the extent that there is an evident lack of unity among the federating units in the country. The expectation soon after independence that, with time, a common political culture or platform would emerge in the country has so far not been achieved. To this can be added the continuing weakness of national authority, as component units are discouraged to transfer their loyalty to the centre in a manner that encourages the emergence of a strong political authority.

Resulting from the politicisation of identities in the last decade has been the accentuation of the national question. For different reasons, ethnic, regional and sectional groups have been advocating and agitating for re-visitation of the national question through a sovereign national conference with powers to legislate and initiate radical reforms to and restructuring of the Nigerian Federation.

There is agitation for true federalism, resource control, and a conference of ethnic nationalities, among the Yorubas, the Igbos, the Ijaws and most minority groups of the South South region. Apex ethnic associations such as the Afenifere, the Ohanaeze, the Ijaw National Congress and others have been consistently advocating the re-definition of the Nigerian state. Christian groups have also joined the agitation for a sovereign national conference as a medium for resolving the nation's numerous identity-based conflicts.

The colonial origins: State constitution, political engineering and identity formation

From start, the British colonial edifice was not constructed to foster unity and stability among the different groups that eventually formed modern day Nigeria. Indeed, the colonial government was dismissive of the concept of a one and united Nigeria, and made sure that any attempts in that direction in the form of nationalist agitations, was frustrated (Nwosu 1977:28). To ensure that nothing changed regarding this ambition, the colonial government laid the foundation for regional exclusiveness by consciously insulating the northern region from mainstream Nigeria; including ensuring that the intrusive forces of modernisation and social change were kept at bay. Indirect rule and the native authority system sustained this insulation by wedging the north from contact with other provinces, and where this was considered impracticable, ensured that such contacts were few and far apart. Even the celebrated policy of amalgamation in 1914, had little concrete effect as it remained so more on paper. This situation was sustained despite claims to accelerated unification beginning from the early 1920s. For instance, there were no common institutions and frameworks bringing the North and other parts of Nigeria together until much later in the 1940s. Following on this tendency, the constitutional developments initiated by colonial authorities from 1946 onwards reinforced the regionalisation of politics. For example, native authorities formed the recruitment platform for membership of the Legislative Council under the 1946 Richards Constitution, just as the Macpherson Constitution that followed further reinforced the primacy of sub-groups and regional interests by 'the institutionalization of regional political parties and the regionalisation of politics' (Nwosu 1977: 28-30).

Colonialism also engendered uneven development that served as the template for the bourgeoning of sectional identities. Curiously, the northern province was again enamoured from western education and its main harbingers, the missionaries. Instead, the Arabic system of education was kept intact leading to visible and qualitative differences in educational and manpower development across regions between the north and the south. These disparities not only gave the Northern region a slow start in and share of the emerging educated Nigerian elite but also resulted in imbalances in recruitment into important positions in the public sector. These disparities also generated unhealthy and unending competition and distrust, distorted communication between regions, and generated conflict (O' Connell 1971; Melson & Wolpe 1971; Nwosu 1977). In the long run, this divide nurtured and ossified sectional identities along ethnic and region lines.

Colonial officials preferred to align themselves with the aristocratic leadership of the Northern region. Indeed, different colonial policies from amalgamation to indirect rule and the native authorities' systems, to mention a notable few, seemed to have been cleverly designed and implemented by the British 'to favour the relatively dominant North'. Specifically, the colonial policy of indirect rule was designed to prop up the emirate system in the north, and at the same time, to checkmate and possibly destroy other traditional political systems in other parts of Nigeria. While it preserved one therefore, colonial rule worked assiduously to discard others. While colonial officials regarded the south and its educated elements with disdain, contempt and suspicion, the north was considered 'placid and predictable' (Nwosu 1977: 27-28). The colonial officials regarded the northern political leaders and their aristocratic base more highly, and preferred their conservative orientation. They had little or no restraint to put in place structures and incentives favourable to the ruling oligarchy in the north so that they could eventually capture and retain political power in the emergent Nigerian Federation (Mackintosh 1966:34).

Colonial rule also structured competition between north and the south, east and west, and between the main ethnic groups. The size of the north, its slow pace of acceptance of western education and modernization, and the unwritten but strategic pact between the northern elite and British colonial rulers, all combined to create deep cleavages between north and south. Having 'isolated' the northern part of Nigeria, the south became a haven for intense and continuous rivalries, including a cantankerous relationship, between the west and the east, the Yoruba and Igbo, over positions and appointments.

Furthermore, colonial engineering resulted in political inequality and insecurity. It would be recalled that southerners dominated the nationalist movement, while the north was deeply suspicious of the movement and its agenda towards early independence from the British. As noted earlier, there were numerous incompatibilities between the regions besides the geographical fact that the sheer size of the north was more than the other two regions in the south combined. While regional tensions reflected this geographical, the north sought to maintain a firm hold on power. Thus coalesced, at a level, a north versus south clash of identities. The competition for representation, power and resources became more of a one-sided contestation between the Eastern and Western regions on the one hand, and between them and the north, on the other. The unequal tripod and the tensions and conflicts generated remained despite the creation of more states by the military regime of General Yakubu Gowon in 1967; a move calculated to pull the rug off the feet of the Biafra secessionists.

The above was further complicated by the fact that an ethnic majority constituted the nucleus and cultural majority of each region, with the remaining smaller groups existing as marginal minorities (Sklar 1963: 1-4). The majority groups who were numerically superior became the bases of the political parties and power, while the numerical minorities were politically peripheral. The nature of each region initiated a superior-inferior relationship between majority and minority groups, with the latter subordinated, excluded and deprived in the distribution of power, representation and resources. In time, the regional and geographic power differences created and accentuated the basis for identity politics and agitations among minority groups. But then, the initial reaction of minority groups in relation to the redress of their subordination was to struggle for accommodation. One strategy was to clamour for the creation of more regions and the protection of minority rights (Osaghae 2001:2). Unfortunately, the mobilisation of minority ethnic nationalism was not enough to overwhelm the penchant of the British colonial authorities for their own political and administrative convenience pursued at minimum cost. The very failure to succumb to the creation of more regions or states to assuage the fears of the minorities set the stage for some of the imperfections or rough edges in Nigeria's post-colonial experiences.

Colonialism laid the basis for the 'manipulation of ethnic sentiments', and the rise of barriers against inter-regional mobility (Uya 1992; Nigeria 1987). First it prevented the development of national leaderships, integrated national institutions, and national political parties. Political leaders were 'a loose potentially antagonistic coalition of particularistic elites' (Graf 1983:195). No effort was made to weld together and unite the emerging elite for post-independence nation building. Without a national and unified orientation therefore, ethnic, religious and regional identities became the 'most readily available ideological appeal to mobilize and retain' supporters (Graf 1986:195). As a result, the power base of elites was confined to the region, the ethnic group and the community in that order.

Colonialism constructed a terrain in which politics and political control was primary. The colonial state was less concerned with development and welfare as with resource extraction, political control and the maintenance of law and order. The British essentially perceived political power as a veritable resource in itself, and not even as an instrument for development. Because British colonialism was weak in terms of making provision for social infrastructures, industrial and commercial development, public goods were scarce. This created an intense struggle among groups and regions for advantage. By the time it became clear to each group that the state had become a major platform for resource mobilisation and sharing in relation to group development and welfare, it became the central object of competition and violent rivalries. As the struggle to capture the state became inevitable, it became a nagging socio-political problem for each group how to gain advantages over others. In this context zero-sum political competition of the winner takes all, the loser is not only frustrated and disillusioned but marginalised and deprived. As nascent nationalism and nationalist struggles crystallised therefore, the expectation or primary concern was on how quick political power could be wrestled from the British so that most of the anomalies of colonial rule can be reversed.

State consolidation and the accentuation of identity formation 1960-1989

There is no doubt that the kind of state that emerged at the dawn of British colonialism was a very powerful and omnipresent one, especially giving its extensive writ and the vast resources at its command. Unfortunately, the post-colonial state retained many, if not all, of the features of its progenitor, the colonial state. The political class that inherited, or more appropriately captured, the state at independence made little or no efforts to transform it, such that it the state remained essentially a tool for exploitation, repression and domination. Politics, in this regard, generated fierce competition, as political power became the easiest and fastest route for individual and group economic empowerment, accumulation and survival.

The result was an unhesitant and unrestrained struggle for power by a highly fragmented political class which previously formed a coalition, no matter how loose then, just to be able to forge ahead with and consummate the independence project. After independence, the emergent political class turned against each other in a vindictive and vicious competition to retain political relevance in post-independence Nigeria (Ake 1996:27). Such bitter rivalries between the ethnically and regionally based political classes turned governance and government into a feverish theatre of identity-based absurdities. Issues such as census, resource allocation, and elections, turned into political nightmares during the First Republic as the contending regional and ethnic based elites struggled to gain advantage over the others in the search for and retention of state power. As the power of the state over these issues and the control of development and group welfare became more glaring, group resistance became more persistent and more dangerous. These kinds of contentious rivalries for hegemony pervaded virtually all institutions of state, raising the political stakes deriving from them to an unsafe altitude. The politicisation of the military and the hegemonic struggles within that institution opened the way for the military coup and counter-coup of January and July 1966 respectively.

Clearly, military rule was another facet of the struggle for hegemony within the ruling class. Officers of Igbo extraction dominated the first military regime; a situation that was partly responsible for the counter-mobilisation against the regime by Hausa-Fulani elites in the armed Forces. If anything, the eventual outbreak of the civil war in 1967 became an important signifier of the intensity and pervasiveness of identity-based tension and conflict in the country. It also showed clearly how much damage that the poor management of Nigeria's delicate plurality could cause. Although the creation of 12 states by General Gowon just before the Nigerian civil war marked a clever yet desperate attempt to diffuse minority fears, the replacement of regions with states did not thwart the growth and proliferation of dangerous sectional identities. Part of the blame could be that national orientation towards centralized, state-directed development and a strong national government in the 1970s papered over the structural nexus between identity and politics.

At a level, the northern dominance of the army meant that military rule was merely the continuation of northern hegemony by other means. Prolonged military rule, in turn, paved way for considerable appropriation of state resources and power in the hands of an over-bloated Federal Government. The military, these resources and power were deployed to the advantage of the north, and by extension, raised allegations of marginalisation and exclusion from other ethno-regional groupings. In many ways than one therefore, military rule exacerbated identity politics.

The fact that not much changed in the character and form of identities in relation to the nation state project in Nigeria was evident during the Second Republic. In spite of tremendous political re-engineering to prevent the emergence and proliferation of sectional ethnic and religious power bases, the different political parties at that time (and the pattern of alliances they forged between and among themselves) only continued what obtained during the First Republic. For instance, the zero-sum format of identity-based electoral politics of the period re-echoed what obtained during the First Republic. The major parties- the National Party of Nigeria (NPN), the Unity Party of Nigeria (UPN) and Nigeria People's Party (NPP) turned out to be re-embodiments of the old NPC, AG and NCNC respectively. Each of them mobilised the critical mass of their supporters from the different regions: NPN from the Hausa/Fulani north, the UPN from the Yoruba-speaking southwest, and the NPP in the Igbo east. In order to mobilise the potential voters during the General Elections of 1979 and 1983, ethnicity, religion and regionalism were openly touted and exploited. Apart from paving the way for massive electoral malpractices, identity politics eventually undermined the Second Republic.

The period 1984 to 1989 was therefore significant in three interrelated respects. First, the return of the military after a rather short civilian interregnum further strengthened northern hegemony. Second, the period coincided with deepening economic crisis which caused scarcities, poverty, massive unemployment and a general decline in living standards of the people. These factors, in turn, sharpened competition and allowed two major types of identity: ethnic and religious, to assume new social relevance. On the one hand, ethnic identities were accentuated by the struggle to maximise state resource flows in favour of the small but highly privileged social strata and resistance by disenfranchised groups (Jega 2000:24-40). On the other, religious revivalism assumed new and striking social dimensions among Christians and Moslems alike, in reaction to acute economic distress (Muazzam& Ibrahim 2000). While religious fundamentalism in different forms flourished, it coagulated with established ethnic identities to intensify violent conflicts between adherents of different religions. Ethno-religious violence became common- for example, in Kano, Kaduna, Yola and Gombe between 1980 and 1985, and in Kafanchan in 1987.

While economic crisis was deepening religious identity, the state made matters worse by allowing doubts to cast in popular consciousness on the secularity of the state as provided for in the constitution, through the solicitation of membership of the Organization of Islamic Conference (OIC) in 1986. This step was a watershed in the history of state-religion partisanship in Nigeria. Thereafter, religious affiliation was dragged into every appointments, policies and resource distribution.

Two other tendencies that made identity politics more relevant at this period of economic crisis were increasing state repression and a flowering of civil society groups. The Nigerian state became more authoritarian in the 1980s as part of state strategy for the management of harsh neo-liberal economic reforms agenda. This coincided with an unprecedented growth in and proliferation of civil society organisations whose activisms were directed towards the unconditional withdrawal of the military from government and the restoration of civilian democracy in the country.

Persisting state character, identities mobilisation and instability in Nigeria, 1990-2003

The 1990s witnessed both the accentuation of identity crisis in Nigeria, and such other related challenges to the stability of the country. Apart from manifesting in violent inter-communal, ethnic, and religious confrontations, the various crises arising from the politicisation of identities from the 1990s onward also targeted the infrastructure of power and authority within the country. During the period, the state revealed itself further through extreme and often unwarranted authoritarianism and repression. Apart from been extremely corrupt, dishonest, insincere and self-perpetuating, the military fuelled ethnic, religious and sectional hegemony. In order to perpetuate military rule, Generals Babangida and Abacha manipulated religion and sectional sentiments and devised a system of divide and rule, oiled by a structure of graft and co-optation.

Corruption - the appropriation of state resources for personal and prebendal ends - reached an endemic institutionalised proportion. The Abacha regime entered the history books as the most repressive regime in Nigeria. More dangerously, it branded an entire region as the opposition and commenced a brutal regime of intimidation, exclusion and repression against them. The subsequent siege mentality that was created was reflected in the resistance that produced the likes of the Oodua People's Congress (OPC), the Supreme Egbesu Assembly (SEA), Movement for the Survival and Self-Actualisation of Biafra (MASSOB), to name a few. The regime encouraged a north versus south and a Hausa/ Fulani and Kanuri versus Yoruba antagonism. It painted the south as miscreant troublemakers and forcefully projected northern supremacy. In the South-South, Abacha commenced a long-drawn regime of brutal repression against the militant Ogonis and the Ijaws through frequent and large-scale military pacification exercises.

The unending transitions, replete with all the imaginable inconsistencies further exacerbated ethnic and sectional animosities during and after the annulment of the 1993 presidential election results by the Babangida regime- an action which triggered a groundswell of social mobilisation and anomie among different civil society groups. The Abacha transition pursued a northern and Moslem hegemonic agenda, in addition to its totalitarian and corrupt rule. Both the Babangida and Abacha transitions contributed greatly to identity mobilisation and protracted violent conflicts. The already lingering economic crisis made more manifest the crises of governance and of the state in Nigeria under each of the military regimes, and more significantly, raised widespread anxiety over the allocation of resources and the equity, justice and fairness of the process.

There were a number of other notable outcomes of and reactions to this build up of state authoritarianism and repression. First, and perhaps the most concrete was a growing militancy of civil society groups, especially manifested in the minority nationalisms that enveloped the oil-rich but poor south-south region. In the 1990s and afterwards, the campaign for minority rights changed gear from seeking accommodation to demanding self-determination; defined as the re-negotiation and reconstruction of the Nigerian state as a whole (Osaghae 2001:2). The re-democratisation project coalesced around regional agenda (mirroring the depth grievances felt especially by the southerners over the annulment of the June 1993 Presidential election results, and against political misrule and flagrant violation of human rights). These encouraged identity-based movements to team up with civil society groups to pursue the pro-democracy struggle with the vigour deserved. The period after the annulment witnessed increased protests and violent action by different segments of the civil society demanding equity and justice from a pathologically flawed state.

The popular clamour that the different entities making up Nigeria must seat at the table to discuss nagging but substantive national questions also became persistent and loud. Numerous groups became more adept and assertive in demanding greater administrative and fiscal autonomy within a restructured Federation. This is the context within which different calls, particularly for a sovereign national conference, resource control and equitable power sharing among the regions, must be understood. As a consequence, every issue of importance became politicised along different identity lines. Along with the mobilisation of identities began the rise of tensions, antagonism and the increase in the volatility of intra- and inter-group relations. The seeds of the massive ethno-religious riots that broke out from 1999 onwards were sown.

Conclusions

Nigeria today is a deeply fractured and severely divided nation. Ethnic, religious, sectional, regional and other identities have produced pervasive feelings of anxiety and tension. The prominence of the factor of identity in the politics of the country has become an ever-growing and dangerous liability. After more than four decades as an independent entity, there is still a festering assertion of identity and inter-group conflict, increasing segmentation and fragmentation of Nigerian peoples, and an unending clamour to start contemplating, unravelling and resolving the national question. There is also increasing challenge to the state, regarded in many quarters as the institutional agency for unjust and inequitable treatment. Without doubt, identity conflicts have undermined not just political but also slowed the pace of economic development in the country.

At another level, identity has created a citizenship crisis indicated both by overlapping or multiple identities and loyalties with contradicting demands and claims as well as by citizenship polarized along group versus nationality. Second, there is a growing sense inequality between individual and group citizenship and rights. There is indeed a hierarchy of citizenships in which some at individual and group levels enjoy differing quality of citizenship rights and preferential treatment. In the hierarchy, the ethnic minorities and marginalised majorities such as the Ibos, and the Yorubas at certain times, have been subordinated. Third is the crisis of indigeneity, in which national citizenship is denied in preference for (or subservience to) 'indigeneship'. This has created a situation in which the average Nigerian is a stranger, an alien in 35 of the 36 states of the federation (Bach 1997:380).

The identity crisis in Nigeria is largely linked to a state that though constitutionally heterogeneous, has constructed a stratified structure of dominance over the vast citizenry. Clearly, the state has not attempted to build a level playing field for all its citizens. Instead, it has been too partial, too parochial and too partisan in dealing with and accommodating them. It has lent itself to becoming a hegemonic tool for the marginalisation and subordination of large segments of the population. By its centralised nature, the state continues to serve as an instrument of hegemony and resource appropriation, and for the subordination of different groups. The nature of state construction has spawned a deadly competition for hegemony, state power and resources, thereby accentuating the mobilisation and politicisation of ethnicity, religion and region and state (Jinadu 2003: 8).

The paradox, of course, is that frequent resort by the state to the use of force and repression has both weakened and made it vulnerable (Amuwo 1998: 73). It is associated with exclusion and repression of several ethnic, religious, minority and other primordial groupings and formations, inequitable political representation, resource distribution and application of unequal access to power and resources, and the distribution of social amenities and benefits.

Weak and partisan as it is, the Nigerian state has engendered a sense of belonging not to "one nation" but with smaller communities of faith, descent or locale (Ijediogor 2000). The absence of a 'strong sense of nationhood or citizenship' makes the Nigerian state an easy prey to sectional and private interests (Forrest 1995: 3). As Amuwo and Herault (1998: 8) rightly puts it, because the Nigerian state denies Nigerians their civil rightly as citizens, many of them have taken 'refuge in the ethnic right to recover their citizenship. The absence of clearly defined concept of citizenship, the status of non-indigenes and of the laws of ownership, boundaries and control of natural resources further weakens the state'.

Most inter-ethnic and communal conflicts and conflagrations mask the manipulative and unseen hands of the elite, to whom an identity card or base remains a tool in the politics of preferment and incorporation. The manipulation of social cleavages in the elite contention for power has persisted since the colonial period (Diamond 1995), as they fan the embers of discord or capitalise on them for their selfish ambitions. The ruling class and elite, being weak, insensitive, and bankrupt of ideas, have been unable to generate alternative visions or an idea; a programmatic and ideological basis for leadership. They have found identity sentiments as a cheap rostrum for political mobilisation and personal gains.

A combination of poverty, large-scale unemployment, socio-economic scarcity and political frustration has sharpened ethnic differences and divisions. Economic scarcity has accentuated the urge by individuals to take solace in ethnic cocoons and to become hypersensitive towards others believed to be at an undue advantage. Poverty and unemployment have made more glaring than ever the existing inequities, particularly in the oil-rich Niger Delta. Economic stagnation, hyper-inflation, collapse of utilities and infrastructures, have created a large social 'underclass' compromising of the under-educated, unemployed, poor, deprived, and frustrated who are easily manipulated and exploited by different factions of the ruling class (Sankore 2001: 10). Since the return to civilian rule in 1999, the new 'democratic' freedom in place has further opened up new avenues for the expression of long-suppressed social anger. Group resistance to, and the emergence of a new siege mentality, among hitherto dominant groups have further strengthened identity consciousness and mobilisation.

In conclusion, the central argument in this chapter is that the character and behaviour of the Nigerian state, and that of the succession of elites that have captured it from independence to date, should be blamed for the scaling up of identity issues and problems all of which undermines political and economic development, stability and unity of the country. The state and its emergent elites merely built upon the inherited colonial and structures without attempting to reconstruct what was in place or to create an entirely new and all-embracing national identity and the sense of belonging that comes with it. The ensuing identity crisis has become so corrosive and devastating, paving way for the state to assume the form of a ravaging leviathan. The rampages of the mammoth can only be checkmated by the deconstruction of identities away from its contentious utilisation to that of development and peaceful pluralism. But to do so, the state would have to be reformed and its elites that operate it restrained.

References

Ake, C., 1996, 'The Political Question', in Oyeleye Oyediran (ed.) *Governance and Development in Nigeria: Essays in Honour of Professor Billy J. Dudley*, Ibadan: Agbo Areo Publishers.

Amuwo, K., 1998, 'Beyond the Orthodoxy of Political Restructuring: The Abacha Junta and the Political Economy of Force', in K. Amuwo, A. Agbaje, R. Suberu & G. Herault (eds.) *Federalism and Political Restructuring in Nigeria*, Ibadan: Spectrum Books.

Amuwo, K. & Herault, G., 1998, 'On the Notion of Political Restructuring in a Federal System', in K. Amuwo, A. Agbaje, R. Suberu & G. Herault (eds.) *Federalism and Political Restructuring in Nigeria*, Ibadan: Spectrum Books.

Atkinson, R. R., 1999, 'The (Re) construction of Ethnicity in Africa: Extending the Chronology, Conceptualization Discourse', in Paris Yeros (ed.) *Ethnicity and Nationalism in Africa: Constructivist Reflections and Contemporary Politics*, Houndsmill: Macmillan.

Bach, D.C., 1997, 'Identity, Ethnicity and Federalism', in Larry Diamond, A. Kirk Greene and Oyeleye Oyediran (eds.) *Transition Without End: Nigerian Politics and Civil Society Under Babangida*, Ibadan: Vantage Press.

Baker, B., 1999, 'African Anarchy: Is it the States, Regimes or Societies that are Collapsing?', *Politics* 19(3).

Beck, E.M., 1980, 'Labour Unionism and Racial Income Inequality: A Time-Series analysis of Post-World War period', *America Journal of Sociology*.85.

Diamond, L., 1988, *Class, Ethnicity and Democracy in Nigeria: The Failure of the First Republic*, Syracuse, New York: Syracuse University Press.

Diamond, L., 1995, 'Preventive Diplomacy for Nigeria: Imperative for US and International Policy', Paper presented to the House International Relations Committee, US Congress, Washington D.C. 28 November.

Egwu, S.G., 2001, 'Ethnic and Religious Violence in Nigeria', Abuja: The African Centre for Democratic Governance.

Esman, J.M., 1994, *Ethnic Politics*, Ithaca, NY: Cornell University Press.

Forrest, T., 1995, *Politics and Economic Development in Nigeria*, Colorado, Westview Press.

Graf, W.D., 1986, 'African Elite Theories and the Nigerian Elite Consolidation: A Political Economy Analysis', in Yolamu Barongo (ed.) *Political Science in Africa: A Critical Review*, London: Zed Press.

Gurr, T. and Hart, B., 1994, *Ethnic Conflict in World Politics*, Boulder, Colorado: Westview Press.

Hodgkin, T., 1957, 'Letter to Biobaku', *Odu* 4

Horowitz, L.D., 1985, *Ethnic Groups in Conflict*, Berkeley: University of California Press.

Idowu, W.O.O., 1999, 'Citizenship, Alienation and Conflict in Nigeria', *Africa Development*, XXIV (1&2).

Ifidon, E.A., 1996, 'Citizenship, Statehood and the Problem of Democratization in Nigeria', *Africa Development*, Vol. 21 (4).

Ignatief, M., 1999, *The Warrior's Honour: Ethnic War and the Modern Conscience*, London: Vintage.

Ihonvbere, J.O., 1988, 'The "Irrelevant" State: Ethnicity and the Subversion of the Goals of Nationhood in Africa', Paper prepared for the International Conference on Ethnicity and Nationhood in Africa, University of Sokoto, Sokoto, Nigeria.

Ijediogor, G., 2000, 'Militant Groups Only Let off Tension', *The Guardian*, Saturday, July 22.

Ikelegbe, A.O., 2003, 'Civil Society and Alternative Approaches to Conflict Management', in T.A Imobighe (ed.) *Civil Society and Ethnic Conflict Management in Nigeria*, Ibadan: Spectrum Books.

Institute for Democracy and Electoral Assistance (IDEA), 2000, 'Democracy in Nigeria: Continuing Dialogue(s) for Nation Building (Capacity Building', Series 10).

Jega, A., 2000, 'The State and Identity Transformation under Structural Adjustment in Nigeria', in Attahiru Jega (ed.) *Identity Transformation and Identity Politics under Structural Adjustment in Nigeria*, Uppsala: Nordiska Afrikainstitutet and CRD: Kano.

Jinadu, L.A., 2003, 'Democratization, Development and the Identity Crisis in Nigeria', Second Annual Lecture, Department of Sociology, University of Lagos, Lagos July, 30.

Kieh, G.K., 2001, 'Reconstituting a Collapsed State. The Liberian case', in Segun Jegede, Ayodele Ale and Eni Akinsola (eds.) *State Reconstruction in West Africa,* Lagos: Committee for the Defence of Human Rights.

Mackintosh, J.P., 1966, *Nigerian Government and Politics,* London: Allen and Unwin.

Maiz, R., 2003, 'Politics and the Nation: Nationalist Mobilization of Ethnic Differences', *Nation and Nationalism,* 9 (2). p. 197.

Melson, R. and Wolpe, H., 1971, *Nigeria: Modernisation and the Politics of Communalism,* East Lansing: Michigan State University Press.

Muazzam, I. and Ibrahim, J., 2000, 'Religious Identity in the Context of Structural Adjustment in Nigeria', in Attahiru Jega (ed.) *Identity Transformation and Identity Politics under Structural Adjustment in Nigeria,* Uppsala: Nordiska Afrikainstitutet, & Kano: CRD.

Ndikumana, L., 1998, 'International Failure and Ethnic Conflicts in Burundi', *African Studies Review* 1998 (4)(1).

Newman, S., 1991, 'Does Modernization Breed Ethnic Political Violence?', *World Politics* 43.

Nigeria, Federal Republic, 1987, *The Report of the Political Bureau,* Lagos.

Nnoli, O., 1978, *Ethnic Politics in Nigeria,* Enugu: Fourth Dimension Publishers.

Nnoli, O., 1989, *Ethnic Politics in Africa,* Ibadan: AAPS.

Nwosu, H., 1977, *Political Authority and the Nigerian Civil Service,* Enugu: Fourth Dimension.

Obi, C.I., 1997, 'Oil, Environmental Conflict and National Security in Nigeria: Ramifications of the Ecology-Security Nexus for Sub-Regional Peace', University of Illinois at Urbana Champaign.

O'Connell, J., 1971, 'Authority and Community in Nigeria', in Melson, Robert and Howard Wolpe (eds.) *Nigeria Modernisation and the Politics of Communalism,* East Lansing: Michigan State University Press.

Ogachi, O., 1999, 'Economic Reform, Political Liberation and Ethnic Conflicts in Kenya', *Africa Development* XXIV, (1&2).

Olzak, S., 1983, 'The Economic Construction of Ethnicity', Paper Presented at Annual Meetings of the *American Sociological Association,* Detroit.

Osaghae, E., 1994, *Ethnicity and its Management in Africa: The Democratization Link,* CASS Occasional Monograph No. 2.

Osaghae, E., 2001, 'From Accommodation to Self Determination: Minority Nationalism and Restructuring of the Nigeria State', *Nationalism and Ethnic Politics,* 7 (1).

Otite, O., 1990, *Ethnic Pluralism and Ethnicity in Nigeria,* Ibadan: Shaneson.

Ottaway, M., 1999, 'Ethnic Politics in Africa: Change and Continuity', in Richard Joseph (ed.) *State, Conflict and Democracy in Africa,* Boulder: Lynne Rienner.

Post, K. and Vickers, M., 1973, *The Structure of Conflict in Nigeria 1960-1966,* London: Heinemann.

Richardson, Jr J.M. and Sen, S., 1997, 'Ethnic Conflict and Economic Development: A Policy Oriented Analysis', *Ethnic Studies Report* XV, (1) January.

Sankore, R., 2001, 'Politics of Ethnic and Religious Conflict', Lagos, *Thisday on Sunday*, October 28.

Siobhian, H., 2001, 'The Institutional Foundations of Sub-State National Movements', *Comparative Politics,* 33 (2) January.

Sklar, R.L., 1963, *Nigerian Political Parties*, New Jersey: Princeton University Press.

Sundberg, A., 1999, 'Class and Ethnicity in the Struggle for Power - The Failure of Democratization in Congo-Brazzaville', *Africa Development* XXIV, (1&2).

Taiwo, F., 1996, 'Of Citizens and Citizenship', Lagos, *The Tempo*, September-October.

Thomson, A., 2000, *An Introduction to African Politics*, London: Routledge.

Timbiah, S.J., 1990, 'Reflections on Communal Violence in South Asia', *Journal of Asian Studies* 49(4).

Transition Monitoring Group (TMG) and United Nations Electoral Assistance Division 2002. Communiqué: Mechanisms for the Civil Society and the State in conflict management, Abuja, March 6-7.

Uya, O.E., 1992, 'Nigeria: The Land and the People', in Okon Edet Uya (ed.) *Contemplated Nigeria*, Buenos Aires: EDIPUBLI S.A.

Warren, K.B., 1993, 'Introduction: Revealing Conflicts Across Cultures and Disciplines', in K. B. Warren (ed.) *The Violence Within: Cultural and Political Opposition in Divided Nations*, Boulder: Westview Press Inc.

Wilson, R., 2001, 'The Politics of Contemporary Ethno-nationalist Conflicts', *Nations and Nationalism* 7 (3).

5

Drama and the Quest for Democracy in Post-Military Nigeria

Gbemisola Remi Adeoti

Introduction

Doubtless, democracy is a key element in modern theories of development. It is believed to be a necessary system for harnessing social energies and resources towards combating inequality, misery, unemployment, illiteracy and oppression. Diamond (1999: 7) makes the point when he writes that democracies 'appear in the long run to respond better to the needs of the poor and marginalized, because they enable such groups to organize and mobilize within the political process'. The notion of democracy in this paper transcends the formal confines of party politics, elections and the contest for power among elites. It refers to a process and practice of harmonising diverse socio-political interests in society. Supported by a free press and independent judiciary, democracy seeks to guarantee the rights of citizens to participate directly or indirectly in decision-making, and to mobilise human potential towards national development.

Literature, especially drama, and politics are not mutually exclusive, but inherently complementary. Both, according to Ngugi wa Thiong'o, 'are created by the same reality of the world around us' while '[their] activity and concern have the same subject and object: human beings and human relationships' (1981: 71). Ken Saro-Wiwa in his prison diary – *A Month and a Day* – asserts that 'literature must serve society by steeping itself in politics, by intervention, and writers must not merely write to amuse or to take a bemused, critical look at society' (1995: 81). As T.S. Eliot has observed almost four decades ago, a deep political philosophy has its foundation in the realm of the 'pre-political' where seminal works of imaginative literature belong. This, in his words, 'is the substratum down to which any sound political thinking must push its roots, and from which it must derive its nourishment'. The most fundamental question which virtually all political thinking addresses, is: 'What is Man? What are his limitations? What is his misery and what is his greatness? And what, finally, his destiny?' (1968: 144). Different cultures across the world have sought answers to these questions through the arts of drama.

This chapter focuses on the crucial intersection between the goals of politics and drama. While it identifies certain factors militating against the development of a genuinely democratic polity in postcolonial Nigeria, it highlights the prospects for a more democratically engaged dramaturgy and a reformed polity where democracy thrives and endures.

Reflections on Nigerian drama and the democratic imperative

The supposition of an inter-relationship between drama and politics informs the works of many a Nigerian dramatist from the established to the emerging talent. Drama as a social art form is a product of socio-political and historical realities, as well as the human daily condition of existence (Booth 1981; Calinescu 1982; Etherton 1982; Malomo and Gbilekaa 1993; Lihaba 1994; Kerr 1996; Williams 1996; Yerima and Akinwale 2002). While drama can be used in the construction and stabilisation of hegemony, it can also serve the 'marginalized' in the task of deconstructing the dominant power structure and contesting marginality (Gilbert and Tompkins 1996).

From the anti-imperial temper of the pre-independence era, drama has remained a vehicle for the articulation of social content and discontent, being a notable part of cultural assertions in the decolonisation struggles. Here, the opera-dramatic compositions of Hubert Ogunde and his African Music Research Party in the 1940s denouncing the excesses of colonialists readily come to mind. Some of these include: 'Strike and Hunger' (1946), 'Towards Liberty' (1947) and 'Bread and Bullet' (1951). In spite of the hostility with which they were treated by the colonial state, Ogunde and his theatre group made a trenchant 'political statement in favour of self-rule' through the plays (Clark 1979: 43). His political intervention through the theatre, however, did not abate with the attainment of independence, as those who inherited political power from the colonialists could not realise the liberation ideals of self-rule. The political crises that soon engulfed Nigeria shortly after independence imperilled national development as corruption, power abuse, political repression, and nepotism overwhelmed the polity. 'Yoruba Ronu' (1964) and 'Otito Koro' (1965) were Ogunde's stage responses to the acrimonious politics of the Western Region of Nigeria from where he hailed. Both plays were inspired by the unpopular premiership of Samuel Ladoke Akintola, in the Western Region. The pervasive collapse of law and order later culminated in the military coup of January 15, 1966. The intervention by soldiers in politics not only effectively scuttled first attempt at democratic rule in Nigeria but also made the military a permanent feature of the Nigerian political scene.

The development of literary drama in the 1960s was anchored around the personalities of playwrights and dramatists like Wole Soyinka, John Pepper Clark, Wale Ogunyemi, Ola Rotimi and Sony Oti. These authors provided discursive strategies for interrogating, engaging and negotiating the political sphere in a very critical manner. Interestingly, the betrayal too soon by politicians of expectations held out by political independence necessitated a dramaturgy that could not afford insularity from politics as witnessed in the concert tradition of the colonialists or the literary pamphleteering tradition of Onitsha Market Literature.

Soyinka's *A Dance of the Forests*, written to celebrate the nation's independence in 1960, anticipates the early collapse of the democratic experiment after independence as well as the prolonged authoritarian rule that followed. For the playwright, there seems to be nothing in the polity worthy of celebration when all available social indices point to a festering crisis of governance, which the politicians and nationalists hardly attend to with a sincerity of purpose. Whether in the community of the Dead summoned by the human world to celebrate 'the Gathering of the Tribes' or among the mythical dwellers of the forests like *Eshuoro* and *Ogun*, 'The Gathering of the Tribes' refers to Nigeria's independence celebration, amidst unmediated ethno-religious and geo-political differences. Among the participants in the play are characters drawn from Yoruba mythology like Eshuoro who is a fusion of the attributes of *Esu* (the Yoruba trickster deity) and *Oro* (a deity of mystery associated with the ancestral cult), and *Ogun*, the god of iron. In the re-enacted court of a medieval tyrant, Mata Kharibu, intolerance, selfishness and narcissism are the norm. The play alerts its audience to the dearth in the public sphere of consciousness and attitudinal traits necessary for sustaining democratic governance. It warns that a political arrangement founded on such habits is fated to encounter disaster.

Kongi's Harvest and *Madmen and Specialists* depict the evils of tyrannical governance styles. Both plays are imbued with the censuring temper of satire in a manner that makes them fresh and relevant, many years after their premiere. For instance, Kongi, who is the eponymous hero of *Kongi's Harvest* and Dr. Bero in *Madmen and Specialists* ably personify absolutist tendencies of military rulers. The playwright equally portrays in a contemptible and laughable manner the authoritarian ethos foisted on the African polity by the military in *Jero's Metamorphosis* and *Opera Wonyosi*.

Apart from Soyinka, Ola Rotimi engages the stage in the discourse of Africa's post-colonial crisis of governance. For instance, he deplores the shrinking of the democratic space consequent upon the vices of the elite in *Our Husband Has Gone Mad Again*. Earlier, the recurring problem of leadership arising from the challenges of decolonisation and nation building is confronted in two historical plays – *Kurunmi* and *Ovonramwen Nogbaisi*. *Kurunmi* captures the fall of Aare Kurunmi, the Generalissimo of the Oyo Empire who rebels against the Empire as personified in Alaafin. Kurunmi anchors his rebellion on the need to defend the 'sacrosanct tradition' of succession, which Alaafin seeks to alter in favour of his heir, Adelu. The author, however, shows the futility of war as a means of resolving conflict in place of dialogue. The use of history in the play is to provide a detached but topical comment on the Nigerian civil war (1967-1970), the origin of which many writers have traced to the failure of democratisation after independence.

The exploration of African myth, legend and history to make artistic statements is palpable in Ogunyemi's *Obaluwaye*, Duro Ladipo's *Oba Koso*, Ogunyemi's *Kiriji*, Ladipo's *Moremi*, and Sofola's *King Emene*. These plays express the temper of what Osofisan describes as 'our nation's age of innocence' (1997: 11). The dominant trope in each of these plays is a 'mono-archical' figure that embodies power and authority while others are subordinate to him. Thus, a unitary order is subtly created in the universe of the stage.

The perceived polemical limitations of drama written during this 'age of innocence' contribute to artistic revaluations by some writers who believe that the arts should play more intervention roles in national politics. Indeed, the challenges of democracy as a means of addressing the inadequacies of military rule have been more trenchantly dramatised in the closing decades of the twentieth century. The period coincided with yet another fool's errand in the democratic experiment in Nigeria, between 1979 and 1983, and the second full-blown military rule (31 December 1983; 29 May 1999). As the military re-inserted themselves in the nation's politics, Nigerian drama's political engagement assumed a more critical dimension.

In this political/artistic dispensation marked by torrents of creative energies from Esiaba Irobi, Femi Osofisan, Fred Agbeyegbe, Tess Onwueme, Ahmed Yerima, Ben Tomoloju, Stella Oyedepo, Taiwo Oloruntoba-Oju and Chinyere Okafor as well as established playwrights like Soyinka and Clark, dramatists became so-preoccupied with themes relating to authoritarian tendencies in governance and a wish for democratic re-ordering of power relations. In their plays, they urge the expansion of the public sphere to include those hitherto excluded by undemocratic mode of governance. Their plays condemn dictatorship while also projecting the creation of a new political order for the country.

Nigerian writers and performing artists have not only used drama as a scourge of autocrats, but also as a means of canvassing for a democratic culture based on popular sovereignty, equity, equality, the peaceful resolution of conflicts, respect for rule of law and tolerance of dissenting views. In broad terms, the audience is confronted not just with mere 'imitation' or 're-presentation' of action in Aristotelian terms, but with a deeper negotiation of the public sphere by re-constituting real historical events and situations.

Undoubtedly, the most important historic challenge before Nigeria at this particular period was how the country would, after recovering from the adverse effects of military rule, launch itself on the path of genuine democracy and development. Dictatorship tends to deny people's rights and freedom, and when people are not free and their choices curtailed, it becomes difficult to mobilise them for development. In view of this, democratic governance seems to hold a brighter prospect for the actualisation of the visions of independence - especially freedom and empowerment.

To this end, Nigerian playwrights create in different ways, a social space where power use and abuse represent the norm rather than an aberration of social-political interaction, depending on the thematic pre-occupation of their plays. They also lay bare disorder and corruption apparent in a supposedly democratising order. For instance, Osofisan's *Aringindin and the Nightwatchmen* is an eloquent metaphor that depicts evils of dictatorship. In a way that is somewhat reminiscent of Bertolt Brecht's *The Resistible Rise of Arturo Ui*, *Aringindin*...attempts to soothe the people's feelings of helplessness and lethargy induced by prolonged alienation from power. It strives to reanimate their being as individuals and a collective by ridding the society of repressive forces. Osofisan contends in the play that a true match to genuine democracy will begin when people are ready to confront tyranny, dislodge Aringindin (a theatrical anticipation of Late General Sanni Abacha) and the Nightwatchmen from the fortress of power.

In summary, the play enacts the ordeal of an unnamed Nigerian community whose peace is constantly violated by armed robbers. The robbers unleash a spate of violence on the people, claiming several lives and property. At Aringindin's suggestion, the community sets up a night guard squad (vigilante) under the leadership of Aringindin. However, the community soon cedes its liberty to the squad as a result of the latter's arbitrary actions, all in the name of providing security for the people. The community sinks deeper into anarchy culminating in the death of Tisa (Aringindin's arch critic) and the abdication of the throne by the community's traditional head, Baale. The exit of the Baale, in turn, paves the way for full-blown dictatorship, led by Aringindin and Kansillor, his civilian collaborator. It takes the vengeful bullet from Yobioyin (Tisa's fiancée) to end Aringindin's life and his reign of terror.

In terms of dramatic forms and theatrical conventions, a general survey shows that some dramatists provoke contempt at the anti-democratic conducts of the elite, both civilian and military. Through wit and disdain, they censure the will to narcissism upon which military dictatorship and other antitheses of democracy are founded. Again, Osofisan's *Aringindin and the Nightwatchmen*, Soyinka's *A Play of Giants*, *From Zia with Love*, *The Beatification of Area Boy: A Lagosian Kaleidoscope*, and *King Baabu* exemplify this possibility. In another vein, some playwrights adopt a dialectical materialist reading of the nation's socio-political reality. Their experiences in this respect are represented through a fusion of Bertolt Brecht's elements of 'epic' theatre with the communal participatory aesthetics of traditional African performance. Such artistic experiences are found in Osofisan's *Yungba Yungba and the Dance Contest*, Rotimi's *If... a Tragedy of the*

Ruled, and Taiwo Oloruntoba-Oju's *Awaiting Trouble*. Visions of a new democratic Nigeria are articulated through a revolutionary alternative or what Saint Gbilekaa (1997) has tagged 'radical' theatrical discourse.

The perceived marginalisation of women in the polity and the imperative of women's empowerment against the backdrop of democratisation also gain the attention of some dramatists. Expectedly, these thematic concerns have generated their own gender-centred theatrical discourse as demonstrated in J.P. Clark's *The Wives Revolt*, Rotimi Johnson's *The Court of the Queens*, Tess Onwueme's *The Reign of Wazobia* and Chinyere Okafor's *The Lion and the Iroko*.

In *The Wives' Revolt*, Clark shows the limitations of a society that lays claim to democratic culture, yet, excludes a vital segment of its population from decision-making organs- the women. The image of the African woman portrayed in *The Wives' Revolt* is that of a human being who can successfully challenge the mores of patriarchy in order to achieve a genuinely democratic society where the two sexes co-exist as partners and stakeholders. Such a harmonious order will require the removal of socio-cultural encumbrances that account for gender imbalance. The crux of the domestic feud in *The Wives' Revolt* is the money paid by the foreign oil company operating in Erhuwaren. The money is, perhaps, paid in compensation for the devastation of the community's means of livelihood due to oil prospecting activities. The issue in contention is the appropriate formula to adopt in sharing the money equitably among the people. The formula proposed and adopted by the Elders' council sparks a row as it divides the money into three equal parts. One part is given to the elders, one part to men across age grades and the third part to women across age grades. To the elders, it is 'a most fair and equitable settlement'. But to the women, it is not fair and equitable because it privileges men who propose it. They are allotted two-thirds of the total sum, leaving only one-third for the women. The adoption of this proposal queries the democratic claim of the decision-making organs of the community represented in the Elders' council and the General Assembly.

At the basis of the gender dispute are issues of freedom from domination and women's rights to participate in governance in all its ramifications like men. Consequently, in place of the unequal formula, the women demand that the unspecified amount of money should be divided into two equal halves – one for men across grades and the other for women across age grades. This will place both sexes on an equal pedestal. Mutual rejection of the 'other' position clearly shows the conflict as that between advocates of equality and inclusion on the one hand (women) and defenders of domination and exclusion on the other (men). In pressing home their demands, the women abandon their domestic duties and thereby cause a great dislocation in the social order. They quietly walk out on their husbands. But the absence of women threatens the existence of the society itself and men do not have any choice at the end of the day other than to acknowledge the import and role of women in the society. The play among other lessons stresses the importance of debate, respect for people's rights and the virtues of co-operation beyond gender partition.

The same issue is treated in Onwueme's *The Reign of Wazobia*, but from a more radical feminist perspective. Part of Onwueme's theatrical revisionism in *The Reign of Wazobia* is the negation of traditional rites that nurture gender disparity. The play depicts a group of women who join forces to gain political advantage over men, exploring men's perceived obsession with power. Consequently, the women succeed in reversing the culturally erected disequilibrium in power relation within the society. She contends that for democracy to take root and be sustained, the woman's otherness must be properly addressed.

The Reign of Wazobia denounces socio-cultural and political practices that encourage sexual inequality especially in the public sphere. At the centre of conflict is Wazobia, the female regent of Ilaa in Anioma kingdom. Her provisional tenure of three seasons has expired, but she is reluctant to yield power to a substantive male king as demanded by tradition of the kingdom. She is consequently locked in a fierce battle for the throne with male chiefs who are poised to end her allegedly 'terroristic' interregnum. On her part, Wazobia seeks to perpetuate herself in power as a way of rejecting women's exclusion and men's perpetual domination. To her, the custom that prescribes the role of regency for women and limits them to that is discriminatory. It basically ensures that only a man will always become the substantive king and the female regent would have to leave office at the end of three seasons when the new 'male' king would have been installed. She captures the perceived exploitation in a metaphor of fruit which men for ages have 'used, sucked dry and disposed off at will'.

The passivity, which makes women, not actors on political stage but social beings always acted upon is what Wazobia is set to stop and she is stirring other women's consciousness in that direction. The play's prologue indicates this goal as it features a mock battle between the mob of men fiercely demanding Wazobia's immediate abdication and an army of 'naked' women protecting her against men's aggression. What follows is a battle for the vacant throne between the forces of tradition led by Iyase, Idehen and other chiefs on the one side and the forces of female ascendancy represented by Wazobia, Omu and the women folk on the other.

In another category are plays with a similar concern with the travails of democracy and governance, but which defy easy taxonomy, as they are more receptive to various dramatic influences. Such plays as Esiaba Irobi's *Nwokedi* and Ahmed Yerima's *The Silent Gods* adopt the eclectic option in their responses to the project of democratisation. Eclecticism here involves a conscious adoption of multiple artistic forms and styles by playwrights to react to the challenges of democratisation. Its inherent circumvention of notable conventions of play-making carries within it, elements of innovation, reform and renewal.

Consequently, it is a kind of departure from the traditional genres of comedy and tragedy.

However, in spite of this demonstrable identification with the national quest for nationhood and development within a democratic framework, valid contributions and potentials of drama constitute an area of research that is yet to be adequately explored, judging from the extant literature on democracy. This hiatus is particularly registered in the common tendency to treat democracy almost exclusively as a political and economic concept. Meanwhile, the complexity and dynamism of democracy as a human phenomenon demands a broad analytical mechanism, and a multi-disciplinary approach.

Drama and the discourse on democratisation

The character and persistence of political instability that confronted many post-independence regimes in Africa, and pressures arising from the abrupt end of the Cold War, made democracy as a mode of governance, a very compelling option. Fukuyama (1992) is quite right when he submits that:

> the most remarkable development of the last quarter of the twentieth century has been the revelation of enormous weaknesses at the core of the world's seemingly strong dictatorships, whether they be of the military authoritarian Right or the Communist-totalitarian Left (xiii).

It is gratifying to note that another civilian administration has been inaugurated since 29 May 1999. The regime, led by a retired General, Olusegun Obasanjo, was the product of a multi-party election conducted by the military in February 1999 to conclude its transition to civil rule programme. The former military ruler has also been re-elected in the 2003 general elections for another term of four years. However, what is earnestly in contention is whether what obtains now is truly democratic.

At the moment, there seems to be a wide chasm between democratic ideals and the realities of Nigeria's governance since the return to civil rule in 1999. While there is wide room for improvement, it is important to bear in mind that democracy is not about providing immediate solutions to all social problems, but about developing institutions, attitudes, values and procedures that can facilitate the provision of such solutions. It is in this regard, in spite of what is now generally recognized as visible indicators of authoritarianism, like arbitrary increase in fuel prices, declaration of a state of emergency in Plateau State, the suspension of the State Governor without following due process and the withholding of funds meant for local governments in Lagos State in spite of Supreme court rulings among other indices, that there are still some prospects that democracy can thrive and endure in Nigeria. That is given a concerted effort at eradicating corruption, reform of the economy in favour of the well being of majority of citizens and overhauling of the political processes especially the electoral process to ensure that the people's participation and choices actually matter.

In view of its capacity to promptly respond to the changing social tempers, the most defining challenges before Nigerian drama in the 'post-military' dispensation involve creating a template for state reconstruction and national re-birth, completely erasing the unpleasant legacies of military dictatorship and as a replacement, entrenching democracy. Drama can and should contribute to this development by generating – through its aesthetics – useful ideas that can facilitate the enthronement and consolidation of a stable democratic culture. Since a stable polity impacts on the practice of the arts, artists need to partake in the construction of such a socio-political order.

In the last decade or so, dramatists, it is pleasant to note, have been exploring the home video medium to reach a wider audience, apart from the text and the stage. This medium is now very popular in Nigeria today, especially with the South Africa-based Multichoice Direct Satellite Television (DSTV) with its 'African Magic', which features titles from the Nigerian home video films. Apart from this, video shops selling Nigerian films are emerging in major cities in London, and in West Africa – Lome, Cotonou, Ouagadougou, Abidjan, Freetown and Monrovia.

The home video refers essentially to a screenplay made up of dialogue, lifelike characters using remarkable gestures, within a setting that is somewhat life-like. The increasing popularity of this home video entertainment coincides with the decline in the production and patronage of literary drama on the one hand, and live theatre performance on the other. Several reasons can be adduced for this trend. First, a low literacy level, put at thirty percent in the country, inhibits the audience's access to written dramatic texts. Second, stage production is more demanding and not as commercially rewarding when compared with the movie. Third, home video can easily be accessed from the comfort of people's homes, hence sparing the would-be-patrons of live performance the risk of violent crimes like armed robbery, extortion, assassination, kidnapping and ritual murder, which haunt the nightlife of many urban centres.

While there is a lot of mediocrity in the presentation and storyline of many home videos in circulation, this medium seem to have become one that dramatists can explore to the fullest towards realizing a constructive engagement with public policy vis-à-vis democracy and good governance. As we have noted elsewhere, in spite of the organisational problems being encountered in this growing industry, it has a great potential to contribute to the realisation of the overall goal of nation building. The variety of talents available within the industry should be explored in raising awareness in civil society about developmental issues – apart from promoting opposition to authoritarian tendencies (Adeoti 2004).

According to the National Film and Video Censor's Board (2003), well over 4,000 home video-films have been produced in English and indigenous languages like Edo, Yoruba, Hausa and Igbo within the last decade. The dominant subjects among these include bloodletting, murder, sex, witchcraft, rituals, violence, religious bigotry, and the illusion of material success (Ekwuazi 2002). It is important that scriptwriters and producers begin to focus more on contemporary issues of democratic governance and development. The values and facts disseminated through the medium of home video films often have a remarkable imprint on the minds of the growing viewers nationwide, and even outside Nigeria.

This medium cannot afford to be merely for entertainment and remain in the realm of the apolitical. Rather, it should provide a forum for engaged and sustained discourse between the artist and the ordinary people on the imperative of a democratised polity. Already, a few titles have been produced with this pre-occupation in mind. Akinwumi Isola's 'Saworo Ide' (1999) and its sequel, 'Agogo Eewo' (produced in 2002 by Mainframe); Yinka Smart's 'Akobi Gomina' I & II (produced in 2001 by Smart Image Entertainment and Corporate Pictures), Yekinni Ajileye's 'Alaga Kansu' (produced in 2001 by YemKem International), Wemimo Olu Paul's 'Oyato I & II' (produced in 2003 by Wemimo Films)' Abiodun Majekodunmi's 'Her Excellency' (produced in 2003 by Wemimo Films), are worthy examples. Not only do they lay bare the limitations of absolutism of the recent past, but also point the way forward to a democratic order. 'Alaga Kansu', for instance, tells the story of an elected Local Government Chairman who wades through intrigues and corruption to make a difference in governance. His tenure is marked by accountability and probity and he is later elected as a State Governor. His counterparts like Koledowo suffer electoral defeat in their bid to retain their seats as Councillors and Chairmen, largely because they use their offices to accumulate wealth for themselves with little regard for the electorate.

Akinwumi Isola's *Saworo Ide* (Brass Bells) and *Agogo Eewo* (Gong of Taboo) take a backward glance at Nigeria's postcolonial history and conclude that military dictatorship, apart from inhibiting the emergence of a truly democratic polity, stifles national development. These works demonstrate the need to dethrone dictatorship as a precondition for democracy to flourish.

In addition, practitioners of literary drama, especially prominent ones like Soyinka, Osofisan, Yerima and others should also consider the option of video production in articulating their views on democracy and governance. While some of their plays mentioned earlier like *King Baabu*, *Midnight Hotel* and *The Silent Gods* could be re-worked for the screen, new ones can be written for the medium with the same political end. In any case, their intervention becomes imperative in the home video industry that still needs greater artistic competence and intellectual depth. This is with a view to uplifting the quality of thematic engagements and technical output from its present level.

Apart from the video-film, Theatre for Development (TFD) or Community Theatre is another viable artistic outlet that deserves a careful consideration. This is a form of popular drama that draws its subjects, players, costumes, props, stage and audience from a particular community, focusing on certain social problems. Usually, its focus group is the subaltern or the underprivileged in rural areas or city suburbs. Shorn of the trappings of elitist drama, TFD can be regarded as 'the theatre of the people, by the people, for the people' as the theatre goes to the people, identifies their problem(s), dissects the problem(s) and through dramatic deliberation, proffers possible solutions.

This type of theatre where the artists and the audience are united in a common search for solutions to a communal predicament can play a pivotal role in mobilising popular consciousness and action within the civil society on governance and rights issues. Interestingly, TFD is capable of generating ideas that can widen, within a short period of time, the public space in a manner that ensures free and fair participation of citizens in governance issues on equal footing. Nigeria has witnessed, in the twilight of military rule, a remarkable increase in the activities of Non-Governmental Organisations (NGOs), each stirred by different political persuasions. Their foci and target groups notwithstanding, these organisations will find it rewarding to incorporate TFD in their grassroots and community-level advocacy programmes. TFD can also be used to promote accountability in governance, campaign against corruption, enlighten the people on health related issues, eradicate ignorance and promote co-operation across ethno-religious divides, to mention a few.

In conclusion, drama in its various manifestations like the stage, the text and the screen, remains an effective strategy for strengthening civil society toward achieving an expansion of the democratic space to allow for greater participation. Drama can serve to mobilise the people and enlighten them on the ethos and practice of democracy. Nigerian drama recognizes this fact, and much of the genre has been channelled towards the tasks of widening the democratic space. But it is still capable of contributing more towards freeing the polity from the ills of absolutism if it mobilizes appropriate discourse on values and attitudes. Through its consciencitising schema, drama should continue to sensitise the government to the dangers posed by authoritarianism to nationhood and development in post-colonial Africa. It should also educate the civil society on the consequences of lethargy or acquiescence with anti-democratic actions and policies of the government.

References

Adeoti, G., 2004, 'Home Video Films and the Democratic Imperative in Contemporary Nigeria', A paper presented at the Faculty of Arts Weekly Seminar Series, Obafemi Awolowo University, Ile Ife. February 4.

Awa, E., 1996, 'Democracy in Nigeria: A Political Scientist's View', in O. Oyediran, (ed.) *Governance and Development in Nigeria*, Ibadan: Oyediran Consult Int., pp. 1-21.

Booths, J., 1981, *Writers and Politics in Nigeria*, London: Hodder and Stoughton.

Calinescu, M., 1982, 'Literature and Politics', in J. Barricelli and J. Gibaldi, (eds.) *Interrelations of Literature*, New York: MLA, pp. 123-49.

Clark, E., 1979, *Hubert Ogunde: The Making of Nigerian Theatre*, Oxford: Oxford University Press.

Diamond, L., 1999, *Developing Democracy: Toward Consolidation*, Baltimore: The John Hopkins University. Press.

Ekwuasi, H., 2002, 'Towards a Sustainable Motion Picture Industry', Lagos: *The Guardian*, Thursday, May 2, p. 64.

Eliot, T.S., 1968, 'The Literature of Politics', in *To Criticize the Critic*, London: Faber and Faber, pp. 136-144.

Etherton, M., 1982, *The Development of African Drama*, London: Hutchinson University Library.

Fukuyama, F., 1992, *The End of History and the Last Man*, London: Hamish Hamilton.

Gbilekaa, S., 1997, *Radical Theatre In Nigeria*, Ibadan: Caltop Publishers.

Gilbert, H. and Tompkins, J., 1996, *Post-Colonial Drama: Theory, Practice, Politics*, London: Routledge.

Kerr, D., 1995, *African Popular Theatre: From Precolonial Times to the Present Day*, London: James Currey.

Lihamba, A., 1994, 'Theatre and Political Struggle in East Africa', in E. Osaghae, (ed.) *Between State and Civil Society in Africa: Perspectives on Development*, Dakar: CODESRIA, 196-216.

Malomo, J. and Gbilekaa, S., eds., 1993, *Theatre and Politics in Nigeria*, Ibadan: Caltop Publishers.

National Film and Video Censor's Board, 2003, Lagos, April.

Ngugi wa Thiong'o, 1981, *Writers In Politics: Essays*, London: Heinemann.

Ogunbiyi, Y., ed., 1981, *Drama and Theatre in Nigeria: A Critical Source Book*, Lagos: Nigeria Magazine.

Osofisan, F., 1997, 'Playing Dangerously: Drama at the Frontiers of Terror in a Post-colonial State', Inaugural Lecture, University of Ibadan, July 31.

Saro Wiwa, K., 1995, *A Month And a Day*, London: Penguin Books.

Williams, A., 1996, 'Literature in the Time of Tyranny: African Writers and the Crisis of Governance', *Third World Quarterly*, Vol. XVII, No 2, pp. 349-62.

6

National Reconciliation or Polarisation? The Politics of the Ghana National Reconciliation Commission

Kwame Boafo-Arthur

Introduction

Efforts toward national reconciliation aim to facilitate a congenial socio-political and economic atmosphere for qualitative development. Generally, national reconciliation is deemed necessary on account of two specific situations: (a) in the aftermath of intra-state conflict, especially civil war, and (b) after the termination of the reign of a brutal and oppressive regime. In the view of the International Institute for Democracy and Electoral Assistance (IDEA), 'those are the contexts around the world today where the need for reconciliation is most pressing' (Bloomfield 2003: 12).

With these two scenarios in mind, it could be argued that a succession of reconciliation commissions may, in fact, be long overdue in the West African sub-region for several reasons. In the first instance, the sub-region has turned out to be the most volatile and coup-prone on the continent, and indisputably one with the largest number of military regimes since the 1960s. If we accept the premise that military regimes, on the average, are the most notorious for the repression and brutal abuse of the fundamental rights of the people, it becomes clear then that nations in the region have suffered far more several human rights abuses and social polarisations from the first military coup in Togo in the early 1960s. This ground alone justifies the setting up of reconciliation commissions in each and every one of the countries that have experienced military dictatorships in order to reconcile individuals and groups that suffered under them.

Secondly, the sub-region has since the 1990s, experienced some of the worst and most brutal intra-state conflicts, civil wars and armed rebellions in the continent's history. It is difficult to overlook the unpleasant carnage and brutality that attended the Liberian and Sierra Leonean civil wars as well as the on-going rebellion in Côte d'Ivoire that is fast tearing that once peaceful country apart. Unprecedented atrocities were committed by all the factions in those major civil wars in West Africa, leaving open sores on the conscience of many. Against this background, national development is likely to be at bay where peoples and groups are deeply divided on account of deep animosities and acrimonies enlivened by those violent conflicts. Ideally, therefore, concerned efforts should be made to reconcile different groups and to promote a spirit of unity in such divided societies as first steps towards sustainable development. Again, setting up reconciliation commissions appears to be acceptable mechanism for redressing past wrongs with the omnibus objective of ensuring the peace and stability that are necessary for development.

Whereas the general impression is that reconciliation is only required in countries coming out of actual civil wars, the major argument of this chapter is that those that experienced prolonged military rule where opportunities for the expression of personal and civil liberties are severely circumscribed, must also go through this healing process in order to ease the difficult task of national development. With the troubling state of the sub-region as the background, the focus of this paper is the politics of the National Reconciliation Commission (NRC) in Ghana. This chapter outlines the circumstances that occasioned the setting up of the Commission, and the intense debate that arose in its wake especially within Parliament. What different interpretations can be given to the tenor of parliamentary debates on the National Reconciliation Commission Bill? Are there any lessons to be learned from the perceptions of parliamentarians and the larger society with regard to the challenges of reconciliation? The supposition is that given the nature of dictatorial governance, either civilian or military, and the dictates of democratic accountability, truth and reconciliation commissions are urgently required in many African countries. Whereas the possibility of either facilitating reconciliation or fuelling the amber of national polarisation are real, it is argued, however, that successful reconciliation is relative and can only be gauged in terms of the ability to prevent the occurrences in the future, of those circumstances that led to the setting up of the reconciliation commission in the first place. Whether the anticipated positive outcomes are immediate or not, there is an imperative to carry along on the reconciliation bandwagon the support of a significant proportion of the people but not necessarily everybody. This is because every political decision is bound to have proponents and opponents depending on the context. That is, there cannot under any circumstance be absolute support for any political decision. As the chapter argues, a synoptic historical overview of the political mis/fortunes of the nation would lend support to the timely establishment of a reconciliation commission. The simple fact is that since independence, Ghanaians have suffered from all kinds of oppression through both civilian and military dictatorships that paid scant attention to the rule of law and fundamental human rights.

Is national reconciliation a necessity for developing countries?

National reconciliation tries to bring the past to the present for very good reasons. To some extent, national development is influenced by the collective historical experiences of the people. Thus, the past is of essence not only in sustaining the present and building a strong future but also in the context of serving as an important barometer for policy formulation and implementation. In order to build a viable nation in the 21st Century, against the background of the abysmal failures of the past, there is need for a clear understanding of current events which, to some extent, are informed by lived experiences. On this, Martin Albrow notes: 'A sense of rupture with the past pervades the public consciousness of our time (Duncan 2003: 801). For Daniel Bell, the future 'begins in the present... for in the decisions we make now, in the way we design our environment and thus sketch the lines of constraints, the future is committed' (2000: 17). Reconciliation is therefore necessary for any developing country that has endured authoritarian military rule or civilian dictatorships that traumatised the people. It is also necessary for nations that have just emerged from prolonged violent conflicts.

In the cases of South Africa, El Salvador, Argentina, Chile, and Guatemala, it was found that 'official inquiries into the atrocities of the past seemed the only treatment available to heal the symptoms developed under years of tyranny' (Avruch and Vejarano 2000: 46). Correcting past mistakes that bedevilled national development not only served to ensure that such mistakes are never replicated in future, but also necessitated calls for a clear and collective national memory of how such mistakes occurred, who precipitated them, who became sacrificial lambs or victims due to such mistakes, and how such mistakes serve as veritable lessons for the nation.

Perhaps it is in view of what may be termed correcting past wrongs (which fractionalised the people) to avoid a repetition or reoccurrence in future that reconciliation commissions are becoming a vogue in contemporary times. Gross human right abuses by despotic leaders tend to polarise societies and undermine development. 'Truth Commissions' as Hayner points out, 'can play a critical role in a country struggling to come to terms with a history of massive human rights crimes' (1994: 600). This is because reconciliation aims among others at 'the acknowledgment of the dignity of victims...long ignored. It restores the individual's capacity to live with or alongside the other. It allows us, while remembering, to bring closure to a chapter in our past. It enables us to live in the present, making our life as a nation and our lives as individuals in a shared future. It always remains a never-ending process'. In the view of Lederach, reconciliation 'represents a place, the point of encounter where concerns about the past and the future can meet. Reconciliation-as-encounter suggests that space for the acknowledging of the past and envisioning of the future is the necessary ingredient for reframing the present. For this to happen, people must find ways to engage themselves and their enemies, as well as articulate their hopes and worst fears' (Avruch and Vejarano 2000: 47).

Torpey outlined four parameters for setting up such a commission. They include: (1) the need to make amends to the victims who suffered or their families; (2) the need to put an end to the cycle of impunity and to enhance respect for the rule of law; (3) the need to develop structures that will forestall a future repetition of regime-sponsored crimes; and (4) the need to attend to equality as a value that strengthens the legitimacy of a society and its government (Torpey et al. html). All the grounds they proposed seem to apply in the Ghanaian case as the overall objective is to bring about a peaceful and functional society with minimal political dissensions and recriminations. It must be added, however, that even though 'truth' is not part of the nomenclature of the Ghanaian exercise, a central objective of the NRC remains to establish accurate, complete and historical record of human right abuses (National Reconciliation Commission Act 2002, Act 611, Section 3(1).

In other words, there are nagging doubts about certain historical events in the realm of human rights violations that are brought to the fore, and also accurately recorded. Jose Zalaquett, a Professor of Law and Ethics and a member of the Chilean Commission for Truth and Reconciliation and a former Chair of the international executive committee of Amnesty International, points out the necessity for the truth after prolonged dictatorship. He notes, 'in the stage of a society's recovery and reconstruction after an abusive regime, truth commissions help to create a consensus concerning events about which the community is deeply divided'. This is of great importance because according to him, 'the purpose of truth is to lay the groundwork for a shared understanding of the recent crisis and how to overcome it' (Zalaquett 1996). It must be stressed that those who for one reason or the other have been subjected to unjustified violent attacks tend to have a morbid and lingering fear of the reoccurrence of such traumatic events in the near future. Usually, such fears tend to undermine the building of trust in those who perpetuated such atrocities, and ultimately, lead to the reconciliation in the long run. Under such circumstances, the cliché 'time heals all wounds' loses its meaning. When this happens, bottled-up grievances relating to unacknowledged and unforgivable wrong doings do not only ossify but are also painfully 'passed down the generations, creating a widening gap of estrangement, fear and hatred, which increases the likelihood of further violent conflict and aggravates its intensity' (Lerche, internet page). Thus, unless the people are genuinely reconciled, a vicious cycle of revenge/reprisals through other forms of violent acts may be perpetuated to the detriment of the nation.

The singular importance of reconciliation commissions lie in the fact that public acknowledgment of past wrongs to some extent can reassure victims that their fundamental rights would no longer be violated. The assumption is that this knowledge would equally contribute in no small measure to the healing process among victims, and eventually, facilitate the kind of dialogue leading to forgiveness of crimes committed. The expectation also is that public acknowledgment must move in tandem with contrition or remorse as inclusive steps towards forgiveness. In other words, the consummation of forgiveness may take time but 'true acknowledgment and contrition by the other side will in themselves have a positive effect on relations between the parties' (Lerche, Ibid.).

Emerging democracies can only thrive in an atmosphere of peace and national cohesiveness. Democratic consolidation may thus be endangered if national reconciliation and unity are taken for granted, especially in situations where there have been major assaults on the basic rights of others without concrete attempts at redress. Among other things, therefore, emerging democracies can be nurtured and strengthened only when attention is directed towards the reformation of political institutions in ways that enable them to guarantee and effectively protect and promote human rights. One required step towards this would be to expose past methods used by state agents to infringe on the rights of the people, and take steps towards ensuring that the conditions that allow such impunities to thrive are decapitated. In Ghana, for instance, some of the worse forms of human rights violations and abuses, especially extrajudicial killings, abductions, disappearances, detentions, torture, and confiscation of properties occurred on a proportionally higher scale under military regimes. Indeed, the propensity of Ghana Armed Forces to intervene and meddle in civil administration has become legendary in Africa. Against this background, it seems clear that one effective means of building sustainable democratic governance is to expose the darker sides of the country's political history which allowed people to be abducted and summarily executed, and in many cases, tried in kangaroo courts and tribunals and jailed. With the benefit of hindsight, one major outcome of such extrajudicial acts is that the society becomes unduly polarised. Obviously, nothing entrenches national disunity than the perception that past wrongs can go unpunished, or could be perpetrated again with recklessness. In the end, nurturing and deepening the culture of democracy would be difficult to achieve in any polity distinguished by divisive societal balkanisation inspired by gross human right abuses.

There is a strong temptation to consider Ghana at least, in comparison with other nations in the sub-region of West Africa as an island of peace and political stability. It would appear, in fact, that since there has not been any destructive civil war like those in Liberia, Sierra Leone and Côte d'Ivoire, the setting up of a reconciliation commission is an unnecessary waste of time and scarce resources. It is pertinent to point out that even though there have been no civil wars or large-scale rebellions of a devastating type, Ghana has had its fair share of civilian and military dictatorships whose tenures have left deep and indelible scars in the minds of many citizens. The present global mood in favour of reconciliation offers another opportunity for nations to focus on pressing developmental problems without the distractions arising from the zero-sum politics of disunity and a pervasive sense of injustice. It has become manifestly prudent to re-visit the past, not necessarily for revenge or vengeance, but to draw critical public attention to certain societal wrongs committed in the name of the State, and to face the future with a renewed national purpose, national commitment and national unity. It is important that contemporary and future national leaders should not become prisoners of those past atrocities committed against the people by dictators of different political pigmentations who inflicted personal and collective wounds on their compatriots under the guise of national interest. The political history of instability engendered by unwarranted military interventions with their attendant repression and abuse of human rights, makes such an exercise timely and urgent. In the process, it may be necessary, as has actually been done in the case of Ghana to ensure worthwhile but short-term tradeoffs between reconciliation and justice.

Basis for national reconciliation in Ghana

As pointed out obliquely in the preceding section, there is need for genuine national reconciliation in Ghana, even though the country has not experienced the same kinds of volcanic civil wars as elsewhere in West Africa. Yet, no doubt, the country has had a bitter and continuing political experience. While some may deny that the nation lacks a united political platform to pursue pressing governance reforms and developmental agenda, on account of past mistrusts and suspicions, this denial is a patent demonstration of deeper reluctance within the public to contend with the truth about politics and society in the country. What is also incontrovertible is that a major part of Ghana's history is steep in horrific human right abuses that cannot be ignored or swept aside. In the course of time, different groups, especially those outside of power and the opportunities that come along with such status, tend to read mischievous undertones to any political step taken by governments. This alone, even, could serve as a necessary basis for instituting a mechanism for national reconciliation.

It should be recalled that at independence, politics evoked unprecedented excitement throughout the continent of Africa. In Ghana, however, the eventual 'revolutionary' government that executed three former Heads of States and five high-ranking army generals without due legal processes, turned out to be one of the saddest political footnotes in the country's post-independence history, but also one of lingering bitterness and concern. Obviously, there must have been something fundamentally wrong with a 'revolutionary' leadership which, in one swoop, executed many prominent political figures, including past Heads of State, not to mention the gruesome murder of three judges and many others. Even though the *dramatis personae* of the infamous Preventive Detention Act (PDA) may no longer be alive today, there is little doubt that the harrowing lessons they have bequeathed remains a source of rude collective memory and embarrassment to the citizens. Despite the wise saying that 'times heals any wound', it is still incontrovertible that collective amnesia has failed to reconcile many people, especially those directly affected, by the bitter experiences of those times. Consequently, a process that will expose past wrongs committed in the name of the State in order to enable the larger society share in the unwholesome burden presently shouldered by affected citizens alone is long overdue. Such an exercise, it is believed, will compel the nation to face the unpleasant realities of its past with resolve not to allow a repeat. Exposing the gravity of the crimes would serve, not just to extract remorse from the perpetrators as earlier noted, but also to offer satisfaction and healing, at least psychologically, to the victims of human rights violations and abuses.

Since independence in 1957, Ghana has had four military regimes, all of which trampled and subverted the fundamental rights of the citizenry often without just cause. In the process, those regimes created an unhealthy political climate that, for all intents and purposes, has contributed significantly towards undermining national development. Of course, that is not to say that no forms of human right abuses were perpetrated under any of the past civilian regimes. For instance, the civilian government of the Convention Peoples' Party (CPP) under the charismatic leadership of Dr Kwame Nkrumah could not be fully absolved from human rights infringements and crimes against the people. Indeed, one of the dark moments of the Nkrumah rule between 1957 and 1966 was the passage of the notorious Preventive Detention Act (PDA) only one year after the country attained independence. It was clear from the beginning that the Act, which endorsed detention without trial, was aimed at political opponents. It was recklessly abused by the over-zealousness of the CPP to intimidate and subdue political oppositions, and then to all countervailing forces in the country. After successfully driving the opposition underground, any critic of the CPP government within the party or outside experienced the full weight of the Act. Indeed, the gross human rights abuses during the CPP era in no small measure contributed to the military coup of February 1966 that ushered, for the first time, the military into politics under the National Liberation Council (NLC).

Paradoxically, most of the victims of the CPP misrule who had been imprisoned without trial received a respite from the NLC which opened the prison doors for political prisoners after the coup. On the balance, one may say that the new regime restored some semblance of basic rights where the ousted civilian regime failed. On the surface, this claim is tantamount to a hasty conclusion from the point of view that the military had no business intruding in politics in the first place. More importantly, the NLC and successive military regimes eventually clamped down on fundamental human rights through various illegal means, including the confiscation of properties, the exclusion of the citizenry from governance processes, to name just two. One of the earliest individual infringements was the caging and parading through the streets of Accra of Boye Moses, Nkrumah's former bodyguard.

The restoration of democracy during the 1969 General Elections brought the Progress Party (PP) to power, supposedly on the platform of liberal democracy. Fundamental human rights and the rule of law were restored under the PP government. The main issue under the PP was whether or not the government was under obligation to guarantee and protect the basic rights of all irrespective of nationality. The answer is in the affirmative, especially if other nationals resident in the country conform to certain obligations. However, the passage of the Aliens Compliance Order of 1970 significantly undermined this obligation to foreigners making it one of the memorable blights on the record of the PP. Another complaint against the PP government related to the popular 'Apollo 568' when people were prematurely retrenched from their jobs by the government without due process and/ or compensation. By this action, their economic right to earn a decent living was aborted. Expectedly, the PP government did not last long as the military again intervened, on 13 January 1972, bringing the National Redemption Council (NRC) of General Acheampong to power. It is interesting to note, however, that unlike the CPP government and the NLC, the NRC levelled no accusations regarding human rights abuses against the PP government.

Between January 1972 and June 1979, Ghana was under a military regime whose names changed from the National Redemption Council to the Supreme Military Council (SMC I & II). Precisely on 4 June 1979, and for the first time in the post-independence history of the country, one military regime forcefully removed another from power when the Armed Forces Revolutionary Council (AFRC) under the Chairmanship of Flight Lieutenant Jerry John Rawlings terminated the SMC II. It is generally acknowledged in Ghana, at least, that the worst sides of military rule in terms of the gross violation of human rights abuses, was perpetuated by the AFRC. Among other abuses, men and women were arrested, stripped naked and publicly flogged either for hoarding essential commodities or selling them above prices stipulated by government fiat. Agents of the military government forcefully opened warehouses seized and sold products at rock-bottom prices. Furthermore, the new military regime imposed an indefinite dusk to dawn curfew on the entire country thereby restricting the free movement of people. As noted earlier, the peak of human rights violations and abuses was the arrest and summary execution, without recourse to the law, of eight high-ranking military officers, including the three former Heads of State.

It should be recalled that at the time the AFRC took over the mantle of political power, mechanisms for returning the country to civilian rule were well advanced under the SMC II. The new AFRC junta thus had little or no choice than to reluctantly administer an election that was eventually won by the Peoples' National Party (PNP) led by Dr Hilla Limann. It was an exciting moment for

Ghana as Rawlings AFRC willingly handed power over to the PNP government in September, thereby ending the long period of military rule. Unfortunately, that excitement was short-lived when the army again struck on New Year's Eve in 1981 to oust the PNP from power. Once again, Jerry Rawlings was back in power as ringleader of the coup plotters, but under a new name: the Provisional National Defence Council (PNDC). But then, if pockets of infringements on individual and collective rights marked the previous three-month rule of the AFRC, this took an unprecedented severity under the PNDC despite its revolutionary stance. Essentially, the revolutionary slogans of that period were put in place as a decoy or smokescreen to fool the people. In effect, if the AFRC as the forerunner to the PNDC instituted a decentralised structure of tyranny and violence, the latter gave way to what Rawlings correctly termed as an unprecedented democratisation of violence. The corpus of inquisitorial organs such as the National Investigative Committee (NIC) and the Citizens Vetting Committee (CVC) and other adjudicatory organs of the 'revolution', each with its own detention cells were clear manifestations of the erosion of the fundamental rights and civil liberties of the people. These organs operated alongside several other ubiquitous paramilitary and security organisations that intimidated, coerced and incarcerated real and imagined opponents of the regime. Throughout almost one decade of the PNDC rule, a pervasive 'culture of silence' enveloped Ghana, and became an effective barometer for gauging the level of tension, fear, and uncertainty evident throughout the country (Gyimah-Boadi 1990: 333; Hutchful 1997; Boafo-Arthur 1998). Since the military governed largely through draconian decrees, they paid scanty or not attention at all to the finer models of governance grounded in the rule of law and respect for fundamental human rights.

Due to governmental excesses from independence— in succession under the Convention Peoples' Party, (CPP) from 1957–1966, the Armed Forces Revolutionary Council, AFRC, from June-September 1979, and the Provisional National Defence Council, PNDC, from 1981–1992— numerous human rights abuses were recorded. Although the aforementioned were the most notorious, the other regimes— the National Liberation Council (1966–1969), the Progress Party government (1969–1972), the National Redemption/ Supreme Military Council (NRC/SMC) (1972–1979) and the Peoples' National Party (PNP) (1979–1981)—cannot be completely exonerated of perpetuating human rights abuses, although on a less gruesome scale. But, then, an abuse is an abuse regardless of the perpetrator or the victim.

It suffices to state that as a result of such gross and persistent abuses under successive governments, the Ghanaian society became openly polarised. For instance, by utilising the Preventive Detention Act (PDA) of 1958 as a tool against political opponents the CPP government did not only succeed in ostracising and forcing notable opposition figures to flee into exile, but also deprived the citizenry in general of their fundamental rights to comment and participate fully in national affairs. Under some of the military regimes, especially the AFRC and the PNDC, uncountable human right abuses were perpetrated. Thus, apart from polarising the body politic, other outcomes of the convoluted governance regimes on Ghana includes factionalism, mistrust, suspicion, and revengeful feelings. Indeed, the body politic has been functioning along these lines accentuated, of course, by the inability of the citizens to come to terms with, or forgive and forget some of the heavy-handed human rights abuses inflicted on them by fellow countrymen. In the long run, such deep-seated social fractures are bound to have far-reaching but negative implications for the peace and stability of the country.

In the section that follows, how these seething feelings of injustice served as veritable precursor to the debates on national reconciliation in the Ghanaian Parliament prior to the promulgation of the enabling Act for the reconciliation process, otherwise known as Act 611, will be discussed. In part, some of the vital questions to ask include whether the Parliamentary debates leading to the passage of the relevant Parliamentary Act point to a fledgling national consensus or otherwise? If yes (or no), what are the major lessons from the debate among popularly elected representatives of the people for genuine and durable national reconciliation? Would national reconciliation flow naturally when the work of the NRC is completed? Has the setting up of the NRC in any way closed up the gaps between the diverse socio-political interest groups in Ghana, or on the converse, further alienated them from one another? The important caveat to add here is that it may not be possible to find comprehensive and conclusive answers to all the questions, but at least a useful signpost or insight into the current status of national reconciliation in one of West Africa's most promising countries can be realised.

The politics of the parliamentary debates

The National Reconciliation Commission (NRC) was inspired by Article 278 (1) of the Constitution which granted the President discretionary power to appoint a commission of inquiry into a matter of public interest. The NRC Act (also referred to as Act 611) finally received President assent on 9 January 2002. In terms of details, the Act dealt with matters pertaining to the membership of the Commission, comprising of a chairman and eight other Commissioners, and the mandate of the Commission, which is to seek and promote national reconciliation among the people of Ghana through the establishment of accurate, complete and historical record of violations and abuses of human rights inflicted on persons by public institutions and holders of public office or persons purporting to have acted on behalf of the state during the periods of unconstitutional governments. The specified period notwithstanding, the Commission could entertain complaints from 6 March 1957 to 6 January 1993.

The Act establishing the Commission guaranteed its independence and stipulated its *modus operandi* on various matters ranging from its meetings, duration, publicity, and so on. Part II of the Act dealt with investigations and proceedings, while Part III was on the Completion of Report and Related Matters. The final section, Part IV, concerned matters of Administration, Finance and Miscellaneous Provisions. For the purposes of its investigation, the Commission was empowered, among others, to require a person to furnish any information and produce any document or article in whatever form which is relevant to an issue under investigation. The Commission could hold private and public hearings and information from the former shall not be made public. Witnesses before the Commission had privileges and indemnity from civil and criminal proceedings. Furthermore, any person subpoenaed or called to appear before the Commission at a hearing of the Commission may be represented by a lawyer. And to ensure strict confidentiality, members of the Commission were required to take the Oath of Secrecy set out in the Second Schedule of the Constitution. The Commission was given 12 months for its work and was required to submit its report to the President within three months of the conclusion of its assignment, after which it is required to fold up. Funding for the work of the Commission came from three main sources: that provided for by the Parliament from the Consolidated Fund and any other public fund, donations and grants. The Parliament was empowered to debate the content of bills submitted to it by the executive during the second reading and consideration stages. The debates captured in this paper took place during those stages.

The thinking of both the majority and minority parties on the reconciliation bill clearly demonstrated the inflexible and irreconcilable positions each took with regard to two key issues: (1) the time frame for the National Reconciliation Commission, and (2) the mode of appointing members of the Commission. However, both parties in the parliament, as well as the wider public, agreed on the importance of national reconciliation for national peace and unity, development and the strengthening of democracy. The emotions and passions on display from both sides pointed, in significant part, to the existing fault-lines within Ghana, the broader imperative for national reconciliation notwithstanding. To begin with, one is struck with the omnibus question: why did the ruling and opposition parties, the NPP and the NDC respectively, adopt such inflexible positions on these two key issues? Answer to this question can perhaps be found, in my opinion, by what the leading parties thought could help maximise their ultimate political leverage vis-à-vis the other. Unfortunately, however, where parties take uncompromising positions in such a brazenly partisan manner, it is national cohesion that suffers.

Earlier in 2002, a survey conducted by the Centre for Democratic Development (CDD)-Ghana towards the setting up of the NRC had found strong national support for such an idea across board. But then, the genesis of the NRC could be traced to the electoral manifesto of the NPP which categorically affirmed (and promised the electorate during the 2000 general elections that if voted into office) that the party would initiate and push a Bill setting up a National Reconciliation Committee. On this matter, the NPP manifesto categorically noted that:

> A conscious and systematic search for consensus and compromise will be a feature of NPP rule, so that we can forge a greater unity in the nation and promote a more harmonious society... The festering sores within the body politic must be healed. This is necessary so that the nation can look confidently and boldly into the future and not be dragged back by the past. For this purpose, and as a special assignment, the NPP government will, as a matter of urgent priority, establish a National Reconciliation Committee to consider all surviving cases of human rights abuses and award appropriate compensation for the victims (*Manifesto 2000 of the New Patriotic Party*, p. 37).

From the outset then, it was obvious that the proposed Commission would have a mandate and task that is patently political. On a positive note, the ruling party acknowledged the pressing and dire need for such a nationwide process, more so that one of the existing parties which traces its roots to the AFRC and the PNDC regimes over the previous two decades had just lost political power. In his inaugural address to the nation on 7 January 2001, therefore, President John Agyekum Kufuor reaffirmed his government's commitment to national reconciliation by stating:

> Our greatest enemy is poverty. And the battle against poverty starts with reconciling our people and forging ahead in unity. We have gone through turbulent times and we should not in any way downplay or brush aside the wrongs that have been suffered. I do not ask that we forget, indeed we dare not forget, but I do plead that we try to forgive (Parliamentary Debates, 2001, Column 1283).

To buttress his government's resolve to pursue national reconciliation, the President re-echoed his maiden address to the Parliament on 15 February 2001 by reiterating that his administration would implement the NPP manifesto to set up the National Reconciliation Committee. According to him, this was a means to offer a platform for an increasing number of aggrieved people to ventilate their grievances as a way of promoting the objectives of national reconciliation. Such a step, he explained, was necessary to move forward as a united people. He emphasised:

> But this does not mean that we should forget about the many abuses that have taken place and we should not give the impression that we endorse a culture of impunity. Those who have been wronged need to be acknowledged, and where it is beyond human capability that those wrongs can be reversed as in the loss of dear ones, for example, the least we can do is to publicly

apologise and help in whatever way we can, with their rehabilitation (Parliamentary Debates, 2001, Column 1284).

The Bill was also influenced, again in part, by the transitional provisions contained in the 1979 and 1992 Constitutions specifically foreclosing all avenues for debating and redressing human rights violations or prosecuting the perpetrators. It is important to bear in mind that the indemnity clauses of the two Constitutions differed from those granted under the 1969 Constitution which was limited to amnesty for coup plotting. However, the 1979 and 1992 constitutions went beyond the mere indemnification of coups to prohibit the institution of any legal action(s) in respect of acts committed by military rulers, their assigns, and agents. The indemnity clauses embedded in the transitional provisions of the 1979 constitution as provided in section 15(2) were transferred wholesale to the 1992 constitution. Section 34(3) of the Transitional Provisions of the 1992 Constitution states:

> For the avoidance of doubt, it is declared that no executive, legislative or judicial action taken or purported to have been taken by the Provisional National Defence Council or the Armed Forces Revolutionary Council or a member of the Provisional National Defence Council or the Armed Forces Revolutionary Council shall be questioned in any proceedings whatsoever and, accordingly, it shall not be lawful for any court or other tribunal to make any order or grant any remedy or relief in respect of any such act.

The entire Section 34 of the transitional provisions indemnified any member of the AFRC and PNDC from prosecution; implying that all legitimate avenues for seeking redress in cases of human rights abuses were stopped. Indeed, the transitional provisions was in such a bad taste in terms of purportedly safeguarding the rights of the people, ensuring equity and fair administration of justice, and promoting a social order based on the ideals of freedom, equality, justice, probity and accountability. There is obviously something ominous about a legal framework which permits the prosecution of all manner of people for various petty crimes while prohibiting a similar course of action against other privileged individuals for similar or even worse crimes. In fact, on one occasion, before becoming the Speaker of Parliament, Hon. Peter Ala Adjetey, had cause to take exception to this disturbing constitutional provision by lamenting their negative implications for the promotion and protection of the fundamental human rights and freedoms, justice and fair play, of the ordinary citizenry. Addressing the NPP's Sixth National Congress, he noted further that it is

> [Monstrous] to think that a constitution will contain provisions which nakedly seek to prevent courts of justice from doing justice and providing relief to persons who have suffered without just cause, not for a period, but forever. These provisions run counter to the well known principle of constitutional

law in parliamentary democracies that no parliament can bind its successors (*Joy-FM News on line*, 29 August 1998)

Undoubtedly, the indemnity clauses does not in any significant way reflect the perceptions and aspirations of the average Ghanaian who, if anything, feels a sense of exasperation that the clause provides an escape route for irresponsible past leaders. While the PNDC 'revolution' unjustly consumed the very people it was supposedly meant to empower, a mockery was made of the national motto: Freedom and Justice, by the entrenched clauses exonerating certain categories of the people from trial for past misdeeds. During the Parliamentary debates the Deputy Minister for Energy, Mr. K. T. Hammond and Hon. Nana Asante Frempong alluded to the fact that the transitional provisions were inserted into the 1992 constitution without debate on the floor of the Consultative Assembly (Parliamentary Debates, 2001, Columns 1348-1350). This probably explains their presence in the Constitution despite their obnoxious intents.

Furthermore, the Memorandum on the NRC stressed further the determination of the country to consolidate democracy and promote constitutional rule. For these objectives to be realised, according to the document, the nation should be able to 'deal with *some of the issues from our turbulent past* that risk compromising the forward march of democracy and peace in the country. Considerable anguish and bitterness still pervade many segments of society as a result of the extensive nature of the *human rights violations committed in recent times*' (my emphasis). Yet, certain words and phrases used in the Memorandum instantly raise further questions. One may ask, as indeed those in the Minority in the Parliament tried in vain, why focus on only *some of the issues from our turbulent past* and only *human rights violations committed in recent times?* The well-chosen phrases conform to the time frame proposed in the Memorandum to the Bill. The focus was on all the military regimes the country had endured. It was not deemed necessary to include the civilian regimes.

Areas of agreement and disagreements

The debates that ensued during the second reading of the Bill and at the consideration stage showed beyond doubt that both the Majority and Minority were convinced about the necessity for a reconciliation commission. Among other details, the Memorandum on the Bill noted that: 'It is time we freed, as much as is humanly possible, the future from the debris of the past and thereby enhance the possibilities of consolidating and deepening the hold of democracy and respect for human rights and the rule of law over our country' (Parliamentary Debates, 2001, Column 1290). In one of his several contributions during the Parliamentary Debate on the Bill, Alhaji Muhammed Mumuni (NDC-Kumbungu), stated: 'human rights leaders worldwide have come to the consensus that genuine reconciliation and recovery would depend on confronting the country's past and that silence over the past would normally lead to bitterness and simmering conflicts' (Parliamentary Debates, Column 1309-1310). Another member of the Minority, F. A. Agbotse (NDC-Ho West) noted: 'This has been one Bill which has come to the House and has got the acceptance of the whole society. The whole of Ghana seems to be saying that we want reconciliation' (Parliamentary Debates, 2001, Column 1394-1395).

As noted earlier, the general consensus in the House on the need for reconciliation had wider support nationwide. The need for reconciliation was the clear message obtained by the Committee on Constitutional, Legal and Parliamentary Affairs which embarked on Regional Public Hearings. In addition, the Committee invited several non-governmental organisations and civil society-based organisations to submit memoranda on the Bill and/or attend upon the Committee. Some of the NGOs and civil society organisations that submitted memoranda includes the Trades Union Congress, Ghana National Association of Teachers, Civil Servants Association, as well as notable individuals. Moreover, the vibrant press was agog on the issue. The Catholic Bishops Conference at a meeting in Wa was supportive of the reconciliation idea because they believed it would bring peace and comfort to the numerous victims of injustice (*Daily Graphic*, 14 July 2001, p. 12).

However, there were sticky issues that unambiguously showed that both sides of the House were determined to politicise the passage of the Bill establishing the National Reconciliation Commission. The first was on the issue of time frame which the Committee on Constitutional, Legal and Parliamentary Affairs was constrained to refer to the whole House for a decision' (Parliamentary Debates, 2001, Column 1302). In the Memorandum, only the periods of unconstitutional rule (i) 24 February 1966 to 21 August 1969; (ii) 13 January 1972 to 23 September 1979; and (iii) 31 December 1981 to 6 January 1963 were to be investigated by the NRC. The reasons given by the NPP for the time frame, which encompassed only the military eras or periods of unconstitutional rule, were given as follows:

(a) With few exceptions, most of the victims of political detentions in the First Republic were dead and reconciliation is essentially an exercise involving the living.

(b) Commissions of Enquiry were set up after the fall of Nkrumah and accounts of the events leading to political detentions during the First Republic were comprehensively documented.

(c) Only wounds inflicted during the period of unconstitutional or military rule cry out for healing because no Commission of Enquiry has been set up to attend to them.

(d) Unlike military regimes where people were cowed, afraid, and not able to use the courts, in periods of constitutional rule the political climate is conducive for seeking redress in the courts and this is precisely what happened. For example, there was the *Re: Akoto* case during the First Republic and the *Sallah* case that came out of the Apollo 568 during the Second Republic. These gentlemen exercised their rights during these constitutional eras so there was no need to deal with constitutional periods where citizens had every right to seek judicial redress without fear since 'the courts were not under guard'. Unconstitutional governments suspended constitutions and later used constitutions to indemnify themselves thus making it impossible for anybody to question them (Parliamentary Debates, 2001, Column 1346).

In effect, what the memorandum claimed was that under constitutional regimes, the courts were unfettered and any aggrieved person could seek and obtain redress one way or the other. All Parliamentarians from the ruling NPP were in favour of the limitation of the time frame to only the unconstitutional periods and at various times cited one or two of the aforementioned rationalisations to buttress their positions during the debate. On the other hand, the minority party in Parliament, composed basically of NDC members, were vehemently opposed to the limitations on the time frame as sought for by the Attorney General, preferring instead a mandate that allows the NRC to start its investigations from 1957, embracing all post-independence governments whether military or civilian. Hon. Doe Adjaho, the Minority Chief Whip, poignantly asked those who were opposed to the expansion of the time frame to incorporate all civilian regimes to indicate what they were afraid of (Parliamentary Debates, 2001, Column 1411). The Parliamentary Minority opposed the time frame by debunking its rationale as given by the Attorney General and Minister for Justice and by other majority members in Parliament. They contended that:

(a) The assumption that reconciliation is only for the living but not for the dead is baseless on the grounds that acts of commission and omission under constitutional regimes affected families, siblings and communities. In other words, those hurt most turn out to be descendants who might have lost parents, sources of livelihood, et cetera, and not the victims who might have died. These must be delved into to heal the wounds of such families whether the main victim is dead or not.

(b) The PDA came into being under a constitutional government and many people including the forebears of the NPP suffered under it. It is therefore wrong to limit the reconciliation exercise to only unconstitutional regimes. In other words, human rights abuses were committed under constitutional governments also, and these must not be brushed aside.

(c) It was under a constitutional rule that bombs were thrown at people with the aim of assassinating Dr Kwame Nkrumah. Innocent people including school children lost their lives so periods of constitutional rule cannot be excluded.

(d) Foreigners were deprived of their basic rights through the Aliens Compliance Order when they were expelled and their properties seized under a constitutional government.

(e) Regional tours by the Committee of the House revealed that Ghanaians are in favour of the time frame starting from 1957.

(f) There is unfairness to be seen to be targeting military regimes.

(g) The limited time frame is likely to undermine the confidence and credibility of the entire exercise.

(h) If the time frame is expanded and nobody avails himself of that opportunity, the nation loses nothing.

The question that comes to mind is whether the two opposing parties in Parliament were acting with conviction in canvassing their positions. The Honourable Members raised other issues that throw further light on the politics behind the debates. For instance, members in support of the stipulated time frame felt that the predominantly NDC Minority wanted the expansion of the time frame 'just to dilute the impact of the Bill' (Parliamentary Debates, 2001, Column 1439). That is, the objective of the Minority was to deflect the focus of the Bill. Nana Akufo-Addo, the Attorney General and Minister for Justice, unwittingly underlined this rigid position in his contribution to the debate at the consideration stage of the bill when he noted that periods of unconstitutional rule were the focus of the bill '*and that is the focus that the Bill will continue to retain*' (Parliamentary Debates, 2001,Column 2916). He justified this on grounds of public interest that in his view were determined solely by the representatives of the people in the House. He strongly argued that 'an excursion into our entire history will not serve the public interest in our country and that the public interest is served by maintaining the focus that this Bill has identified'. There is a fundamental fallacy here because even if the House alone determines what the national interest should be, such a determination must be arrived at by both sides, and not only the majority party as the existing position seemed to imply.

The Minority also indirectly taunted the Majority that they were scared to expand the time frame to include civilian regimes because of human rights abuses perpetrated by their progenitors through bomb throwing during the First Republic under Nkrumah and during the Second Republic under Dr Busia when the Aliens Compliance Order was passed and the Apollo 568 affair involving the dismissal of some leading public officials took place. This appears to be the import of the following statement made by Hon. Ken Dzirasah, the First Deputy Speaker.

> There is a philosophy in life that if you do not want to see your father's ghost, you do not open the cupboard. I believe sincerely that that philosophy is weighing heavily on the minds of my Hon. Colleagues opposite. That just explains why they are not desirous of opening and enlarging the period for

the simple reason that there are certain ghosts in the cupboard and if they open, we shall see them (Parliamentary Debates, 2001, Columns 2907–8).

On the other hand, the inflexible position of the Minority was also influenced by the perception (rightly or wrongly) that the target of the Majority in proposing the Bill was to bring J.J. Rawlings to book. Why the Minority should even entertain such ideas when discussing issues of national reconciliation would seem to support the general view that the periods under Rawlings witnessed the most outrageous abuses. Hon. Kosi Kedem (NDC-Hohoe South) noted that after informal discussions with his colleagues in the Majority, he believed 'their main target was ex-President J. J. Rawlings'. For Lt. Col Agbenaza (rtd) (NDC-Ketu South), only two military regimes were targeted – the AFRC and PNDC (Parliamentary Debates, 2001, column 139) – irrespective of the fact that the memorandum made it clear that the focus was on unconstitutional regimes which included the NLC and NRC as well as the AFRC and PNDC. Alhaji Mumuni (NDC-Kumbungu) felt 'it would be perceived to be some kind of a political vendetta weapon used to target political opponents', if the time frame was not expanded (Parliamentary Debates, 2001, column 1311). In my opinion, the most vicious attack came from the NDC member for Biakoye, Dr. Kwabena Adjei. Apart from construing the reconciliation process as a witch-hunt, he noted that the idea of reconciliation was cooked up by 'a small group of politicians who have an agenda' (Parliamentary Debates, 2001, Column 1510). Although he agreed that the future of the nation depended on the Reconciliation Commission, he desperately appealed to the House not to be 'deceived by the ambition or the agenda of a small group of people to lead this country astray' (Parliamentary Debates, 2001, Column 1518). The fact that the NPP underlined their wish for a reconciliation exercise in their Election manifesto, and the President referred to this position during his maiden speech to Parliament, and the Party's position reiterated in the memorandum to the Reconciliation Bill, to my mind, removes every cloak of secrecy. The charge of an ambitious secret agenda by a coterie of people was thus without basis. To be sure, it is always difficult to convince people who for one reason or the other feel that their future is threatened by the promulgation of a particular law to soft-pedal.

Another key issue parliamentarians could not agree on was the composition of the NRC. The Minority was bent on amending the powers conferred on the President to appoint members of the Reconciliation Commission. Some of them felt that if parliament did not play a role in these appointments, its independence would be compromised. In the view of the Minority, the civil society ought to have been involved in the selection of members of the Commission for the sake of confidence-building and overall ownership of the process. There was also the argument from the Minority that the members of the Commission so appointed should be vetted by Parliament as in the case of Ministers and

Judges of the Supreme Court. In the view of Mr. Kofi Attor (NDC-Ho Central), 'the President brings names; Parliament vets' and 'if you do not pass the test of vetting, as a Minister, or Supreme Court Judge, you do not qualify to sit on any reconciliation Commission' (Parliamentary Debates, 2001, column 1435).

The Parliamentary Minority further argued that the President, by not choosing to set up a Commission of Enquiry on the strength of Article 278 of the 1992 Constitution, rather worked towards an Act of Parliament for the Reconciliation Commission, clearly demonstrated the uniqueness of this body. As such, it was necessary to ensure that the reconciliation process commanded widespread public acceptance and ownership and was also seen to be participatory. There was, therefore, the need to appoint representatives of identifiable bodies to serve on the Commission. In the words of Alhaji Mumuni, such a process will bring about the required 'confidence-building measures to convince the Ghanaian people that this reconciliation is truly national and also reconciliatory' (Parliamentary Debates, 2001, column 2880). However, the Majority counteracted these arguments by noting that under Article 70 of the 1992 Constitution the President appoints members of all the very important bodies. References were made to members of the Electoral Commission (EC) and the Commission for Human Rights and Administrative Justice (CHRAJ) who were appointed by the ex-President in consultation with the Council of State. The strength of the argument of the Majority rests on Article 70(1)(e) which states that the President shall, in consultation with the Council of State, appoint 'the holders of such other offices as may be prescribed by this Constitution or by any other law not inconsistent with this Constitution' (*The Constitution of the Republic of Ghana* 1992). By implication, since the members of the bodies listed under Article 70(1)(a-d) appointed by the President in consultation with the Council of State were not vetted by Parliament, there was no basis for asking for the vetting of the members of the NRC. On the need to compose the Commission of representatives of identifiable bodies, civil society, etc., the response of the Majority was that such a body would be unwieldy and would not be able to perform (Parliamentary Debates, 2001, Column 2881). A further argument by extension was that members appointed by the ex-President to sensitie bodies like the EC and CHRAJ were autonomous or independent minded, and members of the NRC could not act differently.

In sum, apart from the consensus of the House on the need for national reconciliation, subsequent debates on the contents of the Reconciliation Bill manifested the depth of partisanship during the debates. Alhaji Sumani Abubakari of the NDC bemoaned the partisan nature of the debates even though he never parted with the trend of the Minority argument for expansion of the time frame (Parliamentary Debates, 2001, Column 2917-2919). This partisanship and the inability to demonstrate the remotest sign of compromise on both sides led to the boycott of Parliamentary proceedings at the tail end of the consideration stage when the Minority lost the vote on the time frame and an attempt by Alhaji Mumuni to make a statement on behalf of his colleagues was not permitted. At that point, it appeared the proposed reconciliation had rather led to unbridgeable polarisation. After the departure from the floor of the House by the Minority, the Majority agreed among themselves to amend clause 3, by adding a new sub-clause that:

> Notwithstanding the periods specified in subsection (1), the Commission may, on an application by any person, pursue the object set out in subsection (1) in respect of any other periods between 6th March 1957 and 6th January 1993 (Parliamentary Debates, 2001, Column 2882).

A statement made in support of the amendment by Hon. Paapa Owusu-Ankomah, the Majority leader, who is now the Attorney General and Minister for Justice during the passage of the bill admonished his colleagues in the Majority to 'recognize that, as a Government, we ought to be sensitive and listen to the views of others' (Parliamentary Debates, 2001, Column 2922). He added that the amendment should satisfy those who strongly felt that the time frame for the Commission should start from 1957. This position would seem to suggest that the Majority carried its inflexibility on this issue too far while the Minority were equally unbending on its position. The fact, however, that the time frame was amended and a ranking member of the Majority chided his colleagues for not being sensitive to the views of other seems to justify the boycott by the Minority.

Conclusion

One important fact that must not be lost is that Ghanaians were overwhelmingly in support of a national reconciliation process. This was demonstrated, in part, by the huge volume of representations, memoranda and appearances before the relevant committees of Parliament and to the NRC. From the analysis above, it is of essence to note that the majority and minority parties in Parliament exhibited extreme partisanship that eventually paved way for further national polarisation rather than the expected national reconciliation. Clearly, the debate on the Bill within the Parliament, and widely within the society, opened an avenue for the country to gauge the general public mood and feelings, especially those pertaining to events that occurred under the AFRC and PNDC. Unfortunately, on this particular issue, Members of Parliament failed to realise that strong nations are not built solely on the strength of emotions and sentiments as collective public interest should have been the ultimate guide. Since Parliament has a role to play in determining the public interest, such a fixation with entrenched positions was unnecessary, diversionary and unproductive. Furthermore, the debates brought to the fore the hypocrisy of some members. The Minority was not bold enough to condemn the Transitional Provisions, but instead advocated its revocation through a referendum, possibly because such a step might have led to further tensions in society. One may, however, question the basis upon which some members were able to convince themselves that the reconciliation bill was tailor-made to bring former President Rawlings to book, instead of assisting groups within the country to reconcile themselves with their pasts. They could not convince themselves that the ruling government would not go after some of the perpetrators of heinous crimes who are occupying top positions in the NDC in the name of reconciliation. On the hand, they were aware that the focus of the bill on the earlier time frame would only put their progenitors in the spotlight and, as it turned out, portend grave dangers for the fragile political landscape.

It is strange that the majority party led Parliament into a long and unhelpful debate and political horse-trading by its singular fixation with an entrenched position only to accede to the demands of the minority only after a threatened boycott of proceedings. It must be stressed that some of the qualities of good leadership includes the capability to negotiate compromise from time to time, the ability to show sensitivity and respect to opposition views, and the readiness to yield positions without necessarily giving everything, to mention a few. The inability of the ruling party to compromise at an earlier and more opportune moment would seem to suggest that their seemingly irrevocable positions had no strong basis. The entire exercise created unavoidable tensions which the nation could ill afford at that time. Indeed, part of the unfortunate public impression that continue to linger is that Parliamentarians on both sides of the political divide merely toyed with the destiny of the nation through political sophistry and grandstanding that served no good.

It must be noted however, that such irresponsible partisanship endangers democracy by overheating the polity, not least a promising yet fledgling one such as that of Ghana. The larger populace expects elected representatives to always keep faith with, and demonstrate commitment towards collective public good and national peace and stability instead of engage in personal feud and party vendetta. At the end of the day, it is the nation that suffered in the wake of Parliamentary inflexibilities and partisan sentiments that almost truncated good governance and democracy in the country. As Freddie Blay's (CPP-Ellembele) rightly noted, 'It takes a very good Government to insist that a country…should be reconciled'. But, then, beyond good governance must be a genuine intention on the part of elected representatives to act according to the will of the people whom they owe their positions in trust for.

References

Avruch, K. and Vejarano, B., 2000, 'Truth and Reconciliation Commissions: A Review Essay and Annotated Bibliography', *The Online Journal of Peace and Conflict Resolution* 4.2: 37-79.

Boafo-Arthur, K., 1998, 'Structural Adjustment Programs (SAPS) in Ghana: Interrogating PNDC's Implementation', *Journal of African Policy Studies*, 4, 2 & 3: 1-23.

Boafo-Arthur, K., 2000, 'The Political Economy of Ghana's Foreign Policy: Past, Present and the Future', *Ghana Social Science Journal* (New Series), 1, 1: 17.

Bloomfield, D. et al., 2003, *Reconciliation After Violent Conflict: A Handbook*, International Institute for Democracy and Electoral Assistance (IDEA).

Duncan S. A. Bell, 2003, 'History and Globalisation: Reflections on Temporality', Review Article in *International Affairs* 79, 4: 801-814.

Gyimah-Boadi, E., 1990, 'Economic Recovery and Politics in PNDC's Ghana', *The Journal of Commonwealth and Comparative Politics* XXVIII, No. 3.

Government of Ghana, 1992, *The Constitution of the Republic of Ghana*, State Publishing Corp.

Hutchful, E., 1997, 'Military Policy and Reform in Ghana', *The Journal of Modern African Studies* 35, 2.

Hayner, P.B., 1994, 'Fifteen Truth Commissions-1974 to 1994: A Comparative Study', *Human Rights Quarterly*, 16: 597-655

Lerche, Charles O., 'Truth Commissions and National Reconciliation: Some Reflections on Theory and Practice' http://www.gmu.edu/academic/pcs/ LERCHE71PCS.html

New Patriotic Party, Agenda for Positive Change, Manifesto 2000 of the New Patriotic Party, p. 37 (n.d.).

Ninsin, K.A., 1998, 'Civic Associations and the Transition to Democracy', in Ninsin, Kwame A (ed.), *Ghana: Transition to Democracy*, Accra: Freedom Publications.

Torpey, J., Railton, P., Cameron M., and Burns, P., 'Panel Discussion on the Concepts: Truth, Justice, Accountability and Reconciliation', (http:/ www.ais.ubc.ca/programs/descothe/papers/marchalk/panel.pdf)

Zalaquett, J., 1996, The Relevance of Truth Commissions to Different Types of Conflicts. Harvard Law School, http:www.law.Harvard.edu/programs

7

Truth Without Reconciliation: The Niger Delta and the Continuing Challenge of National Reconciliation

Kiikpoye K. Aaron

Introduction

The use of uncomplimentary but telling expressions to describe Nigeria by its founding fathers or by some authors suggests that the manifest imperfections that characterise contemporary Nigeria are not in any way new. Eteng (1998) provides a sampling of such descriptions of the political entity that became known as Nigeria is, among others, 'a mere geographical expression' (Awolowo 1947), 'a mere British invention' (Balewa n.d), 'the most artificial of any administrative unit created in the course of British occupation of Africa' (Hailey 1955), and 'a notoriously precarious lumping together of peoples of separate identities' (Emerson 1960). They all agree that what eventually became Nigeria resulted from the colonial project of creating a nation for no other reason than administrative convenience. It is therefore not by accident that Nigeria has had a troubled and uneasy past – from threats of secession by the Northern region, to the 12-day 'revolution' led by Major Isaac Boro and his colleagues in the Niger Delta Volunteers Forces (NDVF), then the series of ethnically motivated coups and counter coups, and the attempted secession by the Eastern region which culminated in a full-blown civil war between 1967 and 1970.

In spite of this chequered history, which stems mainly from the fact that Nigerians never consented to, nor did they have the benefit of, negotiating the terms of their co-existence as one nation, the country recorded respectable economic growth. Due mainly to the practice of federalism, with the principle of derivation as a basis for revenue allocation, each region looked inward and harnessed its potential. Thus the North produced groundnuts and cotton, the

West cocoa and rubber, and the East palm oil. Essentially a cash crop oriented-economy, a fact that is attributable to the structural incorporation of the Nigerian economy into the world capitalist system, Nigeria produced mainly for export and depended on these crops for its foreign exchange.

The discovery of oil in the minority areas of the Niger Delta and its subsequent dominance of the Nigerian economy from the 1970s changed the Nigerian economy from one of dependence on multiple primary agricultural products to one of over-dependence on a single, non-renewable resource, crude oil, for its chief foreign exchange earnings. Oil resources from the minority areas of the Niger Delta, whose people were either *unrepresented* or *under-represented* at the national level, occasioned a transmogrification of the Nigerian federation from one which rested on the basic principles of non-concentration of power and regional autonomy, to one in which every known principle of federalism is conspicuous by its absence. The struggle to control the over-centralised centre mainly because of the implications for control of Nigeria's vast oil and gas resources has also transformed the nature of political competition to something more intense and Hobbesian (Ake 1994).

The patent lack of hegemony on the part of the post-colonial state has earned it several appellations: 'weak' (Jackson 1982), 'prebendal' (Joseph 1988), 'parceled out' (Ibeanu 1997), 'partial in favour of individuals and groups' (Nnoli 1994), 'a means of production' (Ekekwe 1986), and 'a primary instrument of primitive accumulation' (Ihonvbere 1999). The import of these are that the Nigerian state has neither been able to rise above conflicts nor distanced itself from being a major party to several of the major conflicts experienced since independence. Also, the state has been indicted for several cases of anti-people decisions such as the introduction of Structural Adjustment Programmes, SAPs, the annulment of the widely acclaimed free and fair 12 June 1993 elections, and the subsequent death by poisoning of its acclaimed winner, Chief MKO Abiola; the violation of environmental, land and resource rights of minority peoples, mysterious deaths, disappearances, phantom coups, extra-judicial killings *ad infinitum.*

To be sure, at the inauguration of the Fourth Republic, few would have disagreed that Nigeria was on the road to Armageddon. Works on Nigeria such as *A Crippled Giant* (Osaghae 1999), *This House Has Fallen: Midnight in Nigeria* (Maier 2000), 'Nigeria: Inside the Dismal Tunnel' (Joseph 1999), 'Nigeria: Rivers of Oil, Trails of Blood' (Sklar and Whitaker 1995), appear to capture the widespread perception of Nigeria as a failed project. The nation clearly needed healing.

Thus at the inauguration of democratic government in 1999, Nigerians whose human rights had been brutally abused by successive military dictatorships had high hopes for their restoration. This hope was further kindled by the announcement by President Obasanjo, two weeks into office of the establishment of the Human Rights Violation Investigation Commission (HRVIC), popularly called the Oputa Panel, after its Chairman.

In what turned out to be a poor imitation of South Africa's Truth and Reconciliation Commission, proceedings at the panel implicated the state in several cases of human, environmental and minority rights abuses. The Ogoni ethnic nationality alone brought before the commission over 10,000 petitions. The Commission brought into clearer relief the deprivation of the indigenous people of the Niger Delta of their land and resource rights, state terror directed at the Ogonis and other minority groups of the oil-rich, yet impoverished Niger Delta and the ecological devastation unleashed on the region by the environmentally unfriendly activities of oil Transnational Corporations (TNCs). With the conclusion of the Oputa Panel, the successful completion of Obasanjo's first four-year term, and now the second term of democratic rule, can anything be said to have changed? In other words, could we reasonably argue that there is healing or reconciliation in the land?

The central argument that runs through the chapter is that though Nigerians, generally, currently enjoy greater freedoms, nothing has changed in the gross violation of the 'right to health', the 'right to a healthy environment', and the 'right of indigenous people to control their natural resources' of the Niger Delta people, all enshrined in the *African Charter on Human and People's Rights*, to which Nigeria is a signatory.

To the extent that genuine steps have not been taken to right these wrongs against the Niger Delta people from whose region the wealth of the nation is generated, the Oputa panel is at best an attempt at confusing the symbolism of reconciliation with its substance. The implication of this gestural politics to the consolidation of Nigeria's nascent democracy will be examined. The rest of the chapter is divided into four parts. In the first part we examine some of the theoretical statements that have attended 'transitional justice' as a mechanism of ensuring national healing or reconciliation. This is followed by a chronicle of the various manifestations of the injustices done to the Niger Delta people before the inauguration of the HRVIC. In the remaining sections, we attempt an examination of the reconciliatory value of the Oputa panel, especially as it relates to the Niger Delta peoples.

Theoretical statement

One of the major concerns of societies emerging out of dark pasts is how to heal the society of historic evils and fashion a present and a future devoid of such dark moments. Until the South African experience with the Truth and Reconciliation Commission (TRC), there had been two broad mechanisms for dealing with perpetrators of human rights violations: the criminal trial (retributive justice), and the 'restorative justice' approach.

The criminal justice mechanism, usually the choice of Western nations, requires 'formal rules of evidence and procedure and due process guarantees for defendants including the need for proof beyond reasonable doubt' (Garkawe 2003). This is usually followed by appropriate punishment or compensation for the wrong done. The idea of punishment or compensation is predicated on the legal maxim *ubi ujus ubi remedium*, that is, for every harm there must be a remedy. This not only compensates the victim but it serves the additional purpose of being a disincentive to those who may contemplate committing similar offences in the future. In spite of this perceived strength, this accountability mechanism applied to transitional justice has its drawbacks, chief among which is the fact that the demand for strict rules of evidence may actually exonerate some perpetrators of crimes, especially in societies with discredited criminal justice systems, and in which the offences were committed in the name of the state and in which evidence may have been destroyed. It was because of a weakness such as this that the South African Minister of Defence, Magnus Malan, and others secured acquittal in the court, much to the dissatisfaction of many South Africans. Besides, even when the perpetrator is given the appropriate punishment, it is debatable if this could lead to reconciliation.

But perhaps because of the drawbacks inherent in the criminal trial approach, most nations of Africa and Eastern Europe opt for the restorative justice mechanism. This brought about a proliferation of 'Truth Commissions' in Africa. McGreal (2001), citing *Human Rights Watch*, points out that by 2001 Africa had about 20 Truth Commissions and around another four were in the offing. But just as multi-party elections were embraced by African leaders who lacked a genuine commitment to democracy, African states are now 'jumping on the human rights bandwagon without any real interest in genuinely respecting them'.

Matters are not helped by the fact that with the exception of South Africa's Truth and Reconciliation Commission, these African Truth Commissions provided blanket amnesties for alleged violators of human rights. It is on the basis of this feature that Truth Commissions have faced strong criticisms from human rights theorists and practitioners. Robertson (cited in Garkawe 2003) commenting on the amnesty statute in South Africa, for instance, argues that 'the real purpose of an amnesty statute is not to diminish in a new democratic society the debilitating desire for revenge, it is to enable government officials and military and police officers, to escape responsibility for crimes against humanity which they ordered or committed'. Garkawe (2003) summarises the criticisms of international human rights lawyers on amnesty from South Africa's TRC as follows: that the amnesty breaches South Africa's international obligations, it contributes to the climate of impunity by allowing violators to 'walk freely', and it violates the rights of victims of repression and apartheid. After a thorough study of the process of granting amnesty in South Africa, Garkawe submits that none of these criticisms stands up to scrutiny; for, given the South African situation where violators and victims have to continue to live together and where amnesty was not blanket but conditional on 'full disclosure', the TRC was 'the superior and more culturally appropriate method of accountability'.

In what appears an ill-digested imitation of South Africa's TRC, President Obasanjo, by diktat, impaneled the Human Rights Violation Investigation Commission with a mandate to investigate cases of human rights abuses from January 1966 through June 1998, and to recommend ways that would bring about healing and national reconciliation. But without the requisite constitutional and legal backing, the Commission did not get off to a good start.

First, unlike Nigeria's HRVIC, the TRC in South Africa was passed into law by the South African legislature. Second, the HRVIC had neither the power to grant amnesty to proven violators of human rights, nor could it offer immunity to those regarding whom investigations were carried out. Besides, it lacked the legal teeth to invoke appropriate penalties for those who contemptuously turned down its invitation.

It is these fundamental flaws that may be held responsible for the impunity with which some *dramatis personae* of Nigeria's darkest moments failed to honour the invitation of the Commission to appear before it. Even those who did could not be said to have volunteered the truth of their roles. In fact, they exploited the constitutional inadequacies of the Commission and instead of admission of guilt and pleas for forgiveness, Nigerians witnessed denials and arrogance that smacked of remorselessness. But why was Nigeria unable to adopt the 'stick' and 'carrot' approach of the South Africa's TRC? One explanation may well be that the president, who had been one of Nigeria's military dictators, allowed the constitutional loopholes to escape accounting for his past misdeeds. Another explanation may be that constitutional and legal loopholes were deliberately allowed to ensure that some powerful interests, who played less than noble roles in the past, but who also threw their weight behind Obasanjo's presidential bid, were not offended.

In spite of the denials, Nigerians were able to establish the truth. Through testimonies of victims and in some cases backed by documentary evidence, it was apparent that the state was involved in incidents of extra-judicial killings, murders, the disappearance of elements opposed to it, the destruction of oil-bearing communities through 'wasting operations' and so on.

Going by the gory details of human rights abuses, some have argued that retributive justice through criminal trials would have been appropriate for the Nigerian situation, especially for those involved in heinous crimes. In this case, some compensation, even of a symbolic value would have been necessary to atone for the past (Ikhariale, 2002; Odion 2002). Others hold the view that restorative justice in which admission of guilt should be followed by forgiveness holds the key to Nigeria's effort at reconciliation. This chapter adopts an analytical framework, which posits that national reconciliation is predicated on justice. This may take the form of admission of guilt, a demonstrable expression of remorse, and a renunciation of the old evil ways. But where the alleged perpetrator is unrepentant, then criminal justice should take its course. This calls for a combination of the two transitional justice mechanisms, namely, the retributive and restorative. We now turn to Nigeria's gestures at reconciliation against the background of persistent injustices in the Niger Delta.

The same old song?

Since the production of oil in 1958, when it accounted for only one percent of national revenue, until the present, oil has contributed several billions of dollars to Nigeria's foreign exchange earnings. Tamuno (1999:11), citing *Time Magazine* puts the figures earned between 1974 and 1999 at about $300 billion. The July/August edition of the *National Agenda* (1995) reports that between 1990 and 1993 alone, Nigeria earned at least $199.3 billion. Today, oil and gas resources from the Niger Delta account for over 85 percent of the nation's GDP, over 95 percent of foreign exchange earnings, over 90 percent of the national budget, and 80 percent of the nation's wealth (Tamuno 1999; Owugah 2000; Obadan 1998). It is with the oil, and more lately the gas resources, of the Niger Delta that important national projects have been executed, including the Third Mainland Bridge in Lagos, the building of a new Federal Capital Territory, the construction of a N38 billion stadium in Abuja and much else.

Paradoxically, this significant contribution to national revenue by the oil-bearing communities of the Niger Delta region has not translated to any transformation of the region. The words contained in the *Willinks Commission* report of 1958 that 'The Niger Delta is poor, backward and neglected' remain the fitting description of the state of the Niger Delta today –except to add that the ecological devastation unleashed on the region is life-threatening (World Bank 1995; Ibeanu 1997; I-IDEA 2000). The region has witnessed the worst forms of environmental degradation – seismic blasts, dumping of untreated waste into bodies of water and land, and gas flaring and pollution from decrepit pipelines. These pollutants released into the environment have had adverse effects on resource flows- fishing and farming, the inhabitants' primary occupation- have been rendered fruitless (Harmon 1997; Clark et al 1999; Human Rights Watch 1999; ERA/FoEN 2000; Da Costa 2001). The people's sources of drinkable water have been routinely polluted. Lacking any choice, the inhabitants consume this polluted water with adverse effects on their health. Little wonder that the region's inhabitants are experiencing all sorts of strange diseases.

Largely shut out of the nerve centres of power, where important decisions concerning their oil wealth and well-being are taken, and deprived of any tangible benefits as producers of wealth, the Niger Delta people feel marginalised and alienated from their vast oil and gas resources. Indeed, the Niger Delta represents the greatest paradox of all time: the region produces the wealth of the nation but it remains the most neglected region in the country. On some critical indicators of development, the region lags far behind other parts of the country (I-IDEA 2000:50).

How did the region find itself in this state of affairs? At independence in 1960, Nigeria ran a three-region federal structure dominated by the majority ethnic groups of the Hausa/Fulani, the Ibos, and the Yorubas in the North, East and West respectively. The North produced groundnuts and cotton, the West, cocoa and rubber, and the East, palm oil. A principle of derivation, in which the regions retained 50 percent of their earnings, was adopted as the revenue allocation formula.

However, the advent of crude oil, discovered in the minority region of the Niger Delta, as the nation's major revenue earner changed all that, as derivation as a revenue allocation formula witnessed a progressive decline from 100 percent (1953), 50 percent (1960), 45 percent (under Gowon in 1970), 20 percent (under Murtala/Obasanjo in 1975), 2 percent (under Shagari in 1982), 1.5 percent (under Buhari in 1984) to 3 percent (under Babangida). Recently, the 13 percent constitutional provision has been implemented by the Obasanjo administration. Even so, there are widespread allegations that through the application of the offshore/onshore dichotomy, the central government pays only 7.5 percent, and not the 13 percent as provided by the constitution.

Aware of these injustices, due largely to the consciousness-raising activities of NGOs, environmental rights activists, youths, and opinion leaders, the people of the region have expressed their protest in various forms, including seizure of oil company workers, vandalisation of oil equipment, and the killing of security operatives (Aaron 2003). On such occasion, the state has responded by deploying its instruments of violence to kill, maim and destroy. At Umuechem in 1990, 20 persons including the Community Chief were shot and killed by the Nigerian Police after Shell invited the police to crush a demonstration. Similar incidents of repressive activities of the state have been reported at Obagi, Brass, Nembe and Rumuobiakani (Human Rights Watch 1999). The case of human rights abuses in Ogoni land by agents of the state is so well publicised that we need not be detained with further details.

The above-mentioned cases took place when Nigeria came under the suffocating grip of military authoritarianism. In post-military Nigeria and with the conclusion of the proceedings of the Human Rights Violation Investigation Commission, has anything changed for the Niger Delta people? In what follows, we attempt to address this question.

National reconciliation: Beyond slogans and symbolism

Reconciliatory effort in Nigeria is not new–it dates back to post-civil war Nigeria when the need arose to put the country together again. In what was called the

4Rs (Reconstruction, Rehabilitation, Reconciliation and Reintegration), the Gowon administration made feeble attempts at reconciling the nation. By the popular slogan of 'no victor, no vanquished' it was hoped that the wounds of the past would be healed. But those were slogans. In actual fact, it is debatable if the Ibos could not be said to be the vanquished and if the efforts to reintegrate them were genuine (Odion 2002).

As it relates to recent efforts at healing past wounds, doubts still linger on. In terms of a general respect for civil and political rights, no one doubts that today's Nigeria is better than Nigeria under the military regime, especially the Abacha regime. There have been few cases of arbitrary arrests of real or imagined enemies by the state. This should surprise no one, for we expect no less than this in a democracy.

However, as far as the Niger Delta is concerned, it has been the same old song. There is a continuing violation of the 'right to health' and the 'right to a healthy environment'. Old patterns of environmental despoliation by the ecologically unfriendly activities of oil TNCs persist—untreated waste and refinery effluents are still routinely released into the environment, gas flaring, in spite of its confirmed dangers, is still a regular feature of oil production in the Delta, and there is a greater incidence of oil pollution than ever before. It was during this democracy that the state, in an attempt to protect an American pipeline-laying company, Wilbros, unleashed terror against the protesting community, Choba. It was during the first term of this administration that Odi, an oil-producing community, was destroyed, in what, in terms of intensity and ferocity of application of violence, may be said to be Nigeria's 'Second Civil War'—the houses in the community were destroyed except for a church building! It is this democratic government that refused to honour the ruling by the African Commission on Human and People's Rights to the effect that the Ogonis be compensated by the Nigerian state for the large-scale violation of human and environmental rights (Lobe 2002).

In terms of equitable distribution of oil revenue, the central government maintains a tight grip on oil revenue and continues to frustrate legislation intended to ensure equity. The Obasanjo government resurrected the once discarded 'On-shore-offshore' dichotomy principle in sharing the oil resources. In the end, some Niger Delta States whose oil is mainly offshore could not even pay Civil Servants' salaries. These actions or inactions by the state have generated a pervasive feeling of marginalisation and alienation among the Niger Delta people. These deep feelings among the Niger Delta people cannot be reasonably expected to strengthen national reconciliation. If anything, they raise the question whether the Niger Delta People are citizens of Nigeria or whether the Niger Delta is a colony of Nigeria and its inhabitants, subjects of the Nigerian State.

Conclusion

After Nigeria failed in its earlier attempts at national reconciliation at the end of the Civil War, a second opportunity presented itself with the inauguration of the Fourth Republic and the subsequent setting up of the Human Rights Violation Investigation Commission. Some years after the conclusion of the panel, the hopes of Nigerians have again been dashed. The government could not act on the recommendations of the Oputa Panel. Worse still, some former military oligarchs who refused to appear before the commission have gone to the Supreme Court to secure a judgment that has set aside the findings of the Oputa Panel. For some strange reasons, the Nigerian leadership jumped on the bandwagon of a truth commission without learning some valuable lessons from the South African example. Thus the Commission lacked some basics that were required to make it work – it was not backed by law, and it had no power to grant immunity or amnesty to its witnesses. More fundamentally, it could invoke no sanctions on alleged human rights violators who turned down its invitation.

The reality was that witnesses, some of whom were still facing trial in criminal proceedings, for fear that their confessions could be held against them during their trials, decided to be economical with the truth. Some of those who turned up demonstrated unprecedented arrogance that smacked of remorselessness, and those who refused to turn up roam freely in the land, even seeking elections to the country's highest office.

Even when some of the truth could not be hidden, for instance, that the state was implicated in the gross violation of the human rights of the Niger Delta people, that its unholy alliance with oil TNCs has aided the ecologically unfriendly activities of such TNCs, and that the peoples' right to health, a healthy environment and resource rights have been compromised by the environmentally unfriendly activities of oil TNCs and state policies, nothing has changed.

The deepening sense of alienation among the Niger Delta people poses a continuing challenge to national reconciliation. As marginalised groups continue to be mobilised against a state seen essentially as serving sectional interests, the acclaimed project of expanding and deepening democracy would remain an unserious one. Just as much, the unending and brutal suppression of the collective aspirations of the inhabitants of oil-producing communities using sophisticated weapons acquired with resources generated from crude oil indicate clearly that the government is less than sincere about public gesture of reconciliation. There cannot be genuine national reconciliation without justice, giving that genuine national reconciliation can neither come from military tanks nor from a foundation of injustice. The path to national reconciliation begins with addressing the crucial national question whether the component units prefer to continue as bedfellows, and on what terms. How do we create the sense of belonging for all through the enthronement of justice and good governance? The enabling environment for such questions to be asked cannot be created by rulers whose interests are well served by the existing order. The way forward remains the convocation of a Sovereign National Conference. This is the truth that Nigeria's ruling elite has chosen to bury; but as Shakespeare (cited in Odion 2002) tells us, 'truth buried to the earth shall rise again'.

References

Aaron, K.K., 2003, 'Human Rights Violation and Petroleum Pipelines Vandalization in the Niger Delta Region of Nigeria', in *The Nigerian Social Scientist*, 6(2) 14-20.

Ake, C., 1994, *The Democratisation of Disempowerment*, CASS Occasional Monograph.

Brume, F., 2000, 'Oil pipelines Vandalization: The Wayout', Paper delivered at the Annual Dinner of the National Association of Niger Delta Professionals, Bauchi, December, 2000.

Clark, H., et al., 1999, 'Oil for Nothing: Multinational Corporations, Environmental Destruction, Death and Impunity in the Niger Delta'. A US Non-Governmental Delegation Trip Report, 6-20, September.

Da Costa, 2001, 'Oil Pollution in Nigeria'. www.greennature.com / articles 266.htm\; accessed 01/25/03.

Ekekwe, E., 1986, *Class and State in Nigeria*, Lagos: Longman.

ERA/FOEN, 2000, 'The Emperor Has No Clothes', Report of the proceedings of the conference on the peoples of the Niger Delta and the 1999 Constitution, held in Port Harcourt Nov. 2-4, 1999.

Eteng, I., 1998, 'The National Question and Federal Restructuring in Nigeria' in *The Challenges of African Development: Tributes and Essays in Honour of Claude Ake*, Port Harcourt: CASS.

Garkawe, S., 2003, '"Amnesty for Truth"– A Violation of Human Rights by South Africa's Truth and Reconciliation Commission?', Paper presented at the Activating Human Rights and Diversity Conference July 1–4, 2003, Byron Bay, Australia.

Harmon, Z., 1997, 'World Bank, Big Oil and the Niger Delta' (http.www.waado.org/Environment/Oil Companies/World Bank-Bigoil.html (accessed 3/11/03).

Human Rights Watch, 1999, *The Price of Oil: Corporate Responsibility and Human Rights Violations in Nigeria's Oil Producing Communities*, New York.

Ibeanu, O., 1997, 'Oil, Conflict and Security in Rural Nigeria: Issues in the Ogoni Crisis', Harare, African Association of Political Science, Occasional Paper Series 1 (2).

Ibeanu, O., 2002, 'Democracy, Environment and Security in Nigeria: Reflections on Environment and Governance in the Post-military era', Paper presented at a Conference on Assessment of Nigeria's Democratic Journey So Far', Organised by the Centre for Advanced Social Science with the support of the Open Society Initiative for West Africa, Abuja, February 18–21, 2002.

Ihonvbere, J.O., 1999, 'Federalism, Power Sharing, and the Politics of Redistribution in Nigeria', Paper presented at the International Conference on Consolidating Democracy: Nigeria in Comparative Perspective, Lisbon, September 21-25, 1999.

Ikhariale, M., 2002, 'The Oputa Reports: An Unfinished Job'. Available on the internet on http://www.nigerdeltacongress.com/oarticles/oputa_reports.htm

International IDEA, 2000, *Democracy in Nigeria. Continuing Dialogue(s) for Nation-Building*, Stockholm, Capacity Building Series 10.

Jackson, R. H., 1982, 'Why Africa's Weak States Persist. The Empirical and the Juridical in Statehood', *World Politics* 27 (1-24).

Joseph, R., 1991, *Democracy and Prebendal Politics in Nigeria: The Rise and Fall of the Second Republic*, Ibadan: Spectrum Books.

Joseph, R., 1999, 'Nigerian: Inside the Dismal Tunnel', *Current History* 95, 601:193-200.

Lobe, J., 2002, 'People Versus Big Oil. Rights of Nigerian Indigenous People Recognized', www.africaaction.org/docs02/nig0207 a.htm (accessed 03/01/03).

Maier, K., 2000, *This House Has Fallen: Midnight in Nigeria*, New York: Public Affairs.

National Agenda, Lagos July/August 1995.

Obadan, M., 1996. *The Nigerian Economy and the External Sector*, CASS Occasional Monograph No. 8, Lagos: Malthouse Press.

Odion, L., 2002, 'Reconciliation: Between Substance and Symbolism: The Bottomline', *THISDAY Online*, http://www.thisdayonline.com/archive/2002/05/31/

Owugah, L., 2000, 'The Political Economy of Resistance in the Niger Delta', in ERA/FOEN 'The Emperor Has No Clothes', Report of the proceedings of the conference on the peoples of the Niger Delta and the 1999 Constitution, held in Port Harcourt Nov. 2-4, 1999.

Sklar, R. and Whitaker, C. S., 1995, 'Nigeria: Rivers of Oil, Trails of Blood, Prospects for Unity and Democracy', *CSIS Africa Notes*, 179: 1-9.

Tamuno, T., 1999, 'The Niger Delta Question', A public lecture organised by the Rivers State College of Arts and Science and the Rivers State University of Science and Technology, Port Harcourt, September 30.

World Bank, 1995, *Defining an Environmental Strategy for the Niger Delta*, Vol. 1. Washington D.C: The World Bank.

.

Part II

The Contradictions of Regionalism
in West Africa

8

From Economic Cooperation to Collective Security: ECOWAS and the Changing Imperatives of Sub-Regionalism in West Africa

Charles Ukeje

Introduction

The inauguration of the Economic Community of West African States, ECOWAS, was done in May 1975, almost one and half decades after most West African countries achieved political independence. Without any doubt, the formation of ECOWAS was the product of a global mood, which believed that economic integration was a feasible adjunct towards the realisation of the nationalist goal of self-reliant growth and development. In other words, the architects of ECOWAS envisioned a transcendental sub-regional institutional framework to complement the various national developmental initiatives of West Africa states towards accelerated and sustainable growth and development. This expectation matured against the background of a felt-need or agenda on the part of the nascent elites who captured political power in the post-independence era that their newly won independence and political victories would be worthless without bonding with neighbours across national boundaries.

Beyond this reality check on the part of member, the formation of ECOWAS was also stimulated, if not significantly boosted, by three other external factors. First were the intrusive and negative impacts of global political and economic policies external to Africa but affecting the continent in fundamentally disruptive ways. This came out more boldly in the wake of the oil crisis of 1973 precipitated by the Arab-Israeli war. For many African countries the four-fold increase in the price of crude oil during the war imposed severe constraints on national budgets, and convinced them of the urgent need to warm towards each other to weather the turbulent global storms. The second factor that encouraged economic regionalism in West Africa resulted from similar successes in more developed regions of the world. Most prominent was the remarkable progress made in Western Europe since 1957 when the Treaty of Rome establishing the European Economic Community (EEC) was adopted. In the light of the trend in Europe and other parts of the world, there was an evident desire among those who initiated ECOWAS that the mostly weaker and smaller economies in the peripheries of the world had little choice than to move in the same direction. Third was the reluctance of the developed and powerful countries in the western hemisphere to lend a helping hand to African countries, especially during periods of economic decline and unforeseen turmoil. Despite these odds however, the conscious will to create a functional sub-regional cooperation and integration arrangement never diminished. Rather, such a will became accepted as a fundamental ambition of first generation nationalists that spearheaded the independence movements in West Africa. Overall, both internal and external factors and events clearly served as a wake-up call for political leaders in West Africa to start thinking seriously about alternative paths to sub-regionalism and cooperation.

Today, after close to three decades of its continuous existence, the ECOWAS project has turned out to be a mixed grill of expectations, challenges and misfortunes. In terms of expectations, for instance, several decisions and protocols have been adopted relating to the progressive elimination of custom duties and charges; the abolition of quantitative and administrative restrictions on trade among the member-states; the establishment of common custom tariffs and commercial policies; the removal of obstacles to the free movement of people, services, and capital; the harmonisation of the economic and industrial policies of member states; the elimination of disparities in the level of developments; the harmonisation of monetary policies; and the establishment of a fund for cooperation, compensation and development. Unfortunately, a recurrent concern within the sub-region and outside is that the observance of these far-reaching decisions and protocols has mostly been in the breach, thus short-circuiting the qualitative attainment of this pioneering nationalists' dream.

Despite the plethora of problems mitigating the successful achievement of the primary goals of economic integration, ECOWAS by a curious twist of fate has scored higher on average in terms of mapping out the parametres for politico-security relations within the sub-region of West Africa – perhaps even to the envy of other sub-regions in Africa and beyond. This was achieved against the background of unprecedented armed conflicts, civil wars, complicated humanitarian emergencies, and outright state collapse for the better part of the 1990s. The outbreak of civil wars in Liberia and Sierra Leone, coupled with the grave security implications for sub-regional peace and stability, reinforced the concern that the ideals of economic integration might prove impossible to realise without also tackling the myriad politico-security problems threatening member states, individually or collectively. Indeed, it was specifically the perceived shortcomings in the implementation of the ECOWAS mandates, with regard to harmonising political, security, social and economic concerns, that prompted the Authority of Heads of States and Governments of West Africa to authorise a process of self-evaluation by the early 1990s culminating in the adoption of the Revised Treaty of the ECOWAS.

As pointed out earlier, almost three decades is sufficient to evaluate the progress thus far made by ECOWAS, the various challenges facing it, as well as the most innovative ways to tackle such problems. But it must also be made clear that the nagging questions confronting the Community at this important juncture in its life are many and complex. Certainly, there are no longer concerns about the relevance of ECOWAS, but about the extent to which the canonical ideals behind this initiative can be achieved within specified time frames. In taking stock of its achievements and problems therefore, the following questions are very pertinent. What are the most significant highlights of the internal self-assessment processes embarked upon by the Community in the beginning of the 1990s? What are the substantive factors and forces, internal and external, driving the rethinking and repositioning of ECOWAS to be able to meet new and unanticipated challenges emanating from cooperation and integration? How best can ECOWAS prepare itself to meet the ever-increasing needs and expectations of the peoples of the sub-region? Does the Community in fact have the necessary resources and political goodwill to meet the myriad existing and new challenges facing it? What are the alternative futures facing ECOWAS in the 21st Century and beyond, and how can these be effectively managed?

To address these important concerns, this chapter is divided into three sections. The first, 'The Making of a Dream: Reflections on the Formative Years of ECOWAS' provides a short synoptic background. This is followed by 'From Dreams to Disillusionment: ECOWAS, Economic Cooperation and Collective Security in West Africa' focusing on transitional concerns and challenges. The third part is on 'Re-Inventing the Nationalists' Dream: The "New" ECOWAS and the Challenges of Integration in West Africa in the Twenty-First Century'.

The making of a dream: Reflections on the formative years of ECOWAS

On 28 May 1975, the heads of states and governments of the fifteen independent countries in the sub-region of West Africa signed the Treaty establishing the Economic Community of West African States (ECOWAS) in Lagos, Nigeria. The inauguration was a landmark in several important respects, but overall, it marked the first successful attempt to foster, on a broader sub-regional scale, cooperation and integration among disparate sets of newly independent but weak states. It must be recalled that for much of the period preceding the independence of these countries, the metropolitan colonial powers, principally Britain and France, determined the tempo and degree of cooperation among their respective colonies–most especially by creating harmonised structures and institutions for the delivery of common services. Since those initiatives were essentially designed to foster colonial extraction and accumulation on national and sub-regional scale, however, only a few of them survived after independence.

But the failure of these colonial arrangements in the post-independence era did not deter the already popular idea that regional integration was a critical factor towards achieving economic development and collective self-reliance. Sesay (1985: 125-128) has identified at least three major expectations that stimulated the integration wave in West Africa during the decade of 1960s. These include the belief (i) that individual markets were too small to promote accelerated development in most countries in the sub-region in particular, and Africa at large; (ii) that integration would help in far-reaching ways to consolidate newly won political independence; and (iii) that many lessons can be learned from the demonstration effects of successful regional economic integration in Western Europe under the framework of the European Economic Community (EEC). The first generation of West African leaders must have hoped that these colonial arrangements would ultimately form the basis for the construction of a better and more beneficial institutional arrangement; hence, the various initial steps they took to construct different types and degrees of cooperation and integration schemes in the sub-region immediately after gaining independence.

Elsewhere, Sesay (1980) catalogued some of these pioneering post-independence initiatives and the various challenges that marked their rather unstable existences. In 1964, for example, Sierra Leone and Guinea attempted to work out a Trade and Financial Agreement, culminating in the visit of Sekou Touré to Freetown in June of that year, and an agreement later in October. This bilateral agreement between two neighbours centred primarily on the reciprocal exchange of 'most favoured nation' treatment on trade, transport and customs, as well as reciprocal payment for facilities up to 500,000 Pounds Sterling. This project eventually collapsed, in large part, due to a range of what looked like irreconcilable political, economic and security-related differences between the two countries. Among these problems were the strains on the Guinean economy occasioned by a thriving smuggling trade, frequent border skirmishes and closures, raids into Sierra Leonean border towns by Guinean frontier guards, and finally, lack of money. The arrangement ran into troubled waters and became moribund in 1965 after only about one year of its existence.

After that collapse, President Tubman of Liberia sponsored a quadripartite meeting involving his country, Sierra Leone, Ivory Coast (now Côte d'Ivoire) and Guinea–all countries sharing contiguous boundaries. Again, the major rationale behind this effort was to create a larger and stronger market in West

Africa that could attract foreign investment, promote intra-African economic cooperation and integration, and enhance self-reliance and friendly relationships among participants. That initiative, again, died prematurely as a result first, of persistently bitter and rancorous ideological and personality rivalries between two of the leaders, Houphouët Boigny of Côte d'Ivoire and Sekou Touré of Guinea. The festering ideological differences between the conservative, pro-western and extremely capitalist Liberia and Côte d'Ivoire versus the radical, anti-colonial and anti-West Guinea and Sierra Leone, coupled with complaints of unequal distribution of power and influence among the constituent parties, placed the initiative on a path of inexorable decline. This relationship worsened further after the Ghanaian coup of 1966 which saw the overthrow of Nkrumah and his exile in Conakry in Guinea. Having shown warm hospitality towards the radicalism-inclined Nkrumah, Touré's relationship with Boigny worsened to the point that Guinea threatened to invade Côte d'Ivoire.

Another attempt towards economic cooperation and integration came in March 1971 when Sierra Leone and Liberia agreed to take 'a number of positive steps towards economic cooperation in specific areas of trade and social services'. By October 1973, William Tolbert and Siaka Stevens, leaders of Liberia and Sierra Leone respectively, signed the Mano River Declaration, and in 1976, liberalised trade in local products, and adopted policy to harmonise external tariffs in respect of goods from third countries. By July 1980, however, the process that should have led to the final consummation of cooperation was stalled after the coup d'état by non-commissioned officers led by Master Sergeant Samuel Doe which ended over a century of Americo-Liberian rule. With the ascendancy of Doe to power, the delicate centre could no longer hold in the fragile relationship between Monrovia and Freetown.

During the 1970s also, with the significant lessons from past initiatives in mind, a series of meetings were held throughout the region to drum up support for the idea of broader pan-West African economic integration scheme, beginning with the call for the establishment of a free trade zone covering the entire sub-region by President William Tubman of Liberia. The Togolese President Gnassingbe Eyadema, and his Nigerian counterpart, General Yakubu Gowon, also pledged steadfast support towards the creation of an embryonic West African economic community between their respective states in diverse spheres such as trade, industry, currency, and the movement of persons and goods. They were however prompted, unofficially, by prominent private sector operators who were members of the Federation of West African Chambers of Commerce. This latest effort was almost marred by the fierce and bitter rivalries and enmity between Francophone and Anglophone countries, magnified by France which instigated the establishment of the Communauté Economique de l'Afrique de l'Ouest (CEAO) to serve as a countervailing institutional framework against the increasingly popular Nigeria-led ECOWAS project (Onwuka 1981).

The original Treaty establishing ECOWAS sought broadly to 'promote coop-eration and development in all fields of economic activity'. To achieve this objective, the Treaty–and the various Protocols annexed to it–provided for the progressive elimination of custom duties and charges; the abolition of quantita-tive and administrative restrictions on trade among the member states; the es-tablishment of a common custom tariff and commercial policies toward third countries; the removal of obstacles to the free movement of persons, services and capital; the harmonisation of the agricultural policies and the promotion of common projects in the member states notably in the fields of marketing, re-search, and agro-industrial enterprises; the harmonisation of the economic and industrial policies of the member states and the elimination of disparities in the level of development of member states; the harmonisation of the monetary policies; and the establishment of a fund for cooperation, compensation and development. In pursuance of these laudable but obviously ambitious goals, the original Treaty established the following institutional frameworks: the Authority of the Heads of States and Governments, which serves as the highest decision-making organ; the Council of Ministers; the Tribunal of the Community; the External Auditor, the Technical and Specialised Commissions; and the Execu-tive Secretariat. As a tribute to the subtle Francophone-Anglophone undertone in West Africa politics, and of the significant roles played by Nigeria and Togo in the formation of ECOWAS, the Executive Secretariat as well as the head-quarters of the Fund for Cooperation, Compensation and Development (popu-larly called 'The Fund') were sited in Lagos (now Abuja) and Lomé, respectively.

What is incontrovertible in the light of the significant milestones highlighted above is that the idea of sub-regional cooperation and integration in West Africa never really died out before the establishment of ECOWAS. Indeed, one of the recurrent challenges facing the Community has been how best to transform the commitments of member states into concrete and viable action plans that can withstand the test of time. This difficulty is compounded by a legion of struc-tural, resource and institutional constraints and problems which have been the subject of many insightful discussions and literature. Briefly, they include the fact that the Community has been a victim of the existence of parallel, highly parochial and ultimately divisive allegiances, especially among Francophone member countries. Besides, since most member countries are weak and de-pendent on external resources and support for a wide range of national and collective sub-regional needs, they are usually hamstrung by or prone to undue and excessive external pressures and manipulations, ideological incompatibilities, political instability, the differences in as well as inherent weaknesses of national currencies, the existence of competitive rather than complementary economies, the persistence of structural colonial problems, and a legion of other qualitative and quantitative barriers to sub-regional cooperation and integration.

There is no doubt therefore that those who superintended the birth of ECOWAS were precise and correct in their assessment of the need for cooperation and integration in the sub-region. With hindsight however, they seemed to have been carried away by the excitement of converting their dreams into reality by pursuing sometimes over-ambitious targets and losing track of important but low profile matters. Indeed, one of the banes of the Community has been that of setting unrealistic targets, underestimating the utility of taking modest and incremental steps one at a time, and by so doing, overlooking practical complications that might be triggered in the process of working towards achievable targets. A very good example is the somewhat mechanical expectation with regards to the establishment of a unified custom union – involving the abolition of tariffs, liberalisation of trade, etc. – within only 15 years from the adoption of the 1975 Treaty. In 1983, also, the ECOWAS Authority established a monetary zone to address the problem of convertibility and uniformity of currencies. Twenty years after, little of substance or significance has come out of this celebrated ambition. The real problem, then, could be the tendency on the part of ECOWAS to follow the bandwagon by taking cues from more advanced and better-designed integration schemes, most especially in Europe and North America. It seemed also that the architects of ECOWAS underestimated the sheer enormity of the political, economic, social, technical constraints to cooperation and integration in the sub-region.

In '*The Future of Regionalism in Africa*', Ravenhill (1985) drew attention to some of the general problems making the African environment a less than suitable one for cooperation and integration. These include the low level of intra-African trade, the non-complementarity of African economies, poor physical infrastructure, diverse languages, currencies, persistence of colonial ties, shortage of manpower, and so on. Unfortunately, rather than follow a people-oriented path towards integration, ECOWAS has instead shown a preference for an elitist, top-down agenda. It is as a result of this shortcoming that Abass Bundu, former Executive Secretary of ECOWAS, reportedly insisted, about a decade ago, that the integration culture is yet to be conspicuous in the region in spite of the political noises. Presently, the volume of recorded intra-West African trade has remained abysmally low, with figures hardly exceeding 5-6 percent at any given time. Much of the trade between and among member countries has predominantly centred on informal, unofficial, unrecorded and illicit transactions. Little wonder then that the trade liberalisation scheme that was supposed to have kicked off in 1977 was stalled until 1990.

Even then, its eventual adoption was not a result of any qualitative improvement in sub-regional economic potentials and opportunities, but merely the urge to cash in on the contemporary global trend in favour of economic liberalisation under the broader neo-liberal economic reform agenda of the Bretton Wood institutions. Even the West African Monetary Union (WAMU) that was supposed to lead progressively to the creation of a common currency with a common central bank, a common convertible currency (to replace national currencies), and a common guarantee of convertibility of ECOWAS currency vis-à-vis major international currencies, remains a forlorn expectation despite the obvious benefits. There is a sense then, in which one can be tempted to believe that the long-term existence of an economic grouping is testimony to its resilience and continued relevance to member countries. In the case of ECOWAS, the point that can be made more persuasively is that the institution may be alive but certainly not in sound health. Whereas the Community is expected to create a basis for closer and horizontal integration among member countries, this drive has been severely hampered by complications arising from the intensification of vertical ties with the West in general, and with the former colonial powers in particular.

It is certainly not by coincidence that some of the most successful of ECOWAS' decisions relate to the empowerment of citizens of member countries as contained in the Protocol on Free Movement of Persons, Rights of Residence and Establishment adopted in May 1979. Although the Protocol may never be able to achieve the goal of creating an all-embracing 'community citizenship', or even remove the stumbling blocks to free movement of persons and goods as envisaged, it has nevertheless made it possible for peoples across national borders to live, work, trade and forge other socio-cultural ties with one another than would ordinarily have been possible. There is, of course, a lot of room for improvement; especially as trans-border movements are still known to trigger other needs that can catapult cooperation and integration from its present low level. In this regard, one direction that the Community can take instead of following the present path of making unenforceable decisions that do not percolate downwards and impact positively on the lives of the ordinary ECOWAS citizens, would be to concentrate on developing and improving transportation and communication infrastructures such as the trans-West African highways linking countries. Air transport along the west coast of Africa is also a nightmare as it sometimes takes a whole day of frustrating journey from Dakar to Lagos. Although a decision was reached in May 1980 on the important matter of improving the infrastructure for land, water and rail transportation, very little has been achieved in this area beyond the fact that exactly two years after, in May 1982, the ECOWAS Brown Card Motor Insurance was adopted. No doubt the flagship of ECOWAS, the Protocol on the Free Movement of Persons, Goods and Capital has frequently been hamstrung by the imposition of different forms of barriers, accentuated by xenophobia and other forms of intolerance. As most of the itinerant traders along the west coast of Africa would readily grumble, there are several nauseating difficulties constraining the movement of persons and transportation of goods across borders- roadblocks, customs and police posts, differences in tariffs, paper works, not to talk of the physical dangers to persons as a result of the activities of criminal bandits.

It is never explicitly stated that part of the structural problem that confronted ECOWAS during its formative years (now recognised and attended to in the Revised Treaty adopted in 1993) related to the Community's top-down approach to cooperation and integration, as well as the creation of a patently elitist institutional arrangement, instead of one that would be responsive and closer to the ordinary citizens of member countries. Arising from this is the frequent complaint that ECOWAS had become an over-centralised and over-politicised bureaucracy, alienating and widening, rather than closing, the gaps between governments and the governed. Those who argue along this line claim, with justification, that rather than become the platform for qualitative improvement in the welfare of the citizens of member countries, ECOWAS has been groomed into an extension or appendage of post-colonial state formations with their notorious pathologies. This could be seen, for instance, in the fact that too much power resides with the Authority of Heads of States and the Council, and very little or nothing is left for the Secretariat which is mandated to conduct the day-to-day affairs of the Community. This apart, there is awareness that even though the Community has made important strides in terms of adopting various decisions and protocols, very few substantive changes have truly taken place by way of enhancing the quality of life of ordinary citizens of member countries. This indictment goes further by insisting that ECOWAS has failed woefully to promote the kind of broad-based and integrated development that is people-friendly both in terms of cultivating the active involvement and participation of ordinary citizens, and in making them the ultimate beneficiaries of collective sub-regional progress. If the abysmal low level of citizen participation in the affairs of ECOWAS is anything to go by, it is doubtful that any reasonable degree of support can be mustered at the grassroots level in support of ECOWAS' activities. In many countries, people only know of ECOWAS vaguely, most especially during major summits of the organisation.

The outbreak of large-scale hostilities and civil war in Liberia in 1990, and later on in neighbouring Sierra Leone, brought to the fore the security dimensions of sub-regional cooperation in West Africa. The outbreak of these civil wars radically transformed the fortunes and focus of ECOWAS. The original ECOWAS Treaty was silent on conflict management and prevention - much like the United Nations Charter which made no direct provision for peace-keeping operations, currently its most prominent global engagement. Perhaps the underlying supposition was that such a purely economic-oriented scheme should not dabble into politically sensitive matters of conflict prevention, management and resolution. The architects of ECOWAS appear to have given little thought to the serious implications of violent conflict in the region on the construction of economic cooperation arrangements- despite the nightmarish experience of the

Nigerian civil war. Perhaps, even, the founding fathers of ECOWAS by design opted to downplay the matter of conflict and insecurity because of the concern that the sub-region might never be able to muster the necessary potential for effectively managing them. With the benefit of the twist of events that plunged some member countries into prolonged theatres of violent civil war, and of the far-reaching humanitarian emergencies they created within the sub-region, these implicit assumptions and the neglect of the conflict dimensions to economic relations show a clear error of judgment on their part (Nnoma 1999).

As if to reverse the obvious shortcomings of the Treaty, the Summit of the ECOWAS adopted a Protocol on Non-Aggression in Lagos in 1978 which enjoined members to constantly seek the option of peace than take the costlier recourse to armed hostilities. In 1981, the Community again adopted a Protocol Relating to Mutual Assistance on Defence in Freetown, Sierra Leone, which placed emphasis on the so-called 'trigger clause' policy that any attack on a member state would be deemed as an attack on all others who should respond in kind to assist the affected state.

From dreams to disillusionment?

Enough attention has already been drawn to the myriad problems facing the Community, most of which are still relevant today. But then, there is even greater need to acknowledge the double jeopardy facing those countries that have recently experienced prolonged civil wars: they are not only caught up in the web of heavy indebtedness; in the case of Sierra Leone, one of the 41 Heavily Indebted Poor Countries (HIPC) according to the World Bank and the IMF, but now find their situations further compounded by the far-reaching effects of bloody civil wars. Even the United Nations acknowledged the grim situation of such countries in Africa. According to the world body, more than two-thirds of the countries in dire need of humanitarian assistance – especially emergency food, medical supplies and other assistance – are located in Africa. Unfortunately, other conflict zones outside the continent of Africa, including Afghanistan, have attracted more attention from the international community. As relief agencies have pointed out, Africa received less than half of the $1.6 billion requested for the year 2001 from the international community. This is a cause for grave concern as the international community is inclined to give assistance based on 'the strategic importance governments place on particular operations and crises', rather than the urgency of needs. Thus, whereas the UN High Commission for Refugees reportedly obtained 90 percent of the funds it needed for Yugoslavia, it only managed to receive about 60 percent for Angola and the Democratic Republic of Congo. Also, of the estimated $2.5 billion humanitarian aid appeal for 2002 to help alleviate the plight of about 33 million people all over the world, only about $1.2 billion was earmarked for Angola, Sudan, the DRC, Eritrea, Burundi, Sierra Leone, Somalia, Uganda, Guinea, Liberia, as well as the Great Lakes and West Africa despite the fact that they account for more number than other parts of the world put together.

Giving the puzzling statistics above, it is something of a paradox that ECOWAS was able to achieve success, not in the sphere of economic cooperation and integration, but in the more volatile political and security sphere. There is no point here repeating the circumstances that led to the outbreak of civil war in Liberia and Sierra Leone. What is more important is to emphasise that the Community seized the major initiative by playing a leading, even though controversial, role in the management and resolution of the civil wars. This it did by raising a multinational peacekeeping force, the ECOWAS Monitoring Group, ECOMOG, to mediate between the warring rebel factions (Adeleke 1995). Despite various constraints and scathing criticisms, the general consensus favoured the retention and improvement of ECOMOG's operational mandate.

Less than three months after the ECOWAS Summit met in Banjul in May 1990 to adopt the Nigerian proposal to set up a Standing Mediation Committee on the Liberian crisis, a cease-fire monitoring group was despatched to that country (Iweze 1993; Fawole 2002). As Cleaver (1998) noted, that decision ultimately had two repercussions on the entire operation. In the first place it brought to the fore the endemic rift between members of ECOWAS as witnessed not just in the open suspicion of Nigeria's intentions by certain Francophone countries (Côte d'Ivoire, Senegal and Burkina Faso), but also in the belief among them that ECOMOG was another diabolical attempt by Nigeria to construct and impose a *Pax-Nigeriana* project on an unwilling sub-region. This division accounted for the open flirtation between the governments in Abidjan and Ouagadougou and the National Patriotic Front of Liberia (NPFL) led by Charles Taylor. The support extended by these two countries to Taylor included providing the rebel group with fall back positions, logistics, and resources, all of which no doubt helped the rebel faction to prolong the conflict, and, more importantly, for Taylor to shun sub-regional entreaties towards the restoration of peace in that war-torn country. The second problem that ECOMOG faced related to the inability of the Forces to obtain the consent and commitment of all the fighting factions. The implication of this, again, was that ECOMOG found itself in the uncomfortable position of war fighting rather than peacekeeping (Kuffor 1993). The wisdom here, according to Cleaver, is that although very difficult, 'unanimity amongst the member states of any organization sponsoring a peacekeeping operation is essential' (Cleaver 1998: 224-26).

With the benefit of hindsight, the initial peace that culminated into the poorly conducted elections that brought Taylor to power was achieved at a painful cost. This explains why it was not much of a surprise to close observers that the country was headed in the direction of another catastrophic political misfortune. Indeed, a lot of cogent issues were swept under the carpet only to rear their ugly heads at a later date, as happened with the outbreak of hostilities by the Liberians United for Reconstruction and Development (LURD) that finally set the stage for the forced exit of President Taylor from power and his exile in Nigeria. In the first instance, the entire process leading to the electoral 'victory' of Charles Taylor was fraught with serious complications and problems. Understandably, given the long and painful seven years of cold-blooded civil war, the sub-regional guarantors of peace to that country were very eager to reach a hasty if inconclusive termination of the civil war. There was therefore a measure of willingness to condone evidently blatant electoral malpractices perpetrated by the Taylor camp to win the first post-war General Elections in 1997. It was the same situation with regards to the disarmament and demobilisation exercises which the various warring factions only partially observed. By allowing Taylor's fraudulent electoral victory to stand, major stakeholders in the Liberian peace process perhaps assumed that once Taylor was saddled with the onerous task of governing his country, he would become sober enough to reconcile different groups and interests and pursue genuine post-war reforms. That, of course, was not to be, since Taylor never really made that expected transition from a warlord to a statesman, nor was he humbled by the overwhelming challenges of post-war reconstruction, rehabilitation and reconciliation.

As the Liberian peace process stumbled along from Bamako (1990) to Yamoussoukro (1991), Geneva (July 1993), Cotonou (July 1993) to Akosombo (September 1994), Accra (December 1994), Abuja (1995, 1996), each of the phases was punctuated by several frustrations. Apart from its inability to effectively facilitate peace among the different rebel factions, the various agreements served to deepen the fractionalisation of rivalries among them, as well as magnifying the rancour within the membership of ECOWAS. It will be recalled that at every stage in the long and difficult search for peace in Liberia, Taylor never hid his contempt for, and mistrust of, the Nigeria-led ECOMOG (Iweze 1993; Aning 1999). Following the Bamako Accord of 1990 when ECOWAS sponsored an interim government for Liberia for example, Taylor counteracted by installing a parallel government in Gbarnga, his de facto capital, with control over virtually all parts of Liberia except the capital, Monrovia. During the negotiations in Yamoussoukro (1991), he again undermined ECOMOG by pushing the clearly unacceptable idea that each faction should be allowed to disarm itself and store its own weapons. Unthinkable in the context of the insincerity in that country, such an idea would certainly have caused more damage not only in terms of making those weapons available at very short notice, but also because such a move would not have changed anything fundamental in the structure of command and control put in place by the factions. All that would have happened is that the rebel groups would have been able to simply fall back to their arms depots as and when the need arose, as vividly demonstrated once again in the resurgence of the LURD rebellion in Liberia. Later that same year in Abidjan, Taylor again called for an all-inclusive interim national government, but repudiated this pledge by insisting that 14 of the major stakeholders be disqualified from participating in his envisaged arrangement.

The ECOMOG initiative almost destroyed the fragile consensus that held ECOWAS together up till 1990 (Mitchelle 1999). If there ever were any enduring lesson from ECOMOG's interventions to bring peace and stability to Liberia, and later Sierra Leone, it would be the need for extreme caution any time the organisation is called upon to play the difficult role of honest peace broker (Kofi 1993). At one level, for instance, the ECOMOG initiative dented, if not shattered, the kind of neutrality that an organisation such as ECOWAS should be seen to represent. Apart from allegations that it was a wholly-owned subsidiary of Nigeria, ECOMOG brought to the fore the irritating Anglophone-Francophone suspicions and rivalries that have traditionally slowed or subverted progress towards economic cooperation and integration. This leads us to another criticism levelled against ECOMOG's military operations–that the hurried deployment of troops was not preceded or immediately followed by the activation of a functional central command and control system with superior civilian oversight within the ECOWAS Secretariat. The implication of this shortcoming, according to critics, was not only that the pressing needs of the troops were not promptly attended to, but also that the troops constantly received conflicting instructions from their respective countries. Reminiscing on this, the first ECOMOG Chief of Staff, C.Y. Iweze (1993), rightly noted that the situation represented a classical paradox in military operations reflecting the dilemma that faces a general who goes into battle without intelligence, much like a blindfolded boxer in the ring. The last but certainly not the least complaint was that ECOMOG was hampered by the importunate Anglophone-Francophone rivalries, and the even deeper suspicion of the true intentions of Nigeria, the main sponsor of ECOMOG and a major sub-regional power broker. As pointed out earlier, the initial hindrance that ECOMOG faced was that of dousing the political suspicion that it was not another surreptitious or backdoor ploy by Abuja to push forward *pax Nigeriana* in the sub-region (Walraven 1999; Sesay 1999).

All said, it is undeniable that ECOMOG was crucial in stabilising and reversing the deteriorating situations in Liberia and Sierra Leone. The Force was certainly crucial in facilitating the delivery of vital humanitarian and relief materials, especially to Monrovia at a very critical phase whence not to have done so would have caused irreparable long-term damages. All the same, the intervention created and expanded the corridors and zones of order, stability, and safe haven in and around Monrovia for the teeming population fleeing the unstable countryside. The intervention also considerably pushed forward the difficult peace process indicating that with the necessary political will, a supposedly weak sub-regional grouping such as ECOWAS could independently initiate, maintain and enforce peace. Although the intervention became a huge drain on human and material resources, especially for Nigeria which bore over two-thirds of the costs, it has nevertheless opened a wider window of opportunity for creating new institutional partnerships for role and cost-sharing with other organisations, especially the OAU and the UN (Adibe 1997). This latter point is more pertinent against the background of complaints that the United Nations is biting off far more than it can chew in terms of meeting the demands of maintaining global peace and security, as well as against the background of the declining global attention to African issues and concerns in the post-Cold war era.

Re-inventing the nationalists' dream: The 'new' ECOWAS and integration in West Africa in the twenty-first century

Given the structural, institutional, political and global constraints facing ECOWAS today, the next critical step would be to interrogate the alternative futures facing the sub-regional organisation. Fortunately, by the end of the 1990s, ECOWAS was already under pressure to make itself more relevant in managing the myriad challenges facing the sub-region in the post-Cold War and globalisation era. From that period, there arose a heightened and legitimate concern that focusing on economic cooperation and integration alone might not be enough in the face of socio-economic and political upheavals, the explosion of armed conflicts and civil wars, as well as the unprecedented humanitarian problems arising from the conflict. On 30 May 1990, therefore, the Authority of ECOWAS endorsed Decision A/DEC.10/5/90 inaugurating a Committee of Eminent Persons, including the former Nigerian Head of State and major initiator of ECOWAS in 1975, General Yakubu Gowon, to submit proposals for the review of the Treaty against the background of fundamental and irreversible changes that had taken place on the international scene, and the need to change strategies towards accelerated economic integration in the region in the light of these developments. The outcome of that exercise culminated in the adoption of the Revised Treaty of the Economic Community of West African States at Cotonou, Republic of Benin, on 24 May 1993.

In the Preamble of the Revised Treaty, the new Community spirit was unequivocal, since 'the integration of the Member States into a viable regional community may demand the partial and gradual pooling of national sovereignties to the Community within the context of a collective political will', and the establishment of 'Community institutions vested with relevant and adequate powers'. To give practical expression to this shift in orientation and commitment, the Authority endorsed the establishment of three new institutions: the Community Parliament, the Economic and Social Council, and the Community Court of Justice. In similar vein, the Revised Treaty endorsed the creation of new, more streamlined technical commissions to forge cooperation on agricultural development and food security, industry, science and technology, energy, environment, hazardous and toxic waste, natural resources, transport and communication, post and telecommunication, tourism, liberalisation of trade, customs duties, common external tariff, and community tariff treatment. Finally, it called for a renewed focus on cooperation in political, judicial, legal affairs, regional security and immigration, as well as in the area of human resources, information, social and cultural affairs, women, population and development.

Desirable as those new structures may be, it is still clear that ECOWAS has not learnt much from the sad experience of maintaining over-bloated institutional structures without any commensurate increase in the resources available to the Community. Indeed there is a legitimate fear that these new creations would exacerbate the financial burdens for the organisation, as seen for instance in the difficulties of convening the meeting of the 120-member Community Parliament in Bamako, Mali, in 2002. Since it was inaugurated in November 2000, the Parliament has not been able to meet due to lack of funding. It is even suggested that the ECOWAS Secretariat may be shopping for financial and logistic assistance from major western donor agencies and governments in order to be able to jumpstart and sustain the Community Parliament. Clearly, then, ECOWAS still has a lot to learn about the wisdom of setting incremental and achievable goals and objectives, and also in abandoning its tired top-down approach to sub-regional integration in favour of a more creative, people-oriented style. After all, in the final analysis, it is the peoples of West Africa, not the political and economic elites that should be the beneficiaries of this enterprise. The Community could cash in on the fact that at no other time during its long attempt to forge regional integration, has it been as well-positioned efficiently to respond to the myriad socio-economic and politico-security challenges arising from integrating the sub-region. Today, there is now a pervasive awareness that a large number of the problems believed to be localised within member countries can only be better handled and resolved through collective sub-regional efforts and initiatives.

The point has been made earlier that although the intentions of the founders of ECOWAS were noble and future-oriented, the problem really has been that the translation of these intentions has sometimes caused unintended consequences. Yet, ECOWAS still holds the key to qualitative sub-regional economic cooperation, prosperity, stability and collective security in the present global order. But that will only become possible in the context of an improved and significantly reformed ECOWAS which places the people at the epicentre of sub-regional initiatives.

It is encouraging to see that already several steps have been taken in this direction. At the continental level in July 1999, the Summit of the defunct OAU adopted Decisions 141 and 142 concerning the principles of good governance, transparency and human rights – all issues now recognised as essential ingredients for building representative and stable government, and for conflict prevention, management and resolution. Within the sub-region of West Africa, a newly adopted Protocol of Good Governance has insisted on zero tolerance for political succession and transfer of power achieved through or by coups d'état instead of free and fair multi-party elections. It is hoped that this will serve as a deterrent to those political elites who would stop at nothing to impose themselves on their countries without popular consent. If the spirit of this Protocol is implemented to the letter, it will make political leaders accountable to the people, and not the other way round. It will also help in many ways to improve, expand and consolidate the democratic space that has so far been stifled by tyrannical regimes.

Perhaps more than any other region of the world, the termination of the bitter Cold War rivalries between the two major superpowers has triggered fundamental political, economic and social changes in Africa. With the Cold War safety valve gone, the urgent imperative to look inwards in order to find solutions to major problems has become even more pressing and acute. This has encouraged a return to the once abandoned principle of 'Try Africa First'. In terms of the opportunities, the new era has paved the way for new thinking about some of the sacrosanct assumptions underlying the post-1648 Westphalia system of inter-states relations. Indeed, among the distinctive patterns developing as a result of globalisation is the convergence of opinion on notions of statehood, sovereignty, citizenship and non-interference in the internal affairs of independent states. A whole new chapter has opened challenging in fundamental ways such important principles. Increasingly, there is the recognition among states that events within national boundaries (for example, the harsh treatment of citizens and opponents) ought no longer to be tolerated by the international community. In the same manner, states can no longer hide behind the cloak of these canonical principles to perpetrate human rights abuses and violations.

There is a need to elaborate on the advice that ECOWAS must take incremental steps towards economic regionalism in West Africa. With hindsight, placing more serious emphasis on developing infrastructures at the initial period would have gone further in bridging gaps between member countries, and in fostering closer trans-border contacts and exchanges. The Community, for instance, could begin by paying more attention to one of the biggest impediments to cooperation and integration, that is transportation and communication, rather than struggling to manage an over-bloated bureaucracy and mandate. It is precisely the centrality of joint mobilisation and development of infrastructures that makes the New Partnership for Africa's Development (NEPAD) a unique mechanism for providing essential regional services and facilities in the areas of transportation, energy and water resources, information and communication technology, disease control and eradication, environmental preservation, regional research capacity, alongside the promotion of intra-African trade and investments. The NEPAD recognises also the need to rationalise the institutional framework for economic integration by identifying common projects compatible with integrated country and regional development programmes, and the harmonisation of economic and investment policies and practices. Finally, the Partnership calls for action towards effective coordination of national sector policies and monitoring of regional decisions. The new African Union initiative has also seen wisdom in accelerated economic integration and political solidarity in order to cushion the adverse effects of globalisation and its various undersides.

The civil wars in Liberia, Sierra Leone and now Côte d'Ivoire, have amplified the notoriety of West Africa as one of the unstable regions in Africa (Adebajo 2002). Ultimately, these conflicts will have far-reaching impacts on human survival and development as well as on the productive sector, not just in countries directly affected, but also further afield. Unfortunately, again, ECOWAS has never really invested directly in the ordinary citizens of the Community by way of cushioning them from the possible effects of acute and prolonged poverty and violent conflict. How to reverse this evident shortsightedness in the ECOWAS project so as to make the institution people-friendly is of the utmost priority and concern henceforth.

In a broader theoretical context, it is possible to discuss security in the context of individuals and collectives, not necessarily in conflict with, but outside state security. At a level, it is possible to justify that individual and group security represents important reality distinct from what is usually articulated by states. If this important point is clear, the logical step for ECOWAS in order to reclaim the long elusive nationalists' dream is to reverse the disharmony between individual, national, and ultimately, sub-regional security. To buttress this assertion further is to draw attention to the fact that the absence of a functional relationship between the twin notions of human and state security may be responsible for the shortcomings in the process of implementing Community decisions. This is particularly the case when either human or state security is under threat; the predicament of one directly affects the other in far-reaching ways. On the one hand, states constitute an important agency for promoting individual and collective security, while on the other, problems affecting individuals or groups within a defined national boundary affect the stability or otherwise of states. It is in this respect that many of the ferocious conflicts in the sub-region festered as a result of the escalation of individual and group conflicts either against one another, or in reaction to exclusion and marginalisation traceable to the actions of states.

It does seem that beyond passing the acid test of maintaining sub-regional security, therefore, the intrusive impacts of globalisation have again provided ECOWAS with another window of opportunity to re-enact and vigorously pursue the nationalist dream of qualitative economic cooperation and integration. Today, the diversity of issues and problems facing member states of the Community range from cross-border criminality to the proliferation of illegal small arms and weapons, drugs and human trafficking, the spread of infectious diseases, including HIV/AIDS, environmental and resources problems, to mention a few. All these, either singly or collectively, contribute towards insecurity and instability in many regions of the world, with particularly negative impacts on development. In July 1992 the ECOWAS Summit adopted convention A/P.1/7/92 on Mutual Assistance in Criminal Matters. The Convention covered a range of issues including 'the widest measure of mutual assistance in proceedings or investigations in respect of offences the punishment of which, at the time of the request for assistance, falls within the jurisdiction of the judicial authorities of the requesting Member State'. This was followed in August 1994 with the adoption of the Convention on Mutual Assistance on Extradition, stipulating that members of the Community must facilitate the extradition of convicted criminals to the original country where they had committed the offence for judicial trial. It is hoped that similar efforts will be geared towards addressing the other important issues and problems highlighted.

In the political sphere, the ECOWAS Declaration of Political Principles was adopted in Abuja, Nigeria, on 6 July 1991, with a special focus on three fundamental issues: freedom, people's rights and democratisation. The Declaration affirmed 'full adherence' to the principles of democracy 'in order to enhance the prospects of advancing our economic cooperation and integration in a political environment of peace, security and stability'. It called for the creation of an enabling 'environment in which our peoples can live in freedom under the law and true and lasting peace, free from any threat to or attempt against their security, in which we can pursue a speedy and effective realization of the objectives of ECOWAS'. The Declaration also called on members to 'refrain in our mutual relations... from any threat or use of force, directly or indirectly, against the territorial integrity or political independence of any Members State'. Again, it reiterated the '... determination to settle all disputes... by peaceful means in such a manner as not to endanger peace, security and stability' within the sub-region as well as to respect human rights and fundamental freedoms, to promote and encourage the full enjoyment by all peoples of their fundamental human rights. The Community also noted its support for the liberty of individuals and their inalienable right to participate by means of free and democratic processes in the framing of the society in which they live. The Declaration made it clear that member countries were determined to speak with one voice under the umbrella of ECOWAS in all international issues which touched on the vital interests of development and prosperity, and by extension, resist any attempt by forces outside the sub-region to frustrate the expression of collective will and determination. Lastly, the Community re-dedicated itself to its collective determination to take all necessary measures to ensure speedy and effective realisation of the aims and objectives enshrined in the ECOWAS Treaty.

In 1999, the Mechanism for Conflict Prevention, Management, Resolution, Peacekeeping and Security was adopted. Among its objectives, the Mechanism was to prevent, manage and resolve internal and inter-state conflicts; implement provisions of Article 58 of the Revised ECOWAS Treaty on regional security; implement provisions of the Protocols on Non-Aggression, Mutual Assistance on Defense, Free Movement of Persons, the Right of Residence and Establishment; strengthen cooperation in the areas of conflict prevention, early warning, peacekeeping operations; establish institutions and formulate policies that would allow for the organisation and coordination of humanitarian relief missions; promote close cooperation between member states in the areas of preventive diplomacy and peacekeeping; constitute and deploy a civilian and military force to maintain or restore peace within the sub-region whenever the need arises; set up a framework for the rational and equitable management of natural resources shared by neighbouring member states which may be cause of frequent inter-state conflicts; protect the environment and take steps to restore the degraded environment to its natural state; safeguard the cultural heritage of member states, and finally, formulate and implement policies regarding corruption, money laundering and the illegal circulation of small arms. An important supplement to the above is the Protocol on Democracy and Good Governance following earlier initiatives by other international organisations in calling for the imposition of sanctions against the unconstitutional accession to power.

The impetus from the adoption of the above protocols is that ECOWAS seems to be making concerted efforts towards positioning itself at a vantage point where the Community can respond decisively and adequately to new challenges confronting it. Yet, it is still valid to ask the same crucial question that Ravenhill (1985: 205) posed in his critical assessment of ECOWAS after one decade of its existence: is there a future for sub-regional integration in West Africa? The search for an answer to this poser remains as relevant as ever, three decades afterwards.

References

Adebajo, A., 2002, *Building Peace in West Africa: Liberia, Sierra Leone and Guinea Bissau*, Boulder: Lynne Rienner Publishers.

Adeleke, A., 1995, 'The Politics and Diplomacy of Peacekeeping in West Africa: The ECOMOG Operations in Liberia', *The Journal of Modern African Studies*, 33, 4: 573.

Adibe, C., 1997, 'The Liberian Conflict and the ECOWAS-UN Partnership', *Third World Quarterly*, 18, 3.

Fawole, A. W., 2002, *Military Power and Third-Party Conflict Mediation in West Africa: The Liberian and Sierra Leone Case Studies*, Ile-Ife: Obafemi Awolowo Univ. Press.

Iweze, C.Y., 1993, 'Nigeria in Liberia: The Military Operations of ECOMOG', in M.A. Vogt and E.E. Ekoko (eds.) *Nigeria in International Peacekeeping, 1960-1992*, Lagos: Malthouse Press Limited.

Kwesi, A. E., 1999, 'From Eco-pessimism to Eco-Optimism: ECOMOG and West African Integration Process', *African Journal of Political Science*, 4,1.

Kofi, O. K., 1993, 'The Legality of the Intervention in the Liberian Civil War by the Economic Community of West African States', *African Journal of International and Comparative Law*, 5, 3: 525-560.

Kornfield, P., 1990, *ECOWAS, the First Decade: Towards Collective Self-Reliance, or Maintenance of the Status Quo?*, in Okolo, Julius Emeka and Steven Wright (eds.) *West African Regional Cooperation and Development*, Boulder, Co.: Westview Press: 87-114.

Nnoma, V., 1999, 'The Civil War and the Refugee Crisis in Liberia', *Journal of Conflict Studies*, XVII, 1: 101-125.

Onwuka, R. I., 1981, *Development and Integration in West Africa: The Case of the Economic Community of West African States*, Ile-Ife: University of Ife Press.

Pitts, M., 1999, 'Sub-Regional Solutions for African Conflicts: The ECOMOG Experience', *Journal of Conflict Studies*, XIX: 1.

Ravenhill, J., 1985, *The Future of Regionalism in Africa*, in Onwuka, R.I. and A. Sesay (eds.) *The Future of Regionalism in Africa*, London and Basingstoke: Macmillan Publishers Ltd: 205-224.

Sesay, A., 1980, 'Conflict and Collaboration: Sierra Leone and her West African Neighbours, 1961–1980', *Afrika Spectrum*, 80/2, January 12.

Sesay, A., 1985, 'The Mano River Union: Politics of Survival or Dependence?' in R.I. Onwuka and A. Sesay (eds.) *The Future of Regionalism in Africa*, London and Basingstoke: Macmillan Publishers Ltd.

Sesay, A., 1999, 'Between the Olive Branch and the AK-47: Paradoxes of Recent Military Intervention in West Africa', University of Pretoria, *ISSUP Bulletin*, 6/99: 1-21.

Walraven, Klaus van., 1999, *The Pretense of Peacekeeping: ECOMOG, West Africa and Liberia (1990–1998)*, Netherlands Institute of International Relations, November.

9

Taking Regionalism a Step Further: The Need to Involve the Household in the Development of the West African Region

Yomi Oruwari

Introduction

What researchers on African problems have observed is that the continent is not only the largest regional subsystem in terms of size, but also the least industrialized and the worst in terms of socio-economic inequalities (Shaw 1985). Also, its future prospects are rather grim, due in part to its baggage of colonial inheritances of dualistic economies and decades of reckless civilian/military authoritarian regimes that made the meeting of basic human needs difficult. Be that as it may, the continent has emerged as an important actor in the contemporary arena of world politics. Interdependence based on integration in Africa remains largely an aspiration rather than a reality. Despite resolutions, declarations, constitutions and diplomacy, integration as measured in terms of economic, communications and social transactions remains at a stubbornly low level. This worldview of integration in Africa will continue for as long as we continue to accept the orthodox view that integration takes time to consummate.

This chapter aligns with the radical scholarship that posits that Africa's economic dependence is an essential characteristic of, and the fall-out from the operations of the global capitalist system. It insists that Africa cannot expect high quality integration as long as it remains incorporated in the present manner as a weak member within the global capitalist networks. In other words, continental and sub-regional self-reliance in Africa are incompatible with global capitalist preferences; hence the frustrating hiccups experienced in the long and tortuous process of achieving this important nationalist aspiration. The major thrust of this chapter is that while focusing on the experiences of regionalism in West Africa, there is a need also to start a rethink seriously about regional cooperation and integration from the level of households and the vibrant informal activities they have been associated with long before and after formal colonialism. This rethinking would prevent scholars and African policy makers from discountenancing the households (and the informal sector) in preference for sub-regional initiatives that takes the formal, Eurocentric view that has refused to produce concrete results. And, most importantly, since the ultimate aim of integration is qualitative national development, this is meaningful only when the living conditions of the households are qualitatively improved as they gradually move away from poverty to improved lifestyles.

By making the household (and the informal sector) the point of departure for rethinking economic sub-regionalism, some of the most enduring criticisms of economic integration in West Africa can be articulated and addressed. One of the criticisms against ECOWAS is that as it is presently configured and implemented, the initiative has not taken adequate cognisance of and mainstreamed the household – even though they are supposed to be the ultimate beneficiaries of economic integration scheme anywhere in the world. Following from this, is the fact that even though unintended, the ECOWAS project, has triggered a robust informal sector/market, linking ordinary peoples across different national boundaries across West Africa. In this regard, mainstreaming the people into economic regionalism processes offer another angle towards understanding why the informal sector is the real engine driving sustaining ECOWAS and not official trade relations that is never above five percent at any time. How, then, can the people and the informal sector be brought back into the process of reinventing and repositioning ECOWAS towards genuine economic integration in West Africa in the twenty-first century?

This chapter is divided into five parts apart from the introductory overview presented above. The first part is a general consideration of concepts and notions of integration as conceptualised and implemented in the West African sub-region while highlighting the importance of the informal economy and its relationship to livelihood possibilities and the qualitative development of the households in the sub-region. The second part takes a critical look at the nexus between regionalism, gender and livelihood in the West African region. The third part is what is believed to be viable proposals for effective economic regionalism through the activities of a network of indigenous trans-national enterprises serving as the engine of growth and development in West Africa. This then leads to a critical consideration of the informal sector in economic regionalism in West Africa, and, finally are the concluding remarks.

Reconceptualising integration: The challenges of democracy and regional cooperation in West Africa

We would like to adopt two aspects of the definition of democracy by the distinguished political scientist, Claude Ake (1992). First, is the one that sees democratisation in West Africa in apolitical terms as involving accountability, transparency, competitive efficiency and the making of public choices in a free and equitable manner. All of these provide necessary inputs for successful policy reform and sustainable growth. Second, is the other aspect where the majority of the people see democratisation as struggling for material betterment and political freedom and they are convinced and have realized that material betterment and even mere survival requires freedom from political domination and oppression. Also, as we were reminded by Nzongola-Ntalaja (2002), ordinary people in Africa as a whole were not fighting (during independence from the colonial masters) for ideas. They were struggling to win material benefits, to live better life in peace, to see their lives move forward and to guarantee freedom and better future for their children. In addition to seeking freedom from the arbitrary rule of the white man, the ordinary people of Africa as a whole wanted better paid jobs, education, health care, and other amenities of modern living such as pipe-borne water, electricity and durable houses (Ade-Ajayi 1982).

In a sense therefore, democracy in the region should include an expression of the will to enjoy qualitative livelihood and survival. The survival strategies which ordinary people spontaneously devised to cope with harsh economic austerity measures directly or indirectly serve to strengthen the struggle for democracy. Thus, democracy goes far beyond exercising the civic rights of voting during elections, as the consent of the governed is now taken rather than given. In the past decades, politicians have trampled on the rights of the populace with impunity, since they put themselves into power. The people generally did not vote for them.

Although important, the question goes beyond that of the feasibility of democracy, especially in the manner discussed in the liberal West. The trend in the sub-region, unfortunately, is that democracy has become the government by those who gained power by: through default and/or flagrantly abusing democratic procedures. They bully the masses not just to vote for them but also to devise other fraudulent electoral measures to ensure victory without the people. Since they do not require the electorate to get into power, they rule with impunity and loot national resources without concern for the welfare of the people. Because of their fiery accumulation and display of terror, they deal with nascent opposition elements in very ruthless manner, including incarceration, intimidation, harassment, extra-judicial killings and forced exile.

On the question of regionalism, the starting point is the definition by Onwuka and Sesay (1985) who argued regionalism refers to the various forms and contents of economic integration arrangements (common markets, free trade areas and harmonisation of policies) prevailing or proposed at the regional level. A major lesson that has been learnt so far is that there is no ideal community, criteria or size for economic integration. Beneath their apparent similarities are deep-rooted differences in terms of membership and vision of each of the institutions: even the smaller ones, like the defunct Mano River Union (MRU), had problems that multiplied several times over in the bigger grouping, for instance, the Economic Community of West African States, ECOWAS.

However there have existed long-standing networks of informal relations and exchanges between countries and across the boundaries in West Africa. These complex (and sometimes simple) cultural, human and economic relationships, which sometimes predated the wave of independence in the 1960s, underscore the importance of cooperation between and among countries. As generally reported in the statistics on world and regional trade, formal intra-regional trade in the West African region has been at an abysmally low level compared to the unrecorded but substantial informal trade that has become the backbone of economic relations across the sub-region. In truth, it is these informal transactions that ultimately drive cross-border economic relationships among persons and households, as demonstrated shortly by the extensive personal experiences of Madam Bisi briefly documented below. For example, second-hand German (Mercedes Benz) and Japanese (Nissan, Toyota etc) cars are not produced in Benin Republic, but everyone in Nigeria knows that about 90 percent of those driven on Nigerian roads pass through Cotonou Port. About 50 percent of the tie-and-die fabrics used in Nigeria are also from other West African countries, while almost 90 percent of shoes worn in Gambia are from Aba in Eastern Nigeria even though the soles are imported through informal channels from small-scale factories in Côte-d'Ivoire. The big question that still remains is why people-to-people informal networks of trade across national boundaries are ignored by ECOWAS in its drive to accelerate sub-regional cooperation and development in West Africa?

There is little need to revisit the much discussed genesis, mandate and *modus operandi* of the Economic Community of West African States (ECOWAS) now consisting of 15 member states in the West African region after the exit of Mauritania. Established in 1975, the Community was initiated to address the myriad of challenges to regional cooperation and national development in the sub-region by improving relations with and among members, ensuring the free movement of persons and goods within the sub-region, promoting trade liberalisation and monetary union, and sub-regional security. In sum, the community was intended to promote the rapid and balanced development of West Africa in stages. By 1982, however, there were evidences of growing disenchantment over the non-realisation of these important mandates. For example, Nigeria–easily the main engine driving the ECOWAS project–felt strongly that it was making far too much commitments to and sacrifices at its own expense. This negative attitude precipitated the first expulsion of illegal immigrants (most of whom were citizens of ECOWAS states) in 1983, on the pretext that they were taking up jobs that increasingly unemployed Nigerians should occupy. The following year, 1984, Nigeria closed all its land borders on the claim of checking the large scale smuggling of goods and currencies. This situation continued until the palace coup of 28 August 1985 that brought General Ibrahim Babangida to power, and his subsequent acceptance of the Chairmanship of ECOWAS the same year. The new regime promptly extended a gesture of renewed commitment to ECOWAS; first, by reopening all land borders in 1986, and second, by stating its commitment to the full implementation of the second phase of the Protocol on Free Movement of Persons and Right of Residence. The Babangida regime also provided land in the new Federal Capital Territory, Abuja, for the building of a new ECOWAS headquarters and donated 4.5 million dollars towards its construction (Okolo 2002).

Of special note is the fact that from the inception of ECOWAS, successive leaders in the different member countries have pledged to pursue the ultimate goal of the community; that is, to improve the lives of the people i.e. the households. But then, they took only little, if any steps, towards bringing this expectation to fruition. The need to respond to the dire security problems occasioned by the civil wars in Liberia and Sierra Leone through much of the 1990s, also unfortunately shifted the focus of ECOWAS from the pursuit of strict economic integration to security-related matters. With these wars raging, concerns about mainstreaming people in economic cooperation and integration further diminished. In the next section, a real-life example of difficulties encountered at the level of individuals in forging trans-West Africa economic integration through trade is considered.

Madam Bisi: Nigerian trans-ECOWAS trader

A concrete example of the lack of meaningful progress brought about by ECOWAS for ordinary citizens is illustrated by the experience of a trader interviewed during fieldwork. Madam Bisi could be described as the typical 'Nigerian Trans-ECOWAS Trader'. A devout Muslim of about 65 years old, she had been involved in Trans-ECOWAS trade from the late 1960s up until around 1985 when she decided to stop. She had no formal education but remained a very shrewd and successful businesswoman from the Yoruba-speaking southwest of Nigeria. She traded in potash (locally called *kaun*). She resided in Lagos and used to travel to Northern Nigeria to buy the potash in bulk, which she took by road as far away as Monrovia in Liberia. She sold wholesale to her customers, collected her money and returned to Lagos. All these activities took her ten days for the most part. She undertook these trips about six times a year. She said that she inherited the business from her mother who did it for about five years before stopping. From the proceeds of her business, she was able to invest her profits in property development in Lagos, Ibadan and her hometown Ijebu-Ode. Also, she was able to make the holy pilgrimage to Mecca. She refused to accept the fact that she was a smuggler; believing, in fact, there was nothing like that. She also said that she was friendly with the border patrol officers in both Anglophone and Francophone areas along the route and they never demanded or received bribes from her and other traders along the routes. All that the traders did was to give the patrol officers gifts that they (the traders) picked up along the routes. She said that the gifts were part of the general African attitudes to friendship; at least that was the way everyone involved viewed such gifts. Also the routes and borders were then very safe, as she never had any experience of armed bandits attacking or stealing from her throughout her long involvement in the trade.

Unfortunately, she had to stop the business when the border patrol personnel started seizing her goods and demanding exorbitant bribes, and the route became increasingly unsafe because of lack of maintenance and the growing incidence of armed robbery. She boasted that she was able to maintain her three children in the University in Nigeria apart from building her houses and living comfortably with the proceeds from the business. She did not take a loan from any bank to start the business. In fact, being uneducated she did not know about it when she started the business. Her mother introduced her to her regular suppliers in Northern Nigeria who gave her the first consignment on trust. All she had to bring into the business was her transport fare and maintenance allowance for the journey. When she sold the consignment in Monrovia, she went back to Northern Nigeria, paid the supplier and collected a bigger consignment. Things went on like that until she was able to pay for the consignment in advance. She agreed that total trust is not possible at present as people are greedier and very vicious. She blamed the problems of informal traders on the formation of ECOWAS and the leaders who did not in their actions think about ordinary traders who were not only traditionally inter-country entrepreneurs but who used the proceeds from their enterprises to assist their respective families. She did not have opinions about the formation of ECOWAS since she could not understand it, but she concluded with questions. 'What is the use of any union if it does not assist the people to directly improve their lifestyles economically? Are the leaders not there to make their people live better life?' (Fieldwork, January 2003.)

Economic integration in West Africa

We have to accept that regional integration in the West African region must be development-oriented for it to be meaningful to the people. According to Onwuka

(1985), the existing economic interactions in West Africa could be classified into three groups. First, there are cooperative joint implementation programmes and policies, for example the Cocoa Producers Alliance (CPA). The second group comprises of few economic organisations (some of which are now defunct) aimed at promoting intra-regional trade by excluding third parties through the erection of tariff walls, as was the case with the CEAO (Communauté Economiques de l'Afrique de l'Ouest). In the third group is ECOWAS, which was designed to mature into a common market by 1990, but has so far not been able to meet this set target after a decade and a half beyond the deadline.

A very important problem with sub-regional economic groupings is that their operation presupposes the unification of monetary, fiscal and socio-economic measures by authorities whose decisions are presumed to be binding on member states. Thus, the level and scope of economic integration depends upon which restrictions are removed. The more restrictions are eliminated, the higher the level of integration. The experience in ECOWAS is that it is very difficult to remove these restrictions, at the same time the informal economic sector in the sub-region is not brought into the integration scheme at all.

From the personal experiences of Madam Bisi recounted above, the small-scale people involved in the informal economy depend on it solely for subsistence living. In more recent times, however, itinerant traders of her genre have had to continue with their businesses under harsher conditions, or to retire outright from it. But then, with the collapse of the formal economy creating difficult employment problems in many countries, young and energetic adults with entrepreneurial spirit who are unable to find meaningful jobs are increasingly looking towards and relying on trans-border informal sector trading despite its numerous hazards.

On regionalism, gender and livelihood in the West African region

Before going into the discussion on the relationship of 'gender' and 'livelihood' to regionalism, there is a need to define gender and livelihood and the context in which they are used in this chapter. Traditional relationships between men and women vary from one culture to another. The term gender, though abstract, cannot be ignored when dealing with households. In most cases, gender power is central to shaping the dynamics of human interaction from the household to the international level (Cockburn 1999). Gender is expressed in property distribution, resource allocation and economics. It generates initiative in the community and authority in the family. It therefore cuts across all aspects of life. Women and men have multiple and varied needs. Women are less often heard and therefore less often satisfied. Women and men play different roles that are dynamic and constantly changing. There are gender differences in assets, entitlements and the division of activities. The differences are also based on knowledge. This affects the different roles men and women play in policy formulation, and in the implementation and adaptation of strategies to support and sustain livelihood. People have rights as well as needs, and gender inequalities stand in the way of achieving them. In gender transactions, power relations are far from equal as women are not only poorer than men but face social, economic, political and cultural discrimination on grounds of sex. Gender discrimination affects every aspect of women's lives, including the way their needs and rights are addressed in the development process.

According to Chambers and Conway (1992), livelihood refers to the capabilities, assets (both natural and social) and activities required for a means of living. Livelihood encompasses more than work as it also embraces activities that involve assets, entitlements, handicraft and the knowledge base which people engage and use to make their living. Formal employment conventionally accounts for a very small fraction of work in poor countries and the use of the term 'livelihood' is preferable as it encompasses all forms of activities that help ensure survival and improve living conditions (SIDA 1995). A livelihood is sustainable when it can cope with and recover from stresses and shocks, maintain or enhance its capabilities and assets both now and in the future, while not undermining its natural resource base. The key element of livelihood approaches is that people are the beginning and final points. A livelihood approach therefore describes how people obtain and retain assets, what they eventually do with the assets acquired, what gets in their way whilst seeking to obtain them, and who controls the resources on which such assets are based. It includes the notion that assets serve as a buffer for households against unforeseen disasters. Livelihood approaches provide a way of predicting and experiencing vulnerability to shocks and pressures as an integral part of the development process. It allows the linking of micro to macro issues and accessing resources as central to the process of securing livelihood. Finally, livelihood programming has a rural-focused origin that places the question of vulnerability at the centre. In so doing, the aim is to make livelihood priorities among the poorest households sustainable.

Following the Rio 1992 Earth summit, the concern for sustainable livelihood assumed renewed importance. Sustainable livelihoods are those forms of livelihoods that bring about the empowerment of individuals to earn a living sufficient enough to meet basic family needs. Katepa-Kalala (1997) suggests that part of a sustainable livelihood approach is the identification of assets, entitlements, and the knowledge base that people use to make their living, adding that these are embodied in a range of coping and adaptive strategies. The sustainable livelihood framework according to Grown and Sebstad (1989) has the potential to link labour market analysis (formal and informal) and the ability to capture underlying relationships between and within households. It is based on the ideas of capability, equity and sustainability, where 'capability' is the wherewithal to perform certain basic functions such as making use of livelihood opportunities and responding from time to time to social conditions that can impact negatively on livelihoods. Equity on the other hand, refers to income distribution, measurements in assets, capabilities and opportunities.

Regionalism and the informal economy

To protect shared interests, members felt the need for shared security arrangements that transcend territorial borders. Obviously, if economic integration and cooperation are to be meaningful, then they have to be accompanied by adequate defense and security arrangements. As far as the discussion here is concerned, the security arrangements are those that have short and long-term implications for the households in the region and the defense arrangements have only long-term implications for them. However, because of the political developments in some West African countries notably Sierra Leone and Liberia, the defense arrangements through ECOMOG have over-shadowed inter and intra security arrangements.

In the final analysis, what is glaring is the exclusion of informal economic activities in discussions on regionalism in the West African region. Still, it is only by giving adequate attention to the informal economy of households and to their livelihoods, that the poor people in the sub-region are brought back into the discourse and practice of economic integration in West Africa. It is only when households are considered and mainstreamed (and account taken of the far-reaching implications of gender differences to households), that economic regionalism in the sub-region can become appropriately targeted and meaningful.

The role of trans-national corporations

Before independence, trans-national corporations (TNCs) with headquarters in the developed countries of the west engaged in business and economic transactions in many developing countries, including West Africa. They achieved a head start because the major colonial powers in Africa (Britain, France, Portugal and Spain) dominated business activities, particularly in the distribution and industrial sectors, including mining, in their respective colonial domains. Monopoly and super profits were therefore guaranteed for the imperial centres at the expense of the colonies. Thus, the period before the independence of West African states in the 1960s was the high water mark of unequal centre-periphery relationships in virtually all imaginable areas (Onwuka and Sesay 1985).

After the wave of independence that came in the 1960s, non-colonial OECD countries, including Japan, and more recently other Asian powers like Taiwan, became serious competitors to the established colonial powers in London, Paris and Lisbon. Of note is that Japan, as a natural resource-deficient country, concentrated a larger percentage of its direct investment in Africa as a whole on the extractive sector than other European countries. In the early years of independence, the monopoly of TNCs in extractive businesses was first threatened and then broken by most participating governments. In terms of the manufacturing sector, the TNCs usually established subsidiaries in the region that operated within a wider global framework in a vertical, top-down and monopolistic position.

In post-colonial West Africa, the presence and activities of TNCs broadened as they met, in most cases, with favourable investment climates in different countries. This positive condition for investment, even though it had negative impacts on sustainable homegrown development of the private sector, can be attributed to two other factors. First, is that those at the core of the emergent ruling class in the different countries became pliable agents of TNCs in their areas, and by so doing, provided political insurance covers against any attempt to undermine their influence and presence. Second, with a virtual monopoly on critical resources, especially capital and technology with efficient marketing and organisational expertise, TNCs were able to accelerate the deepening of capitalist production in the region on terms favourable to them. Since the *raison d'etre* of TNCs is profit, they concentrated more on high yielding sectors unlikely to add any meaningful value to the lives of the people and accelerate development.

The superior management and distributive network of TNCs, and of their bargaining leverage reinforced their dominance vis-à-vis most West African states. Many of the business activities of these companies were also with states rather than with particular organisations. In virtually every instance, West African countries were forced into accepting technological and financial services as offered them without question. Thus, homegrown and development-oriented independent actions were constrained and undermined by international finance. In other cases, some West African leaders went further by insisting that international finance and technology supplied by TNCs is a necessary requirement for national growth and development. It is difficult to agree with this assertion bearing in mind that the activities of TNCs benefit them more from these partnerships than the different countries and peoples, because in the long run most of the projects were not sustainable. In the long run, moreover West African countries could have benefited more without, rather than with, international finance and technology. This would be truer if the leaders show more commitment towards improving the lots of the people than themselves. In the end, the relationship with TNCs would have been one of interdependence rather than total dependence. To be fair to some of the states, for example Nigeria, TNCs have practically been replaced in the distributive trade sector, but the problem of gaining a hold over the manufacturing sector is still apparent.

Mainstreaming the informal economy in sub-regionalism

Regional infrastructure

The exclusiveness of intra-West African exchange is reflected in the under-developed state of the regional infrastructure. Transportation by land, sea and telecommunications has been improving tremendously over the years but these by no means balance connection within and between West African countries. The recent introduction of GSM technology is appreciated but the initial price of the cheapest package along with the cost of airtime priced the unit beyond the reach of the low-income households in the region. Although projections have been made for intra-regional road networks, such ideas have not been translated to concrete reality on ground. People are still afraid of using the roads due to several barriers placed on the movement of persons and goods throughout the sub-region, and by language, customs and national security exegeses. To ease the stress from road travels, ECOWAS has the responsibility to cater extensively for the informal regular travellers by introducing such things as regular convenience facilities along the routes, security services, and cooperative custom establishments. It is agreed that there cannot be a total elimination of custom services due to the various negative activities of unscrupulous traders across the sub-region. The urgent need to improve existing infrastructures or to create new ones to ease cross-border travels and trade becomes more important given the fact that about 60 percent of those involved in that informal transactions are women.

Mapping of resources and indigenous multi-nationals

There is an urgent need for ECOWAS to produce maps showing the concentration of natural resources in respect to mining, agriculture, labour (both skilled and unskilled) etc. There is also the need to clearly determine areas most conducive to specific crops which can then be made accessible to all end user countries in the region. This is with the view of encouraging indigenous commercial entrepreneurs, especially farmers, who can use the new knowledge to determine where best to plant particular crops and to harness the abundant natural resources available for the well being of the peoples of the region. The ultimate vision then is to breed a crop of indigenous multi-national organisations that look mostly inwards for finance. Even if they have to use international finance, it would be from a position of interdependence rather than total dependence and on favourable terms. For example, an indigenous consortium of Nigerian, Ghanaian and Ivorian entrepreneurs can decide to set up commercial tomato farms in the Mambila Plateau in Nigeria that had been mapped out to be the best for such a project. This will feed a factory in Northern Ghana that has the cheapest source of labour for production and is close to the mining fields in Côte d' Ivoire that produces the containers for packaging. There should be easy means of transportation to carry the finished products to the market in all the states in the region and even beyond. Of course, there would be the need for a strong Research and Development (R and D) within the industry so as to ensure that most of the raw materials are sourced locally. It is much easier for such an indigenous multi-national effort to look inwards in order to raise funds for the financing of such projects. This is possible only if the elites in the different countries of the sub-region desist from siphoning large sums of ill-gotten wealth in foreign banks where it is then lent back to them at exorbitant interest and with so much arrogance on the part of the foreign banks.

It is only when this shift in attitude is consummated that the dependence of ECOWAS states on the industrialised states for vital project funds can come to an end. When an ECOWAS industrialisation programme materialises, the abundant raw materials, human labour and minerals resources available in the region can then be exploited to the benefit of its peoples and governments. Also, with a robust increase in the level of intra-community trade, the traditional dominance by the industrialised nations of traditional markets in the sub-region will also come to a gradual end. The increasing prosperity of the region will also mean a decreased dependence of ECOWAS states on the exploitative external forces that frequently frustrates homegrown development. It is however important to insert the caveat that the gains of such a new orientation may not come immediately or spread evenly across countries. In this regard, only incremental gains should be expected but with the hope that, in cumulative, they can stimulate holistic development in the sub-region.

What is also lacking is a pro-active awareness and information framework within ECOWAS that brings vital community information to the people, in real time. To date, there is no observable information flow framework for the region. Households do not know what is happening. They do not have a channel for contributing to any of the debates. They are not aware of the successes and failures of high-level, official interventions. It is only when borders are closed and their movements hampered, that they become aware of problems. In this regard, the administrators of ECOWAS must make concerted efforts to be close to the people. Obviously, lack of awareness on the part of the people about what their governments and ECOWAS are doing tend to incubate public dissatisfaction and disenchantment. Thus there is need for improved public enlightenment and information dissemination in order to create awareness and mobilise ordinary peoples and households to identify with the programmes and policies of ECOWAS, and in general, provide an impetus for their success.

Conclusion

By agreeing to form an economic community, member states of ECOWAS have demonstrated that they share common economic and social expectations and goals. Even then, there are a myriad of problems and obstacles that must be overcome in order to realise the full potentials of the organisation and its members. To be successful, the central role of the informal sector must be recognised as the backbone of commercial economic activities in the sub-region instead of treating it with scorn and contempt. This is more so when it is realised that the ultimate aim of regionalism is development and it is meaningful only when the living conditions and the livelihood possibilities of households are significantly and qualitatively improved.

In conclusion, the thrust of this chapter is to show that several false steps and approaches have been taken towards economic integration in the West African sub-region going by the blatant exclusion of households and the informal sector from the process. As presently implemented, the West African economic integration scheme cannot promote any genuine growth and development in the sub-region. However, by taking ECOWAS to the grassroots and the households level, recognising the informal economy, adequately informing the people through advocacy and public enlightenment of Community programmes and activities while recognising their voices, by allowing the people to evaluate the policies and programmes of ECOWAS at regular intervals, will successful regionalism be achieved in West Africa.

References

Ade-Ajayi, J. F., 1982, 'Expectations of Independence', *Daedalus*, 111, No. 2, Spring.

Ake, C., 1995, 'Democracy and Africa: The Residual Option', Reprinted in Adetula, Victor (ed.) (1997), *Claude Ake and Democracy in Africa: A Tribute*, AFRIGOV Monograph Series No.4, Jos: African Centre for Democratic Governance.

Ake, C., 1992, *The Feasibility of Democracy in Africa*, Occasional Publication No. 1, Centre for Research, Documentation and University Exchange, Ibadan: University of Ibadan.

Chambers, R. and Conway, G., 1992, 'Sustainable Rural Livelihoods: Practical Concepts for the 21st Century', Brighton, IDS Discussion Paper 296.

Cockburn, C., 1999, 'Gender, Armed Conflicts and Political Violence', Workshop Paper on Gender and Peace Support Operations of the World Bank.

Gabriel, A. O., 1993, 'Women and Nigeria/Equatorial Guinea Transborder Cooperation: Challenges for the Nineties', *Nigerian Journal of Interdisciplinary Studies* Vol. 3.

Grown, C. and Sebstad, J., 1989, 'Introduction: Towards a Wider Perspective on Women's employment', *World Development*, Vol.17 No.17.

Katepe-Kalala, J., 1997, *Sustainable Livelihood Approaches in Operation: A Gender Perspective*, New York: United Nations Publications.

Nzongola-Ntalaja, G., 2002, 'Democracy and Development in Africa: A Tribute to Claude Ake', in Claude Ake Memorial Lecture Series 4, Abuja: Centre for Democratic Governance.

Okolo, J. E., 2002, 'The Babangida Regime and ECOWAS', in Muhammad, Baba Yunus and Amuta, Chidi (eds.) *IBB - A Heritage of Reform Vol 1: Perspectives and Interpretations*, Zaria: Open Press Ltd.

Onimode, B., 1988, *A Political Economy of African Crisis*, London: Zed Books Ltd.

Onwuka, R. and Sesay, A., 1985, *The Future of Regionalism in Africa*, London: Macmillan Publishers.

10

Civil Wars and the Refugee Crisis in West Africa: A Case Study of Liberian Refugees in Nigeria

Sikiru Taiwo Kassim

Introduction

One of the problems facing most countries in West Africa is that internal conflicts are threatening attempts at national building in many significant ways. A notable consequence of internal conflicts is the frequent displacement of people, either within their countries, that is, Internally Displaced Persons (IDPs), or across international borders, as refugees (Cohen and Deng 1998; UNHCR 1992, Stefen 2001). Although both categories of displaced persons have closely similar needs, the bulk of the assistance to victims of war has always been directed towards refugees in countries other than theirs (Ager 1999). The focus of this chapter is on the social status of Liberian refugees in Nigeria, described here as 'citizens without a home'; by virtue of the fact that under the relevant protocols of the Economic Community of West African States (ECOWAS), they are expected to enjoy right of residence in the host country.

Even though the refugee problem is a global one, available figures show that the majority of them are from Asia and Africa. According to the United Nations High Commission on Refugees (UNHCR), the estimated number of refugees worldwide is 12 million, of which Asia and Africa accounted for 6.3 million and 3.6 million respectively in 2001. The figures for both regions in 2002 stood at 5.8 million and 3.3 million respectively (UNHCR 2002). Unfortunately, according to the later figures, only 33, 915 of the estimated 64,956 Liberian refugees, received assistance from the UNHCR. As long as the war in the country lasted, its refugee situation grew progressively worse because more people fled to safety in the capital, Monrovia, and abroad, in neighbouring countries. As at the first quarter of 2003, therefore, there were over 200,000 Liberian refugees in Guinea, 35,

000 in Côte d'Ivoire and 1,792 in Nigeria (UNHCR 2003). Of course, these are conservative estimates as the figures are much smaller than the actual number who fled to safety in those countries. For instance, there are currently over 3,500 Liberian refugees in Nigeria. We highlight some of the major plights of these refugees based on empirical observations from actual visits to their camp at Oru, near Ijebu Ode in Ogun State, southwest Nigeria.

This chapter is based on in-depth interviews conducted with the refugees, the camp commandants and officials, the representative of the Red Cross and the UNHCR, and from direct participants' observations during visits beginning from 1998. The chapter is divided into eight sections, beginning with the first enumerating some of the root causes of the refugee problem in Africa. The second section traces the genesis of the refugee outflow in West Africa from the outbreak of the first Liberian civil war in December 1989, and the second round of hostilities in that country in 2000 which was prompted especially by the rebel activities of a group called Liberians United for Reconstruction and Development (LURD). The third section examines Nigeria's profile as a refugee hosting country, while the fourth explores different theoretical perspectives on the settlement of refugees vis-à-vis the model adopted by Nigeria. The fifth section focuses on the situation at the Oru refugee camp in Nigeria. Sixth, the chapter critically x-rays the nature of relationship that developed between the refugees on the one hand and their host community on the other, and next, highlight the extent and limitations of humanitarian assistance provided for the refugees in the camp. The last section provides concluding remarks and practical suggestions on how refugees can be adequately taken care of during their encampment, as is the case in Oru.

Causes of refugee flight in Africa

The factors that compel departure from one's country on account of man-made disasters are complex, and are not easily separated from other broad causes of refugee flight. In Africa, among the earliest resulted out of the anti-colonial struggles for independence, most especially before the 1960s. During that important epoch, the activities of liberation movements, especially the ones that took the option of armed struggle, were regarded as subversive thus incurring for those involved the wrath of colonial administrations that forced them into exile in other countries that offered them asylum. Although much fewer compared to those refugees that were forcibly uprooted due to civil wars and environmental conditions, this category of refugees became a rarity as most African countries consummated independence over the last three decades.

Another cause of flight is persecution, or fear of it by individuals or group of individuals, by a state or by forces within a given country which the state cannot control or is unwilling to control. The most notorious in this respect is the regime of authoritarianism and repression instituted under one-party civilian regimes and/or military dictatorships that culminated in gross and irresponsible violation of human and group rights. Oppressive government policies combined with economic hardships and other natural or ecological disasters are also known to force small or large-scale relocation of people from their original homes.

By far, the biggest cause of refugee flight in contemporary Africa remains prolonged armed conflicts and civil wars. The factors that ignite such intense and protracted conflicts are diverse: raging from inter-racial and inter-ethnic rivalries to border clashes, and the activities of insurgent movements. Furthermore, institutionalised racism, most notably under the policy of apartheid, which also involved denial, and violation of human rights, precipitated waves of refugee flights into exile. The destabilising policies of the South African regime against its neighbouring states, are already well-known to the international community as major causes of huge population displacements in that sub-region. Although it assumed increased significance in Africa in the 1980s, there was a major problem in the lack of recognition of peoples forced to leave their respective countries of origin due to economic deprivation, man-made and/or natural disasters and chronic poverty as refugees by the relevant refugee convention of the defunct Organisation of African Unity (OAU) is a major problem.

Genesis of the Liberian crisis

In our attempt to x-ray the genesis of the Liberian crisis, it is necessary to chart an historic course, in order for us to see how inter-ethnic rivalries resulted into armed conflict in Liberia. Liberia is a multi-ethnic state. The 30 tribes whose diversity immensely contributes to the variety and strength of the country fall into 17 ethnic groups. Out of this, over one-thirds of the population belong to two major ethnic groups: the Kpelle and the Bassa. Apart from these two, other large tribes are the Gio, the Kru, the Grebo and the Mano, followed by the Lorma (BUZZI), the Krahn, the Gola, the Kissi (GISSI), the Mandingo, the Vai and the Gbandi (Vogt and Ekoko 1993). At the broad level however, the major and visible line of classification of the populace has been into the minority Americo-Liberians, descendants of freed slaves who dominated society and politics for over a Century until the 1980 coup d'etat by Samuel Doe, and the majority indigenous population who historically suffered marginalisation, domination and exclusion. As Vogt and Ekoko (1993:197) have argued, '[The] conflict in Liberia has its genesis in a complex history of relationships between settlers and indigenous communities, low level of literacy among the latter, crushing poverty in the rural areas and a perception that benefits accrued primarily to the population in Monrovia.'

Until April 1980 when a military coup overthrew the dominant True Whig Party (TWP) government, Liberia's history had exhibited remarkable continuity, and occupied a unique place in the political history of Africa for several reasons. First, it is the oldest Republic on the continent, dating back to 1847. Second, until 1980, the country boasted of the oldest de facto one party political system in Africa as the ruling party had been in power continuously since 1877. Thirdly, the country did not experience classical European-style colonisation like its neighbours (Guinea, Côte d'Ivoire and Sierra Leone) or indeed, the rest of the continent. Instead, it had experienced 'black-on-black' domination or imperialism having been colonised by a handful of free American slaves in 1822, under the auspices of the American Colonisation Society. Arguably, then, it shared a similar history with Sierra-Leone in that both owe their contemporary existences to the emergence of the so-called 'philanthropic' movements in Europe and America in the wake of the abolition of the slave trade. Such movements were eager to find a permanent haven for freed men and women of colour in Africa, who had become a serious social and economic burden on the white dominated societies of Europe and North America at the time (Sesay 1992).

Prior to 1980, Liberia experienced serious political and socio-economic problems which caused internal rifts between the government of Williams Tolbert and members of the opposing parties, the People's Progressive Party (PPP) and Movement for Justice in Africa (MOJA). This rift led to the successful coup of 12 April 1980, by Master Sergeant Samuel Doe and a small group of non-commissioned, and hardly literate, officers within the Armed Forces of Liberia (AFL). Initially, the People's Redemption Council (PRC) under the chairmanship of Doe was broad enough to include the political bases of the coup leaders, and to present itself as a populist regime by evolving into a government of alliance involving elements of the deposed True Whig Party, the original opposition party, the People's Progressive Party, and the Movement for Justice in Africa (MOJA) from whom Doe received his political education.

Apart from Tolbert, who was killed during the coup, Doe's government afterwards executed 13 key members of the former administration, including the Chief Justice, the Speakers of the Senate and Tolbert's brother, Frank, who was the leader of the House of Representatives (Vogt 1995:196; Sesay 1992). At the global level, the coup and the chain of murders that followed were not only strongly condemned by, but also alienated the new government, the international community. To that extent, for instance, the then civilian government of Alhaji Shehu Shagari in Nigeria not only refused the Liberian delegation to seat at the OAU Summit that was held in Lagos but also aborted Doe's quest to complete Tolbert's Chairmanship of the Organisation. Internally, however, the coup was welcomed and celebrated by the majority of Liberians who saw the event as a major milestone and inevitable step towards the termination of the dominant lordship of and misrule by the Americo-Liberians.

No sooner had the PRC regime settled down into government that the delicate coalition that was constructed after the coup collapsed as a result of factional politicking, deep-seated ideological differences and conflicts between the various coalition partners. This came to a head when Doe's trusted second-in-command,

Sergeant Thomas Weh-Syen was executed in 1981 on the charge of treason for attempting to topple his boss. Increasingly dissatisfied with this situation, the radicals who initially provided the intellectual backbone and legitimacy for the Doe regime withdrew from the government to form the core of the opposition movement. President Doe, in turn, seized the opportunity of their withdrawal to tighten his grips on the country- in the process, appointing men and women from his ethnic group, the Khrans, into very sensitive positions in government and in the Army. This was the genesis of Khran dominance of the government and the armed forces, and of ethnic rivalries, tensions and violent conflicts with other ethnic groups.

By 1983, the commander of the Armed Forces of Liberia (AFL), and one of the groups of 17 that overthrew the government of Sir William Tolbert, Sergeant Thomas Quiwonkpa went into voluntary exile to join the swollen ranks of former loyalists and colleagues of President Doe who had fled the country to avoid incrimination and victimisation. Having silenced or forced his enemies, perceived or real, to flee for their lives, Doe began what was widely believed to be a kangaroo civilianisation programme in 1981 that would ensure a mere change of wardrobe as a military head of state to a civilian president. A new Constitution was adopted by referendum on 3 July 1984 and presidential election scheduled for 15 October 1985. The President then formed his own political party, the National Democratic Party of Liberia (NDPL) and followed the announcement to contest for the Presidency by putting in place draconian decrees to prevent any credible opposition from registering a political party not to talk of emerging and contesting the proposed election. One such decree was 'Decree' 75which gave the government blanket powers to ban people with 'un-Liberian' political beliefs from forming political parties (*West Africa* April 1990: 612). It was under this Decree that one of the most prominent opposition figures ever to emerge in post-TWP era, the Liberia Peoples Party, LPP, under Amos, was disqualified for what was described as his advocacy of ideologies foreign to Liberia. The election held in October 1985, but amidst widespread irregularities and malpractices that ensured 'victory' for Samuel Kanyon Doe with a very narrow margin of votes, just a little over fifty percent. According to the Constitution, his victory conferred a six-year mandate as President of Liberia.

The transition from military to civilian rule was a contrived window dressing. Apart from the fact that the leadership remained the same, the style of governance also remained intact: patently autocratic and corrupt, with public disenchantment reaching the highest level. It was under this ominous political climate marked by heightened uncertainty and insecurity that Quiwonkpa launched a coup from exile on 12 November 1985. Unfortunately for him, however, the coup failed and he was captured, butchered and his badly mutilated body placed on display for the public to view. Another of Doe's former colleagues was on record to have claimed that what was left of his body after the macabre public display was devoured by Doe's men (*Patriot Magazine* May – June 1991:26).

The fighting that ensued between the supporters of Doe and those of Quiwonkpa resulted in the merciless killing of Gio and Mano ethnic extraction from Nimba Country, Quiwoinkpa's home base (Vogt 1993:197). It was in that circumstance that Charles Taylor, a closer associate of Quiwonkpa fled Liberia, first sought political asylum in United States, then made his way into Ghana, Sierra-Leone, and finally, Côte d'Ivoire. During his sojourn in exile, Taylor recruited young and evidently disgruntled Liberians mainly from Nimba Country whose victimisation and brutalisation in the hands of Doe provided every reason for them to plot his downfall at all costs. On the eve of Christmas in 1989, Taylor and his National Patriotic Front of Liberia, NPFL, loyalists slipped into Liberia from across the Ivorian border, and launched several devastating attacks against security posts. The NPFL assaults threw Doe's ill-equipped and increasingly demoralised army into complete pandemonium and a hasty retreat. Thus, within six months of launching the first attack, Taylor was already clearly in total control of about seventy-five percent of the entire country, including the strategic port of Buchannan and the town of Gbarnga which later became the headquarters of the National Patriotic Front of Liberia (NPFL).

Significant milestones in that brutal civil war have been well documented (Sesay 1992; Reno 1996; Adibe 1997; Alao, Mackinlay and Olonisakin 1999). What is perhaps worth reiterating further is that the civil war unleashed an unprecedented level of carnage and devastation on the country, particularly on the non-combatant civilian population many of whom were wounded, killed or forced to flee to other countries in the sub-region, including faraway Nigeria, as refugees. During that period, the population of Monrovia, the capital, reportedly doubled from 400,000 to 850,000 (perhaps even exceeded the one million mark at some point during the prolonged civil war) as it provided a safe haven for those fleeing the unsafe countryside. War-related casualties have been estimated as high as 150,000 – an overwhelming majority of them are young people under the age of 18 years. By February 1990, more than 30,000 people had fled to Côte d'Ivoire and 12, 000 to Guinea (*Newswatch* February 1990). Nigeria hosted over 141,000 out of the 600,000 Liberian refugees (*The Guardian*, 23 January 1991; Vogt 1992:59).

As the war progressed and hardship increased, discipline and respect for the laws of war broke down completely among the different warring factions, most notoriously the AFL and the NPFL. Both sides conducted themselves with unprecedented impunity, including kidnapping and killing foreign citizens and those sheltered in sacred places such as churches and embassy grounds (*Newswatch*, Lagos, 14 May 1990; October 1 1990). All these factors put together not only invariably intensified the civil war but also weakened Samuel Doe's tenacious hold on power. He eventually met his waterloo in the hands of a break away faction of the NPFL, the Independent National Patriotic Front of Liberia (INPFL), under the leadership of Prince Yedduo Johnson, in early September 1990 (Sesay 1992:47). By the time he met his untimely death however, the Liberian civil war had developed a vicious dynamics of its own that was difficult to reverse or control. Beyond him, the rebel war not only broadened in scope but also in intensity. For example, new factions emerged besides the NPFL and the AFL. The war also exacerbated the ethnic fractures within the country with the emergence of the United Liberation Movement of Liberia (ULIMO), dominated by remnants of Doe loyalists mainly of Khran descent. From ULIMO emerged tow splinter groups, ULIMO K and ULIMO J led by Alhaji Kromah and Roosevelt Johnson respectively. Other minor factions were the Liberia Peace Council, (LPC), Lofa Defence Council, etc.

Despite a series of peace meetings initiated by ECOWAS from May 1990 onwards, the civil war lingered until the various warring factions signed the Abuja Peace Accord in 1997, just before the general election of that year. The Abuja Accord stipulated, *inter alia*, that there would be (a) disarmament (b) demobilisation (c) restructuring and retraining of the Liberian army and security by ECOMOG, and (d) elections and the installation of a civilian government in Liberia. The Accord clearly showed that the legitimacy of any government in Liberia could only be considered and respected based on these important prerequisites or yardsticks. Finally, it was hoped that the post-war stability envisaged in Liberia would impact positively on the dire situation in neighbouring Sierra Leone.

Unfortunately, what obtained in the post-1997 general election years in Liberia contradicted the spirit and intentions of the Abuja Accord, leaving horrendous consequences for the Liberian people. Firstly, the disarmament process turned out to be an embarrassing fiasco as the warring factions simply dismantled and buried about 65 percent of their weapons (Wilson 1998). The largest and the most powerful warring faction, the NPFL led by Charles Taylor, was the most culpable as it buried large caches of arms and ammunitions in the vast countryside where it enjoyed effective control. Secondly, there was no effective demobilisation and no one knew the exact number of fighters each of the factions had recruited. Thirdly, and most importantly, the AFL was not restructured and reformed as envisaged in the Abuja Accord, with far-reaching consequences for peace and security in the country.

It was against all of these backgrounds, especially of the non-compliance with the Abuja Accord, that elections were held in 1997. The elections which brought Charles Taylor into the Executive Mansion, the once imposing seat of government in Monrovia, were widely believed to have been singularly distinguished by fraudulent electoral practices. In the absence of a neutral armed force before and after the election, President Taylor relied almost exclusively on his former fighters in the NPFL to secure himself and his regime.

After the election, there was relative peace in the country, which necessitated the repatriation of nearly 230,000 Liberian refugees in 1988, scattered all over West Africa, out of an estimated 500,000 displaced (Stromberg 1988) Although this repatriation exercise was slow and incomplete, owing largely to inadequacy of funding and other logistic problems, there was still a pervasive sense of anxiety and uncertainty among the refugees about where to start picking up the pieces of the broken lives on their return. But then, even though relative peace was restored in Liberia at the initial period, it was also clear that what was achieved was an unstable peace. Another insurgent movement, this time under the banner of Liberians United for Reconciliation and Democracy (LURD), began another round of civil war by attacking from Guinea, and with time was joined by another, the Movement for Democracy in Liberia (MODEL). Their major demand was the removal from office of President Charles Taylor; an insistence that, in turn, led to renewed escalation of violence in the country with thousands of people displaced or dead. By this time also, it was clear that Charles Taylor was living on borrowed times, a fate that was sealed during the special summit on Liberia held in Accra Ghana, on 31 July 2003. Apart from condemning the renewed hostilities, the Summit called for an immediate ceasefire and the deployment of the 3000-troop Vanguard Interposition Force under joint ECOWAS/ United Nations supervision also otherwise known as ECOWAS Mission in Liberia, ECOMIL. With the deployment of ECOMIL Forces, a negotiated exit was arranged for President Charles Taylor who was not only expected to relinquish power but also to depart into exile in eastern Nigeria. Out of the Special Summit in Accra, Ghana, also came the appointment of an interim government with a mandate to initiate and consummate a transition to civil rule by 2005.

Profile of Nigeria as a refugee hosting country

Although Nigeria produced the bulk of refugees in Africa consequent upon its 3-year civil war between 1967-1970, it was not until 1990 that it became itself a refugee hosting country. Most of those who sought refuge in Nigeria were fleeing wars in different parts of Africa, but especially, those from West Africa such as Liberia, Sierra Leone and later, Côte d'Ivoire. Prior to the 1990s, the influx of aliens into Nigeria was dominated by indigenes of West Africa attracted by the fabled oil boom of the 1970s and the early 1980s. Although no known measures were taken to grant them this category of people asylum or to regard them as refugees, it was only in 1989 that the Federal military government enacted Decree 52 establishing the National Commission for Refugees. The new Commission was saddled with the responsibility, along with other government agencies, of collaboration with the UNHCR, for the purpose of granting asylum to refugee.

This decree adopted the legal definition of refugees as provided for by the 1951 Geneva Convention relating to the status of refugees and the 1969 African

Refugee Conventions of the Organisation of African Unity, OAU. According to the 1951 UN Convention, a refugee is a person who:

> owing to well-founded fear of being persecuted for reasons of race, religion, nationality, membership of a particular social group or political opinion, is outside the country of his nationality and is unable, or owing to such fear, is unwilling to avail himself of the protection of that country.

The OAU African Refugee Convention, on the other hand, gave an 'extended' definition of a refuge as a person who

> owing to external aggression, occupation, foreign domination or events seriously disturbing public order in either part or the whole of his country of origin or nationality, is compelled to leave his place of habitual residence in order to seek refuge in another place outside his country of origin or nationality.

The Nigeria government gave practical expression to Decree 52, especially by adopting the settlement approach, with the establishment of a Refugee Camp in 1990 at Oru, to accommodate refugees displaced by the Liberian war. Since then the camp has provided abode to refugees from different parts of Africa. By 1999, the number of refugees according to their nationality was as follows: 355 from Sierra Leone, 369 from Liberia, 11 from Congo, I Somalian, 3 Sudanese, 1 Ghanaian, 3 Rwandans and 1 Chadian (Kassim 1999). The figure continued to increase and by 17 August 2003, there were over 5500 African refugees in the camp out of which 3500 came from Liberia. This figure is expected to increase as Nigeria's 'big brother' role in the sub-region continues to attract refugees to it.

Approaches to refugees settlement

The increasing growth of refugees in Africa since the mid 1960s raised the issue of how to accommodate and provide for them during the period that they are displaced, without worsening the living conditions of the residents of the host community (Ford Foundation 1983, Gorman 1987, Stein 1980, United Nations 1981, Walker 1978 and Winter 1984). Over the years, two long-term settlement options emerged; self-settlement and settlement on government organised around agricultural schemes became popular in Anglophone Africa (Chambers 1969). In self-settlement, sometimes called spontaneous settlement, the refugees live in existing villages among local residents or form their own villages, encouraged or welcomed by existing inhabitants and authorities. Sometimes these refugees have kinship or friendship relations with local people and rely on that initial hospitality for information that helps them find food and work. These refugees usually subsist on their own little or indirect government assistance (Batts 1980; Cato 1967; Gould 1974; Hansen 1977 and 1982; Mageed and Ramaga 1986; Zartman 1970).

For the second option, the government acquires a large block of land, usually with the permission of local authorities. The land is often unoccupied or sparsely populated; as the original residents may have been displaced or alienated from the land due to different circumstances, including protracted conflicts. With international aid, the government establishes a smallholder agricultural settlement project and allocated plots to refugees; or less commonly, a mixture of refugees and residents. The government builds access roads in the scheme, built and staffed the schools and clinics. When refugees arrive, they are given plots to farm, food rations (usually for years), blankets, clothing, and sometimes tools (Hansen 1979c; 1980a and 1980b; Rogge 1981). Scheme-settled refugees are expected to become self-sufficient (in terms of their staple food requirements) through farming. Although in Nigeria, there is a slight modification to this, refugees are allowed to farm on any portion of land within the camp and there is no formal allocation of plots for farming.

Furthermore, the argument has emerged in the literature about the consequences of self-settlement in favour of scheme-settlement. One strong argument against self-settlement is that it leads to the deterioration of the quality of live of both the refugees and their local host (Hansen 1979; Muzur 1988; Rogge 1981; Chambers 1979 and 1986; Kirby 1985, cited from Hanson 1990). This is especially as many refugees tend to suffer unrelieved poverty without direct governmental or international assistance. Although self-settlement takes the pressure off governments and international agencies in terms of responding to the needs of both the refugees and their local hosts, they tend to be invisible enough to receive adequate attention and care from government and the international community. At the same time, the local hosts suffer, because the refugees make heavy demands on existing medical and educational facilities, and refugees compete with local residents for scarce food stocks, medical supplies, arable land, and wage labour opportunities. This drives wages down and prices up. Those changes affect mostly the poorest local residents who have little or no land, and who buy their food with income from wage labour, or who exchange labour for food. Self-settlement therefore leaves most refugees physically vulnerable, sometimes over an unduly long period of time. Since refugees tend to settle closer to national borders, their presence in those areas where the writ of government is minimal, in some cases non-existent, can become treacherous as they are exposed to all kinds of insecurity problems, including cross-border raids (Harrell-Bond 1986). Local residents sometimes also get caught in those attacks. Eventually, for all of these problems, local people sometimes attack the refugees with the intention of driving them away for causing their woes by their presence. In so far as the above argument may look genuine in its analysis, the basic fact remains that, Nigeria, the 'big brother' in the West Africa sub-region established camps to provide settlement for the legally recognised refugees and established a commission (the National Commission for Refugees 1989) to cater for the needs of these refugees. This camp provides avenues through which government assistance is channelled to the refugees through a collaborative scheme managed by the UNHCR, Red Cross and other NGOs. This assistance varies from food rations, tents and buildings for accommodation, mats, cloths, blankets, and primary education facilities.

Situation at the Oru Camp

The refugee camp for Liberian refugees in Nigeria is situated in a rural area of the Ijebu speaking community (ORU) in Ogun State, South Western Nigeria. The community is predominantly rural and the majority of inhabitants engage in farming as their main occupation. The camp has clusters of buildings, which include a residential building, an administrative block, which also houses the camp clinic, a primary school building, and a hall for social activities. Also, there is a football pitch, for the recreational activities of the refugees. The buildings that are occupied by refugees are partitioned into small units with planks or for each family to reside. The rooms are poorly ventilated and the refugees only have mats to sleep on. The electricity supply into the camp is faulty so the refugees use lanterns. Only a few of the refugees are provided with mattresses especially those with babies less than one year old. With more refugees arriving from Liberia into the camp in June 2003; the available accommodation could no longer cope with the large influx of refugees, hence the need to provide more shelter. In response to this shortage, 24 tarpaulin tents were provided for the refugees each housing a minimum of 30 inhabitants irrespective of age and sex, with no ventilation and electricity supply. These tents were erected on grasses covered with tarpaulin so the refugees, had to spread their mats and blankets. The situation in the tents is so bad that there is no form of privacy for occupants. The refugees have to cook and eat outside the tents. Some of the tents were named 'New Liberian', 'Mamba Point' and 'Pentagon' among others. The primary school building located within the camp and the open hall meant for social activities, have been converted to shelters by the refugees. Some of the refugees have had to sleep on a bare floor. Since the place is open, they are subjected to harsh weather that tends to make them prone to ailments such as catarrh and cough.

Regarding the sanitary and health situation within the camp, there are two forms of toilet facilities, the pit latrine dug near the tents and the water system which have been overstretched due to heavy usage and abuse. In fact refugees resort to 'bush-attack' (defecating in a nylon bag and throwing it into the nearby bush). Since the bushes where these human excreta are thrown into are also within the camp, the sanitary situation can expect to worsen, and to pose a serious health hazard to the refugees themselves. Also most of the refugees complain of malaria fever resulting from mosquito bites, because the bush and the swampy nature of the camp provide a good habitat for mosquitoes to breed. It is therefore necessary to clear the bush in and around the camp to discourage the breeding of mosquitoes and also to fumigate the camp.

With regard to health issues, there are cases of sexually transmitted diseases among adolescents within the camp. Although the Nigerian Red Cross continues to preach the gospel of safe sex, it is unlikely that the refugees are listening or practising that. As a result of uncontrolled movement in and out of the camp, adolescent females engage in clandestine prostitution in order to earn a better living within the camp. Most weekends, for instance, visitors hang around the camp gate in their cars soliciting female refugee companions. One of the female refugees involved informed this author that:

> I have to survive, we are only given foodstuffs in the camp on a monthly basis and this cannot last us for one month, so how do I get money for myself and survive for the remaining period of the month if the food finishes.

On further enquiry on whether she insists on the use of a condom by her partner, she said:

> I don't decide that! If he wants to use it I wont stop him, and if he decides otherwise,
> I will not disturb him either so long as he pays me at the end of the show.

This kind of attitude raises the propensity for a range of sexually transmitted diseases, including the dreaded HIV/AIDS, to spread like bushfire. Furthermore, the camp clinic only operates on Monday, Wednesday and Friday, attending to illnesses like malaria, catarrh and colds while complicated cases are referred to the General Hospital in Ijebu-Ode, a nearby town. Apart from the fact that drugs are in short supply in the camp clinic, most of the refugees reported that important prescriptions given to them are usually not available in the clinic, and sometimes, too expensive for them to buy outside. Undoubtedly, the facilities in this clinic cannot adequately cater for the growing number of refugees in the camp.

Another problem faced by Liberian refugees is idleness. They roam around the camp during the day without doing anything tangible to sustain themselves. In fact two of the refugees interviewed pleaded with this author to help them find jobs, even as casual, daily paid farm hands. They are also not sure of continuing their education even though the Nigerian legislation on refugees adopted article 22 (I) of 1951 UNHCR Convention relating mainly to primary education. The article states that 'the contracting states shall accord to refugees the same treatment as is accorded to nationals with respect to elementary education'. The Government's efforts do not go beyond this, but most of the refugees are adolescent and high school graduates who need college and university education for their personal fulfilment and usefulness to the host community.

Relationship with the host community

The relationship between the refugees and the local community has been cordial, perhaps due to the fact that the Liberian refugees are black and they speak English, the lingua franca in Nigeria. There is even a form of trade going on between the refugees and the host community, as some refugees trade their food ration for cash with some members of the host community. In this case, some of the locals depend on the refugees for supply of some food items. Furthermore, if there is going to be any form of traditional activities that is to take place within the village, where foreigners were not permitted to attend; the traditional ruler will inform the authority in the camp so that refugees can be aware of these and abide by them. This shows that there is a harmonious relationship between the refugees and the host community.

There is also the religious web that brings the refugees and the members of the host community together. Both worship in the same churches and mosque. Through these religious interactions, the local people offer regular assistance to refugees, including sundry items such as clothing and jobs.

Humanitarian assistance

Humanitarian assistance is vital in order to assist refugees cope with the traumas of flight and impoverishment; and to address their immediate shocks, stresses and traumas. This has been the focal point of the intervention strategy of the Nigerian government. Although, provision of humanitarian assistance to the refugees has always been the preserve of the office of the United Nations High Commissioner for Refugees and its implementing partners like International Committee of the Red Cross, the Nigerian government through agencies such as the National Commission for Refugees (NCFR) and National Emergency Management Agency (NEMA), are playing a pivotal role in the provision of humanitarian assistance to the Liberian refugees in Nigeria, and internally displaced persons (IDPs) in Liberia. The reason for this is because Nigeria is still looked upon as a benevolent 'Big brother' throughout the West African sub-region.

The UNHCR through its implementing partners also complemented the Nigerian government's efforts in improving the plight of the refugees. The International Committee of the Red Cross, (ICRC) through its Nigerian office was responsible for the movement of new refugees from the UNHCR office in Lagos to Oru camp. It also provided the tents and funding for the purchase of prescribed drugs. ICRC distributed relief materials to the refugees and carried out a health campaign to forestall the outbreak of epidemics in the camp.

Conclusion

Much as refugees live a relatively peaceful life in the country of refuge (such as Nigeria), the facilities provided for their basic comfort in the camp are far from adequate, especially giving the recent increase in the camp population in 2003. There is therefore need for a concerted effort by the host government to improve the facilities in the camp so that the 'visitors' can live a relatively more comfortable life. Also the host government and UNHCR should provide educational opportunities and scholarships for the refugees. This will help the refugees to further their education and become more useful to their host country, and to their country of origin when repatriated. More relief materials should be provided and facilities within the camp improved. In as much as efforts have been made to make refugees comfortable in the host country. It is obvious that conflicts and its attendant refugee problems retard the process of nation building, as societies are dislocated and people generally disorganised.

References

Adibe, Clement, 'The Liberian Conflict and the ECOWAS-UN Partnership'. *Third World Quarterly*, 18: 3, 1997.

Ager, A., 1999, Perspectives on the Refugees Experience: in A. Ager (ed.) *Perspectives on the Experience of Forced Migration*, Guildford and King's Lynn U.K: Bibbles Limited

Alao, A., Mackinlay, J. and Olonisakin, F., 1999, *Peacekeepers, Politicians, and Warlords: The Liberian Peace Process*, Tokyo, New York, and Paris: UN University Press,

Betts, T., 1980, *Spontaneous Settlement of Rural Refugees in Africa*, London: Euro Action.

Cato, A., 1967, 'Refugee Problem in Southern Africa', in S. Hamell (ed.), *Refugee Problems in Africa*, Uppsala: Scandinavian Institute of African Studies.

Chambers S. R., 1979, 'Rural Refugees in Africa: What the Eye does not See' *Disasters* 3:4.

Chambers, R., 1969, *Settlement Schemes in Tropical Africa: A Study of Organisation and Development*, London: Routledge and Began Paul.

Cohen, R. and Deng, M. F., 1998, *Mass in Flight. The Global Crisis Internal Displacement*, Washington D.C.: Brookings International Press.

Ford Foundation, 1983, *Refugees and Migrants. Problems and Program Responses: Working Paper*, New York: Ford Foundation.

Gorman, R. F., 1987, Taking Stock of the Second International Conference on Assistance to Refugees in Africa (ICARA II), *Journal of African Studies*,14:1

Gould, W. T. S., 1974, 'Refugee in Tropical Africa', *International Migration Review* 8.3.

Hansen, A., 1990, Refugee Self-Settlement Versus Settlement on Government Schemes. The long-term Consequences for Security, Integration Economic Development of Angolan Refugees (1966-1989) in Zambia, A United Nations Research Institute for Social Development, *Discussion Paper No 17*.

Harrell-Bond, B. E., 1990, Breaking the Vicious Circle: Refugees and Other Persons in Africa, in *The African Social Situation. Crucial Factors of Development and Transformation*, Oxford: Hans Zell Publishers.

Kagan, M. and Doctor, S., 2002, 'Assessment of Refugee Status Determination; Procedure of UNHCR; Cairo Office 2001-2002' A Working Paper for Forced Migration and Refugee Studies, American University, Cairo.

Kalyango, R., 2003, 'Challenges of Integration Faced by Urban Refugees: A Case Review of Cairo and Kampala', Paper Presented at the International Association for the Study of Forced Migration Conference in Changmai Thailand.

Kassim, S. T., 1999, Knowledge, Attitude and Practice of Contraceptives Among Refugees in Nigeria: A Case Study of Refugee Camp Oru, Ogun State, Nigeria. Unpublished M.Sc. Thesis.

Mazur, R. E., 1988, Refugees in Africa: The Role of Sociologist Analysis and Praxis, *Current Sociology, 36: 2*.

Reno, W., 'The Business of War in Liberia', *Current History*, May 1996.

Roger, J.R., 1981, Africa's Resettlement Strategies, *International Migration Review*, 15: 53-54.

Sesay, A., 1992, 'Historical Background to the Liberian Crisis.' in Margaret Vogt (ed.), *The Liberian Crisis and ECOMOG*, Lagos: Gabumo Press.

Sparl, S., 2001, Evaluation of UNHCR Policy on Refugee in Urban Areas; A Case Review of Cairo Evaluation Policy Analysis Unit (EPAU).

Stain, B., 1980, Refugee Resettlement Programs and Techniques, Research Report Submitted To The Select Commission on Immigration and Refugee Policy.

Stomberg, P., 1998, The Year of Return in Liberia, *Refugee Magazines* 112.

The National Commission for Refugees Decree No 52 of 1989.

UNHCR, 2003, *Global Refugee Trend* January–March.

UNHCR, 2002, Refugees, Asylum Seekers and Other Person of Concern. Trend in Displacement, Protection and Solution, *Statistical Yearbook 2001*.

UNHCR, 2003, Refugees, Asylum Seekers and Other Persons of Concern-Trend in Displacement, Protection and Solution, *Statistical Yearbook 2002*.

United Nations, 1981, The Refugee Situation in Africa: Assistance Measures Proposed; International Conference on Assistance to Refugees in Africa (ICARA) (Geneva 9–10 April).

Vogt, M. A. and Ekoko, A. E., 1993, *Nigeria in International Peace keeping 1960-1992*, Lagos: Malthouse Press

Vogt, M. A., 1993, 'Nigeria in Liberia: Historical and Political Analysis of ECOMOG' in *Nigeria and International Peace-keeping*, Lagos: Macmillan

Walker, G. A., 1978, Refugee in Southern Africa, A Report to the Congress on Development Needs and Opportunities for Co-operation in Southern Africa, Annex B: Refugees, United States agency for International Development Washington D. C.

Winker, R., 1984, Refugee Protection in Africa Current Trends, Paper Presented at the Washington Institute for Value in Public Policy Conference on U. S. Policy Toward Africa. Washington D. C.

11

Can ECOWAS Re-invent the Nationalist Dream in West Africa? Reflections on the Protocol on Democracy and Good Governance

Amadu Sesay

... I am convinced more than ever that our long-term salvation lies in cooperation among ourselves rather than in perpetual dependence on factors beyond our control. We can achieve through economic cooperation the self-control needed to prevent external manipulation of our internal policies (Kamara-Taylor 1975: 90).

We believe in regional cooperation with equal fervour, because it is only after developing African states have coordinated their efforts and organized themselves at regional levels, that we can have the strength of purpose, which will make people listen to us not only in the OAU, but also at the United Nations (Stevens n.d. 8).

Introduction

There is no doubt that African leaders, irrespective of their ideological shade, size of their nations and indeed, level of national development, do believe that the futures of their countries lie in collective self-reliance efforts. More specifically, now, as it was in the past, African leaders seem to be convinced that economic integration is the key to solving the problems of nation-building which have bedevilled their countries since independence. This conviction goes beyond the sub-regions to embrace the entire African continent. It explains in part the various attempts at pan-continental integration that have either been suggested, or actually attempted. Two readily come to mind: the elaborate but still-born Lagos Plan of Action of 1980, and the comatose African Economic Community Treaty signed in Abuja, Nigeria, in June 1991. Both schemes anticipated the creation of an all-embracing African Common Market that would pave way for accelerated continental economic development and prosperity, among other things. In short, then, integration is perceived as necessary for realising the nationalist dream of sustainable economic development, stable nations and a prosperous citizenry in the West African sub-region in particular and the continent at large.

Regional integration in West Africa: Past trends and experiences

Efforts aimed at integrating the West African sub-region go back into the colonial period when the metropolitan powers tried to amalgamate the colonies to minimise administrative costs, and to intensify their economic exploitation. The British set up the West African Currency Board for the Gambia, Ghana, Nigeria and Sierra Leone, and the West African Airways Corporation, among others. For the French, the most notable move was the integration of all the French territories into one monetary union, with the CFA as legal tender complete with a Central Bank located in Dakar, Senegal. Indeed, the continuing existence of the CFA no doubt poses one of the most important obstacles to a common currency in West Africa. Many of the colonial schemes did not survive the early period of independence especially in Anglophone West Africa, where the most notable surviving project, the West Africa Examinations Council (WAEC), still conducts pre-university exams for the Gambia, Ghana, Nigeria, and Sierra Leone (Liberia joined the Council in the 1980s).

Several spirited attempts were made to promote regional integration in West Africa soon after independence in the 1960s. A number of important factors were responsible for the 'integration wave'. First, the nationalists saw it as a means of consolidating their hard-won political independence. Second, was the belief that successful economic integration would lead to prosperity and a better life for the citizens of the member states, a fulfilment of the nationalist dream. This belief was based on the fact that their individual markets were too small to promote the much touted rapid economic development and political stability, which the nationalists promised in the run up to independence (Nkrumah 1963). Third, was the demonstration effect of the successful European Economic Community, EEC, which consolidated unity and cooperation among the European states and brought unprecedented prosperity to their citizens. The fact that some of the key actors in the EEC project then were also former colonial powers not only sensitised the newly independent states about the exciting developments in Europe, but also brought home to their leaders some of the gains and possibilities inherent in a successful integration scheme. In short, West African leaders, like their counterparts in other parts of the continent and the Third World, were of the view that pooling their economic and human resources could provide the impetus for rapid economic advancement which would enable them to tackle some of the daunting problems of nation-building confronting them, such as poverty, illiteracy, disease, etc.

It is doubtful, though, if some of the first generation leaders in the sub-region were really interested in integration for its own sake. It is possible that some embraced the idea and philosophy because they saw it as a means of blunting the much more radical alternative of political union among the independent African States proposed by the late Ghanaian leader, Kwame Nkrumah. It was hardly surprising, then, that one of the staunchest advocates of regional integration at the time was also the ultra-conservative Liberian leader, William Tubman. During his inauguration in January 1964, he suggested the creation of a West African Free Trade Area, FTA, embracing all the independent states. He devoted a lot of time to propagating the scheme. In August 1964, for instance, diplomats from four West African countries: Guinea, Côte d'Ivoire, Liberia and Sierra Leone met in Monrovia to deliberate on the possibilities of creating the Free Trade Area. And at another meeting held in February 1965, representatives from the four countries drew up an agreement that would lead to the formation of an interim organisation for West African economic cooperation in Freetown, Sierra Leone.

In 1973, the Mano River Union, MRU, linking Liberia and Sierra Leone was formed (Francophone Guinea joined a decade later in 1983). That same year saw the creation of the Communauté Economique de l'Afrique de l'Ouest, CEAO, among the Francophone countries of the sub-region. Other notable arrangements were the Lake Chad Basin Commission, the Union Monetaire de l'Ouest Africaine, or West African Monetary Union, the West African Clearing House (WACH), the Organisation of Senegal River States, OERS, etc. Many of these organisations have hardly functioned. The Mano River Union, for instance, could not prevent the collapse of its founding members - Liberia and Sierra Leone, and has been stalled by the unprecedented political turmoil within and among Member States. The civil wars in Liberia and Sierra Leone were not only the most protracted in the history of the sub-region but also easily the most notorious, and attracted worldwide attention as a result of the bestialities committed by different warring factions and the armed forces of the two countries (Vogt 1994; Aboagye 1999). In short, then, the West African sub-region has not been short of regional cooperation experiments.

The most significant turning point however came in May 1975 with the formation of the sub-region wide Economic Community of West African States, ECOWAS. For the first time, there was a determined attempt to bridge the colonial, historical and linguistic gap between the Anglophone and Francophone states which the former colonial powers continued to exploit even after political freedom had been achieved. According to Article 3 of the Revised ECOWAS Treaty, the aims and objectives of the Community are presented broadly as the promotion of

> co-operation and integration, leading to the establishment of an economic union in West Africa in order to raise the living standards of its peoples, and

to maintain and enhance economic stability, foster relations among Member States and contribute to the progress and development of the African continent.

Some of the more specific goals of the organisation as contained in the Revised ECOWAS Treaty include,

(i)   the harmonisation and coordination of national policies and the promotion of integration programmes, projects and activities, particularly in food, agriculture and natural resources, industry, transport and communications, energy, trade, money and finance, taxation, economic reform policies, human resources, education, information, culture, science, technology, services, health, tourism, legal matters;

(ii)   the establishment of an economic union through the adoption of common policies in the economic, financial, social and cultural sectors, and the creation of a monetary union.

(iii)   the removal, between Member States, of obstacles to the free movement of persons, goods, services, and capital, and to the right of residence and establishment, etc.

However not much progress has been recorded in the area of economic integration in the sub-region. Over two decades and half of integration efforts have not had any significant impact on trade between Member States which is still less than 10 percent of their global trade. According to a study by ILO/JASPA,

the trade liberalization scheme, the centre piece of the Community's cooperation programme has been characterized by lack of progress. Indeed, the initial steps in this direction have just been taken more than a decade and a half behind schedule (1990: 155).

The study also noted that:

there is yet to be a concrete programme by ECOWAS to achieve harmonious industrial development and integration through specialization and complementarities of production. Similar lack of progress has characterized the Community's agricultural cooperation (1990: 155).

I shall not go into the reasons why ECOWAS is yet to achieve its targets more than twenty-five years after it was formed. Suffice it to note that as a corollary, the Community is yet to make noticeable impacts on the lives of the majority of Community citizens for reasons which are beyond the scope of this chapter.

ECOWAS and sub-regional peace and stability in West Africa

Like other regions in Africa, the advent of independence in West Africa also gave rise to euphoria. This is because independence was expected to usher in peace, stability, economic growth, development and significant improvements in the living conditions of the citizens. The sub-region was also expected to play a constructive role in African and global affairs. Thus, flag independence was celebrated with pomp and pageantry everywhere in the sub-region. However, these expectations turned out to be overly optimistic as the reality of dependent independence soon dawned both on the nationalists and the citizens of the sub-region, as successor elites proved increasingly and hopelessly incapable of holding the liquor of political freedom. The sign posts were many and significant: the inability to conduct violence free and fair elections; creeping and outright dictatorships in many countries, one party systems both *de jure* and *de facto*, ethnically centred regimes, unbridled corruption, economic downturns and/or outright collapse, the breakdown of fragile social infrastructure, coups, civil wars, mass displacements of people and unprecedented refugee outflows, and finally, state collapse. While the Cold War lasted, some of these fissures were papered over only to come to the fore with ferocious intensity with the collapse of bipolarity in global politics and the withdrawal of the Super Powers from peripheries such as Africa. The termination of the Cold War opened a political Pandora's box as competition for power and political control of the state between elites assumed persistently violent and destabilising dimensions. In West Africa, this was manifested in two brutal civil wars and state collapse soon after the demise of communism in the Soviet Union

It could be argued that West African leaders had anticipated some of these developments, so they created ECOWAS as a veritable strategy for confidence building and for promoting the nationalist dream. ECOWAS did make significant contributions to efforts directed at halting the collapse and chaos that characterised West African politics in the 1990s, as witnessed by its unprecedented involvement in conflict management, peacekeeping and peace enforcement in Liberia and Sierra Leone. That is to be expected. For without peace and stability, economic and social development cannot take place and the nationalist dream of creating prosperity for the citizens could not be realised.

It is significant to note that the ECOWAS Treaty did not say anything about conflict management and prevention among its aims and objectives. Paradoxically, though, it is in this sphere that the organisation has made considerable impact and also attracted a great deal of public and media attention not only in the sub-region itself, but also in Africa and the rest of the global system. Surprisingly, for an economic integration scheme, ECOWAS boasts of the most advanced conflict prevention and management mechanism devised by any sub-regional grouping anywhere in the world. Since the Liberian civil war broke out in December 1989 and the Community's involvement in that war via its ECOWAS Monitoring Group (ECOMOG) peacekeeping and peace enforcement operations in August 1990, it is not an overstatement to say that there has emerged what can be called an 'ECOWAS publishing enterprise': academic treatises, projects, books, journal, magazine and newspaper articles, which focus mainly on the successes and problems associated with the peace keeping operations in Liberia and Sierra Leone. In other words, the focus on its activities in the two countries is still alive, while the literature on the operations is vast and continues to grow. That is perhaps to be expected since ECOWAS also rose creditably and in an unprecedented manner to the challenges of conflict management and peace keeping in West Africa at a time when the great powers had literally abandoned the sub-region – and indeed the continent - to its fate and focused their attention on flashpoints in Europe.

Put differently, because of ECOMOG, ECOWAS has rightly or wrongly received unparalleled international exposure and media attention since the 1990s. I shall not go into the politics of ECOMOG's creation and operations in this chapter, for those have been adequately covered (Vogt 1992). What is worth stressing at this point is that it is possible that the founding fathers anticipated some conflict prevention and management roles for ECOWAS, although the Treaty did not make any provision for them, as a way of creating the enabling environment in which development and prosperity could be actualised. Thus as early as April 1978, three years after its establishment, the Heads of State and Government adopted a *Protocol on Non-Aggression*, in the Nigerian capital, Lagos. According to Article 1 of the Protocol:

> Member States, shall, in their relations with one another, refrain from the threat or use of force or aggression or from employing any other means inconsistent with the Charters of the United Nations and the organization of African unity against the territorial integrity or political independence of other Member States.

Three years later, 1981, ECOWAS again adopted the *Protocol Relating to Mutual Assistance on Defence*, in the Sierra Leonean capital, Freetown. Article 2 stipulates that 'Member States declare and accept that any armed threat or aggression directed against any Member State shall constitute a threat or aggression against the entire Community'. It is Article 16 that has however attracted a lot of attention and controversy especially as some prominent members, in particular, Côte d'Ivoire and Burkina Faso, both then staunch supporters of rebel Charles Taylor in Liberia, initially challenged the legitimacy of ECOMOG and boycotted all peace moves by the organisation. Explicitly, the Article states:

> When an external armed threat or aggression is directed against a Member State of the Community, the Head of State of that country shall send a written request for assistance to the current Chairman of the Authority of ECOWAS...

Although late president Samuel Doe insisted that he wrote to ECOWAS for assistance, it is doubtful if he was really in control of Liberia at the time, for he had been holed up in the Presidential Mansion for several months, and his authority and control did not extend beyond the perimeter fence of the seat of power in the country.

Finally, in 1999, ECOWAS once again embarked upon another important conflict prevention and management enterprise, with the adoption of the *Protocol Relating to the Mechanism for Conflict Prevention, Management, Resolution, Peace Keeping and Security*. Space constraints will not allow us to discuss this epoch making document in detail here. Suffice it to say that it contained all the accepted methods of conflict resolution short of war. It is obvious from the foregoing that even at a very early stage, ECOWAS did not want to see itself as an orthodox economic integration scheme, knowing fully well that in a highly volatile socio-political and economic environment like the West African sub-region, economic issues could never be divorced from politics. In other words, West African leaders were simply acknowledging the pre-eminence of politics in intra- and inter-state relations in the sub-region. It was hoped that the organisation would minimise conflicts among its members, and manage them effectively when they broke out. That way, ECOWAS would directly and indirectly facilitate the realisation of the objectives and goals of the nationalists and founding fathers of the respective Member States.

It was in this context that ECOWAS also brought together a group of eminent scholars in Dakar in October 2001 to draw up a *Protocol on Democracy and Good Governance* as an instrument for promoting peace and security in West Africa – not only by engineering convergence in the domestic politics of member states, but also in order to create a conducive atmosphere that would revive the nationalist dreams and aspirations of political stability and economic prosperity for the citizenry.[12] The document, accordingly, sought to address important issues such as political marginalisation and exclusion, free and fair elections, bad governance, corruption, military coups, economic deprivation, gender inequality and development, and youth unemployment that are at the centre of the unprecedented violence and state collapse that have bedevilled the sub-region in recent times.

The rest of this chapter critically examines the possibilities as well as the limitations of the ECOWAS Protocol on Democracy and Good Governance [henceforth simply the Protocol] against the background of the hopes and expectations of both the founding fathers and the citizens of West Africa in the light of developments in member states and the sub-region since the 1990s. It tries to answer several fundamental questions, for instance, can ECOWAS re-invent the nationalist dream in West Africa? What are the possibilities, limitations and challenges in that regard? What were the background conditions in some of the member states that made the sub-region one of the most unstable and notorious in the international system since the end of the Cold War?

The ECOWAS Protocol on Democracy and Good Governance: Analysis of possibilities, limitations and challenges

The Protocol on Democracy and Good Governance that came into force in 2001 is the latest and the most far-reaching attempt by ECOWAS to consolidate peace, security and stability in a sub-region that has witnessed two notorious civil wars. The Protocol is important because it has the potential of impacting positively, directly and indirectly, on the lives of ordinary citizens in ECOWAS Member States. Besides, it has the long-term effect of redeeming the image of the sub-region, which was badly battered during the Liberian and Sierra Leonean civil wars (1989–1997, then 2000–2003, and 1991–2002) respectively. The Protocol covers a wide range of subjects and is divided into three chapters. Chapter 1 deals with the *Principles*; Chapter 2 is on the *Modalities for Implementation*, while Chapter 3 deals with the *General and Final Provisions*. Chapter 1 is obviously the most important portion of the document for it contains 44 out of a total of 51 articles. In all, the Protocol has eight sections each of which is devoted to a topical issue in the politics of the sub-region, and all are located in Chapter 1. Section I deals with the Constitutional Convergence Principles, while Section II is on Elections. Others are Election Monitoring and ECOWAS Assistance, Section III, The Role of the Armed Forces, the Police and other Security Forces in a Democracy, Section IV, Poverty Alleviation and Promotion of Social Dialogue, Section V, Education, Culture and Religion, Section VI, The Rule of Law, Human Rights and Good Governance, Section VII and finally Section VIII, which is on Women, Children and the Youth (ECOWAS, 2001).[14] It is clear from the subjects covered by each of these sections that ECOWAS leaders were determined to address the fundamental issues that were the prime causes of political instability, civil strife and war in the sub-region, especially in the post-Cold War era. Each of these sections presents possibilities, challenges and limitations to Member States individually and collectively, and it is to these that we now turn.

Although the Protocol is made up of three broad chapters, it is Chapter I and its sections, eight in all, which are the focus of this discussion. This is because it reflects not only the concerns but also the efforts of ECOWAS leaders to address all the major issues that have been at the heart of the political, social and economic turbulence and misfortunes in the sub-region. In particular, it tried to address those issues that were at the centre of the political disputes and differences among the elites that eventually led to civil war and state collapse in some member states: political exclusion and marginalisation, denial of access to socio-economic resources, elections, civilian control of the armed forces, and so on. It is premised essentially on the broad assumption that the different political styles and constitutional systems in the member sates were a contributory factor to the sub-region's instability, poor economic performance and the unenviable plight of its citizens. Accordingly, it is assumed that once the entire sub-region is under standardised socio-political regimes and governance systems, all would be well. From such an angle, the section is an attempt to re-invent the nationalist dream, which propelled the first generation of West African leaders to agitate for political freedom from the colonial masters.

Not surprisingly, Article 1(a) provides for the *Separation of Powers between the Executive, Legislative and Judiciary* in all Member States, while 1(c) proclaims 'zero tolerance for power obtained through the use of force or military coup d'état or remaining in power through undemocratic means'. When a Member State violates this important principle, the citizens '... reserve the right to assert their sovereignty...', that is, they are obliged to disobey such a regime using peaceful means. Section I (Article 1(f), deals with religion, another sensitive issue which has led to a lot of bloodshed and horrendous violence in some Member States. Accordingly, it upholds the principles of

> Secularism and neutrality of the State in all matters of religion; freedom for each individual to practice, within the limits of existing laws, the religion of his/her choice everywhere on the national territory. The secularism shall extend to all parts of the State, but shall not deprive the State of the right to regulate, with due respect to human rights, the different religions practiced on the national territory or to intervene when law and order break down as a result of any religious activity.

Section I (Article 1(e) deals with the armed forces, which it acknowledged must be 'apolitical and must be under the command of a legally constituted political authority...' while article 1 (g) stipulates that the 'state and all its institutions belong to all the citizens; none of the decisions and actions shall involve any form of discrimination, be it on ethnic or regional basis'.

To be sure, these are laudable intentions. In reality, however, they present us with what we can call a 'who will bell the cat situation'. This is true not only of this particular section but all the 44 articles in this part of the document. Would ECOWAS, for instance, apply sanctions against offending states promptly, fearlessly and across board? Or would some states be 'more equal than others' in practice? Specifically, while it is possible to harass and intimidate the coup makers in the tiny island state of Sao Tome and Principe to hand over power back to the president, or the coup makers in Guinea Bissau to step down in favour of an interim civilian administration in 2003, would the organisation be bold enough and have the punch to compel a return to the barracks in a country like Nigeria or Ghana, or Senegal for that matter? These questions are pertinent since there is no standing army or court to enforce compliance with the provisions of these articles of the Protocol. It is also doubtful if the fledgling ECOWAS parliament would have enough teeth to bite when called upon to do so. The implication is that ECOWAS will have to rely more on moral opprobrium for compliance with the tenets of the Protocol. The problem though, is how much moral clout the organisation and member states command? Is a public statement by ECOWAS or any of its Members weighty enough to compel the restoration of the *status quo ante* in an erring member State? Is the existence of the Protocol sufficient deterrence?

If past experience is anything to go by, there is not much hope in the efficacy of moral opprobrium or even isolation. For the offending state would always have 'friends' it could hobnob with to 'weather the storm'. Under the circumstances, it would be more beneficial for ECOWAS to enlist the support of much more credible organisations like the UN and the EU, and the great powers, particularly the United States of America. The African Union may also be relevant here. After all it was the combined weight of these actors that forced the 'Charles Taylor Bull' out of the 'Liberian China' shop in early August 2003. He is in forced exile in Calabar, Cross River State of Nigeria, with his family and close aides. However, if ECOWAS is unable to weave such a broad coalition, it might be tempted to opt for selective sanctions against infractions of the Protocol. But that would also negate the spirit as well as the provisions of the Protocol, which is designed to ensure a stable and peaceful environment in which member states would be able to pursue their overwhelming tasks of nation building.

Another central issue tackled by the Protocol is elections. Elections are certainly among the most contentious and destabilising issues in the sub-region. Arguments over the date, modalities, conduct and results of elections have often times threatened the very fragile political fabric of ECOWAS States. Elections generate not only a lot of heat but also violence in some Member States of the Community, and if not properly managed, could wreak havoc in the states concerned and could destabilise the entire sub-region. Indeed, arguments over the conduct and outcomes of elections have led to large-scale violence in countries like Nigeria, Sierra Leone, Liberia, and Togo. It would therefore be in the interest of every member if elections in the community were to be routinely held, and peacefully too. Thus, the Protocol tries to nip in the bud some of the more obvious but also often contentious problems that could arise from the electoral processes. According to Article 3(1), 'the electoral law shall not undergo substantial modification in the last six (6) months before the elections', while Article 3(3) charged Member States to

> take all appropriate measures to ensure that women have equal rights with men to vote and be voted for in elections, to participate in the formulation of government policies and the implementation thereof and to hold public offices and perform public functions at all levels of governance.

Furthermore, voters' lists 'shall be prepared in a transparent and reliable manner, with the collaboration of the political parties' (Article 6). Again, the Protocol enjoined 'the preparation and conduct of elections and the announcement of results shall be done in a transparent manner' (Article 7). Finally, Article 10 stipulates that 'the party and/or candidate who lose the election shall concede defeat to the political party or candidate finally declared the winner, following the guidelines and within the deadline stipulated by the law'. The question that really begs for an answer is: how would the Community ensure that these laudable provisions are complied with by each of its members? What would have been the reaction of ECOWAS if the April 2003 elections in Nigeria had not been free, fair and peaceful, but had led to political violence? Who, among the ECOWAS members, would have 'belled' the 'Nigerian cat'? To be sure, Section III of the protocol provides for election monitoring and assistance by ECOWAS. Would ECOWAS support a credible team in the field given its lean purse? This is an important question given the poor state of the organisation's finances. This is evident in the yawning gaps in Member States' contributions to the ECOWAS Secretariat: 'At the end of September 2000, many member states were owing several years subscription arrears: Liberia (20 years), Gambia, (11 years), Sierra Leone (11 years), Cape Verde, (10 years), and Guinea Bissau (10 years)' (Uche, 2002; Magbagbeola, 2003). Thus, what would be the weight of any Report prepared by an ECOWAS monitoring team that is thinly spread in the field? Would such a report carry the same weight as one submitted by the US, the EU or the UN? Clearly, those whose Reports were reckoned with in the 2003 elections in Nigeria, were external to the Community: the US, EU and UN. From such a standpoint, it is tempting to declare the section on elections as a toothless bulldog or paper tiger. But such a conclusion may also be premature, for it is possible that an ECOWAS Report could add weight to those of other monitors since it is presumed to have the advantage of familiarity with 'street conditions' in the state in question better.

The significance of this Article therefore lies in the fact that majority of ECOWAS members are yet to institutionalise an orderly transfer of political power while politicians are yet to fully appreciate that politics is a vocation, a gentleman's game and not a life and death struggle. Thus the import of these sections of the Protocol is that it is a start in that direction, and an expression of the desire by the Community to remove once and for all those issues that have been the bane of free and transparent elections in Member States, a situation that has been responsible for much violence and loss of life and property in the sub-region. The results of elections perceived by all stakeholders as free, fair and peaceful could contribute immensely to political stability in the state concerned and the sub-region in general.

Another important issue addressed in Section IV of the Protocol is 'The Role of the Armed Forces, the Police and the Security Forces in a Democracy'. It targets a very important segment of the polity whose role in national politics has, to put it mildly, been retrogressively meddlesome. It is important to stress that much of the political instability witnessed in the sub-region, and indeed other parts of Africa, is traceable to the intrusion of the armed and security forces into national politics. The frequent coups, attempted coups and political instability which many states in the sub-region have experienced, some several times, account for many of the most disturbing reversals in the fortunes of those states: Democratic Republic of Congo, DRC, Ghana, Liberia, Nigeria, Sierra Leone, to name but a few. But if accountability, transparency, predictability, and respect for the rule of law, in short, good governance, are the building blocks of the nationalist vision, these instruments of state coercion must remain apolitical and that is exactly what ECOWAS has tried to do in this section of the Protocol. Thus, the 'armed forces and the police shall be non-partisan and shall remain loyal to the nation. The role of the armed forces shall be to defend the independence and territorial integrity of the State and its democratic institutions'. (Article 20(1)). This point is again stressed in Article 21(1), 'the armed forces, the police and other security forces shall be under the authority of constituted civilian authorities'. Finally, Article 20 (3) stipulates that 'the armed forces, police and other security forces shall participate in ECOMOG missions as provided for in Article 28 of the 1999 Protocol'. The significance of this proviso cannot be missed by the perceptive observer, in the light of the historic roles that ECOMOG has played and continues to play in the sub-region, especially in Liberia and Sierra Leone. The critical question however remains, how would ECOWAS act effectively against a breach of these sections?

Chapter II of the Protocol provides the answer to the question: 'in the event that democracy is abruptly brought to an end by any means or where there is massive violation of human rights in a Member State, ECOWAS may impose sanctions'. Such sanctions which significantly, are to be 'decided by the authority may take the following forms in increasing order of severity':

(i)   Refusal to support the candidates presented by the country concerned for elective posts in international organisations;
(ii)   Refusal to organise ECOWAS meetings in the country concerned;
(iii) Suspension of the State concerned from all ECOWAS decision-making bodies.
(iv)   During the suspension the Member State concerned shall be obliged to pay its dues for the period.

It is doubtful if these measures are capable of deterring a determined military dictator from seizing control of the government of a Member State. Even if the section were to do so, this would apply only to the very small and weak members of the Community: Benin Republic, Guinea Bissau, Niger Republic, Sierra Leone, for example, because of their very close ties with Nigeria, the sub-regional Super Power. But what if the coup were to take place in Nigeria itself, ECOWAS' big brother and its most important benefactor? Suspending Nigeria would smack of ECOWAS cutting its nose to spite its face? A worst-case scenario in such a situation would merely bring all the Community's activities to a grinding halt, as the dictator in Nigeria would close the Secretariat and declare the now 'foreign' diplomats and workers *persona non grata*. And once the Secretariat is closed, it is doubtful if there would be coordinated responses to the new regime in Abuja. It is even conceivable that neighbouring states whose economic lifelines are tied to Nigeria, for instance, Republic of Benin, would continue to do business as usual with the new regime. In other words, sanctions would only bite if they have the backing of the international community: the US, Europe, the UN, the AU, etc. A campaign of civil disobedience by civil society forces could also make a difference, as was the case in Sierra Leone during Major Johnny Paul Koroma's coup or, in Nigeria after the cancellation of the June 12, 1993 presidential elections.

Economic deprivation and marginalisation – real or imaginary – access to national resources or what is cynically referred to as the 'national cake', have been at the centre of some of the most violent conflicts in West Africa in the last decade and a half. It is not surprising then, that ECOWAS has tried to tackle this important issue by recognising in the first place, that 'poverty alleviation and promotion of social dialogue are important factors of peace' (Article 26). Accordingly, Member States undertake to 'fight poverty effectively...' by '...ensuring equitable distribution of resources and income in order to consolidate national unity and solidarity', and '[by]... creating an environment conducive to private investment and the development of a dynamic and competitive sector...' Again, the question that begs for an answer here is what would ECOWAS do if this article were violated by a Member State? It would seem to me that it is only in extreme cases that the violation of these provisions would lead to civil strife and the outright breakdown of law and order. Ordinarily, there is no Member State where accusations of marginalisation and exclusion are not made against the incumbent regime. The best safeguard, it seems to me, would be to have leaders who are detribalised, who are honest and committed to uplifting the masses of their citizens to greater economic and political heights irrespective of their religious affiliation, ethnic group or political allegiance. But how many leaders are committed to such laudable goals and objectives in the sub-region? Not many, unfortunately.

Cultural diversity, under normal circumstances, should be a source of strength as it is the case in the United States of America. However for many West African states, it has always been their 'Achilles Heel', a source of political discord and instability. Section VI of the Protocol attempts to remedy the situation because it acknowledges that 'Education, Culture and Religion are essential factors of peace, stability and development in each Member State' (article 31). Accordingly, 'the culture of each section of the population of each Member State shall be respected and developed' (article 33). To give the section practical expression,

> The Executive Secretary shall take necessary measures to organize, within the sub-region, periodic cultural events between/among Member States: festivals of arts and culture, symposia, various cultural events on literature, music, arts, sports and so on (article 32(5).

Again, like previous ones, this Section raises more questions than answers. The first observation is that while mutual respect for the cultural nuances of each Member State is important, it is seldom the cause of misunderstanding and political violence in the sub-region. Rather, it is the perception of cultural marginalisation and lack of respect for each group's culture within states that has often led to communal strife, violence and threats to the integrity of governments and states in West Africa. So the best starting point is the Member States. For how effective will a pan-West African season of arts and culture be in cementing the cultural fissures among the Itsekiris and Ijaws of Nigeria or for that matter the Mende and Temne in Sierra Leone, the Khran and Mandingo in Liberia, etc? Not much. If any thing, such activities would only promote better understanding and respect among the artists directly involved but not much within the Member States. The inevitable conclusion, then, is that the focus must also be on promoting cultural harmony and mutual respect within each of the members. That would complement efforts at the macro level.

Section VII on 'Rule of Law, Human Rights and Good Governance', is at the heart of the turbulence that the sub-region experienced in the aftermath of the collapse of the Cold War. During the Cold War, attempts were made by the great powers to tolerate and indeed accept dictators and presidents for life in many African countries including the ECOWAS sub-region. Bad governments and dictators were seen as bulwarks against communist regimes and were courted by the West while socialist regimes were vilified and isolated. Expectedly, a lot of unsavoury practices and atrocities were swept under the Cold War carpet 'in the interest of sub-regional, regional and indeed, global peace and stability'. The crumbling of the Cold War protective umbrella exposed the underbelly of many of the sit-tight leaders and dictators in West Africa, as business could not continue as usual in the light of the dramatic changes that had taken place in the former communist countries of Eastern Europe. Accordingly, West African leaders must also ride with the wind of change that is blowing across the world if their sub-region, states and citizens are to benefit from it. Thus across board, 'ECOWAS Member States agree [d] that good governance is essential for preserving social justice and for preventing conflict and for guaranteeing political stability and peace; and for strengthening democracy' (article 34). Accordingly, the following steps are to be taken by each state in order to realise this grand dream of a democratic West Africa.

(i)   Member States and the Executive Secretariat shall endeavour to adopt at national and regional levels, practical modalities for the enforcement of the rule of law, human rights, justice and good governance;

(ii)   Member States shall ensure accountability, professionalism, transparency and expertise in the public and private sectors (article 36, 1&2);

(iii)   Member States shall establish independent national institutions to promote and protect human rights (article 37(1);

(iv)   Member States undertake to manage their natural resources in a transparent manner and to ensure that they are equitably distributed (article 39(1).

Certainly, these are laudable intentions and present the sub-region with lots of possibilities. However, in practical terms, their implementation or enforcement at both national and sub-regional levels is fraught with problems and limitations.

To be sure, the end of the Cold War has led to dramatic changes in the political landscape of not only the West African sub-region but also the entire African continent. The phenomenon of presidents for life, one party political systems and rampant coups has been held in check. Now, more than ever before in the history of the sub-region, dictatorships, one party systems and military coups are frowned at not only in the sub-region but by the international community as a whole. Thus, when Major Johnny Paul Koroma overthrew the democratically elected government of Ahmed Tejan Kabba of Sierra Leone, not only was he condemned in no uncertain terms by the international community, ECOWAS, under the leadership of Nigeria, mounted a military operation in Freetown that flushed him and his cohorts out of power. Again, the forced exit of Charles Taylor from Liberia also points to the fact that gross breaches of human rights and other undemocratic behaviour by an African leader would no longer receive the blessing of the region's leaders. Even so, it is pertinent to ask again if such decisive sub-regional action would be possible without the endorsement of the international community. Would ECOWAS muster enough local/internal clout to hound a military or civilian dictator out of power in Nigeria, Senegal or Ghana without concerted international support and involvement? I doubt it.

Be that as it may, it can still be argued that the mere fact that the Organisation has outlawed gross human rights violations in tandem with praxis in the global system since the end of the Cold War is indeed a welcome development. From such a point of view it is plausible that the sub-region, under a determined and fearless leader, could rally international support against a defaulting state. It is to be assumed that once the international community endorses the position of ECOWAS it would be very difficult for the target regime to remain in power for long. It is arguable that such support may now not be hard to obtain. For even before ECOWAS took up the challenge, the great powers and multilateral agencies like the IMF and World Bank were already sanctioning regimes in the sub-region. Even then, ensuring accountability and transparency in the sub-region is not a thing that can be achieved through legal fiat alone. It would require the consolidation of democracy and democratic tenets and culture in each country, although that will of necessity take a much longer time to mature. However, ECOWAS has taken the first step in the right direction and should be encouraged to be bold enough to expose, isolate and sanction offending states and leaders in the sub-region in the future.

The prudent management of national resources is much more difficult to enforce by the Community and international system as a lot would depend on the situation and circumstances on the ground. For instance, the ruthless exploitation of a country's natural resources by warlords is no longer acceptable to the international community. This point was brought home rather forcefully by the UN ban on 'blood diamonds' or 'blood money' from conflict zones. It may however be much more difficult to enforce the Protocol in cases where there is 'relative peace' in the country and where a 'legitimate' government is in control at the centre. A case in point is Nigeria, which has witnessed continuing conflicts in some parts arising from what is perceived as injudicious management of the country's resources and marginalisation. The violence in the Niger Delta is in part informed by the realisation that resources derived from the region are not only used to 'develop' other parts of the country, but also because of perceived large-scale corruption and misapplication of those resources at the expense of the Niger Delta people. Surprisingly, the issue has never been raised at any level within ECOWAS.

It is instructive to also note that West African societies are yet to seriously frown at and reject corruption by political office holders. Government is still seen as a lucrative avenue for getting rich quickly; and that one holding political office must use the opportunity to scale the poverty barrier. In many societies and communities in the sub-region, success is still measured in terms of material well being, irrespective of how it is achieved. For instance, when a former Minister of Finance was accused of corruptly enriching himself while in office in Nigeria, his community bought space in the leading newspaper in the country to literally castigate the government for daring to expose him. The argument was that he is not the first and only one to have done so. Civil society, unfortunately, was also not much interested in the matter, so the matter was swept under the carpet as usual. It is however possible that in the long run attitudes will change, and that civil society in ECOWAS countries will reject and denounce official corruption. This reasoning is much more plausible if there is a strong link between domestic and foreign civil society forces to call attention to ill-gotten wealth. A significant beginning has been made in that regard given the adverse publicity given to the wealth of the late military dictator, Sani Abacha, and the relative cooperation received by the Federal Government of Nigeria from foreign banks and governments in its effort to recover the money. Foreign based financial institutions and governments would also play a critical role here if they openly reject and/or start to query the sources of monies deposited in their banks by leaders in the sub-region in particular, and Africa in general. In short, although this section of the Protocol addresses important issues in the developmental experiences and processes of the West African sub-region, it would be difficult to implement it in the absence of committed leaders and active civil society forces. Nevertheless, it is a significant and positive pointer to the future and I believe that it will mature with time.

The other important issue addressed by the Protocol is Women, Children and the Youth. The marginalisation of women in national life has been a recurring issue in development debate in Africa. Women have been known to contribute, as much as 70 percent of the food produced in Africa (Sesay and Odebiyi 1998). They are also very important agents of peace and development. They have however remained largely marginalised in most societies in West Africa for they are yet to be seen as equal partners in the realisation of the nationalist dream. They are also the victims of several harmful cultural practices in many societies in the sub-region. Again, the existence of an African Charter on the Rights of the African Child not withstanding, children and youths in West Africa are yet to receive relief from its existence. Child labour is still very common in the sub-region. Lately, children are being traded between the sub-region and Central Africa. The matter came to a head in recent times in the wake of the massive use of children and youths in civil wars as child soldiers in Liberia and Sierra Leone. However, it has now been realised that no nation can develop if a segment of its population and citizens remains marginalised or neglected.

Expectedly, the Protocol acknowledges the indispensable role of women in the development process:

> Member States agree that the development and promotion of the welfare of women are essential factors for development, progress and peace in society. Consequently, they undertake to eliminate all forms of discrimination and harmful practices against women (Article 41).

And in an earlier section of the protocol, the Member States pledged to guarantee

> women equal rights with men in the field of education and in particular, shall ensure the same conditions for career and vocation guidance, access to the same curricula, access to opportunities to benefit from scholarships and other study grants. They shall also ensure the elimination of stereotyped concepts of roles of men and women at all levels and in all forms of education (Article 32: 5).

As for children and youths, article 42 implored Member States to 'guarantee children's rights and give them access to basic education'. Further, 'laws shall be enacted in each Member State and at the level of the Community against child trafficking and child prostitution' (article 42:2). Finally, the 'Community shall adopt laws and regulations on Child Labour in line with the provision of the International Labour Organization' (Article 42: 3).

While these provisions hold much promise for the sub-region's children and youths, their impact is yet to be felt by the ordinary child. Education is still a luxury for most children, while child labour, slavery and prostitution are rampant in cities and towns throughout the sub-region. Much more significantly, is the total neglect of the HIV/AIDS pandemic and its devastating impact on children and youths in West Africa in spite of the fact that they constitute the high-risk groups. Nowhere in the document is the issue of HIV/AIDS discussed or even mentioned. This is perhaps the biggest shortcoming of an otherwise important document, for in 2001 the disease was already taking a heavy toll on youths, tomorrow's leaders. The Executive Secretariat is also yet to come out openly with a sub-region-wide policy on HIV/AIDS. Thus, it has been left to individual national governments to tackle the epidemic; and while some countries have made significant progress in that regard, others have not. Unless HIV/AIDS receives the attention it deserves from the Community and national governments, it is doubtful if ECOWAS can truly re-invent the nationalist dream. This is important given the dire predictions for countries in Africa where the pandemic is rife among children and youths.

Conclusions

There is no doubt that the ECOWAS Protocol on Democracy and Good Governance is an epoch-making document. It provides the states and citizens of the West African sub-region with many possibilities for peaceful co-existence at the national and Community levels which is a *sine qua non* for consolidating peace, stability and security in West Africa. The Protocol is a significant document for confidence building within and among the Member States. If fully implemented, it could form the basis for the prosperity which has eluded the sub-region especially since the end of the Cold War. It should therefore be given a chance.

However, for it to have the maximum desired impact on the sub-region's socio-political landscape, West African leaders must seek for its support and acceptance by the international community. ECOWAS must sensitise its citizens and the international community to the existence of the Protocol and the need for them to give the Organisation support in its enforcement. That way, the clout that the sub-region does not presently enjoy in dealing with the 'big fish' in the event of breaches of the Protocol could be facilitated. In particular, it is important to bring the Protocol to the attention of global/regional 'influentials' such as the United States of America, the European Union, the United Nations and even the African Union. These important organisations and states could indeed act as its guarantors and facilitators. That way, it would stand a much better chance of achieving its objectives, as offenders are more likely to be isolated and punished effectively with the support of the major global actors.

References

Aboagye, Festus B., 1999, *ECOMOG: A Sub-regional Experience in Conflict Resolution, Management and Peacekeeping*, Accra: SEDCO Publishing Limited.

ECOWAS, Revised Treaty of the Economic Community of West African States, Abuja: ECOWAS Secretariat.

ECOWAS, 2001, Protocol on Democracy and Good Governance Supplementary to the Protocol Relating to the Mechanisms for Conflict Prevention, Management.

ILO/WEM/JASPA, *African Employment Report*, Addis Ababa: ILO/JASPA, 1990, 155.

Kamara-Taylor, A., 1975, Vice President of Sierra Leone, to the *Second Session of the Mano River Union Ministerial Council, (MRU/MC/2)* Annex 11. Freetown, Sierra Leone, December, p.99.

Magbagbeola, H., 2003, 'The Quest for a West African Monetary Union: Implementation Issues, Progress and Prospects', paper delivered at the 30th Anniversary Sub-Regional Conference of CODESRIA, Cotonou, September 6-7.

Nkrumah, Kwame, *Africa Must Unite*, London: Panaf, 1963.

Sesay, A. and Odebiyi, A., eds., 1998, *Nigerian Women in Society and Development*, Ibadan: Dokun Publishing House.

Stevens, S., *Republican Sierra Leone*, Freetown: Government Printer, no date, p.8.

Uche, C. U, 2002, 'The Idea of a Regional Currency for Anglophone West Africa', Paper delivered at the 10th General Assembly of CODESRIA, Kampala, Uganda, 8-12 December.

Vogt, M. A., ed., 1992, *The Liberian Crisis and ECOMOG*, Lagos: GABUMO Publishing House.

Bibliography

Aaron, K. K., 2003, 'Human Rights Violation and Petroleum Pipelines Vandalization in the Niger Delta Region of Nigeria', in *The Nigerian Social Scientist, 6(2) 14-20*.

Abdul, H., 2002, 'Ethno-Religious Crisis in Kaduna: Impact on Women and Children', in E. Alamika and F. Okoye (eds.), *Ethno-Religious Conflicts and Democracy in Nigeria: Challenges*, Kaduna: Human Rights Monitor.

Aboagye, Festus B., 1999, *ECOMOG: A Sub-regional Experience in Conflict Resolution, Management and Peacekeeping*, Accra: SEDCO Publishing Limited.

Ade-Ajayi, J. F., 1982, 'Expectations of Independence', *Daedalus*, 111, No. 2, Spring.

Adebajo, A., 2002, *Building Peace in West Africa: Liberia, Sierra Leone and Guinea Bissau*, Boulder: Lynne Rienner Publishers.

Adedeji, A., 1999, ed., *Comprehending and Mastering African Conflicts: The Search for Sustainable Peace and Good Governance*, London: Zed Books.

Adejumobi, S., 1999, 'Reconstructing the Future: Africa and the Challenge of Democracy and Good Governance in the 21st Century', *Development and Socio-Economic Progress*, No.75. January/June.

Adejumobi, S., 2001, 'Citizenship, Rights and the Problem of Conflicts and Civil Wars in Africa', *Human Rights Quarterly*, Vol. 23, No.1.

Adekanye, B., 1995, 'Structural Adjustment, Democratisation and Rising Ethnic Tensions in Africa', *Development and Change*, 26 (2).

Adekanye, B., 1996, 'Rwanda/Burundi: Uni-ethnic Dominance and The Cycle of Armed Ethnic Formations', *Social Identities*, 2 (1).

Adeleke, A., 1995, 'The Politics and Diplomacy of Peacekeeping in West Africa: The ECOMOG Operations in Liberia', *The Journal of Modern African Studies*, 33, 4: 573.

Ademoyega, W., 1981, *Why We Struck: The Story of the First Nigerian Coup*, Ibadan: Evans Brothers Nigeria Ltd.

Adeoti, G., 2004, 'Home Video Films and the Democratic Imperative in Contemporary Nigeria', A paper presented at the Faculty of Arts Weekly Seminar Series, Obafemi Awolowo University, Ile Ife. February 4.

Adibe, C., 1997, 'The Liberian Conflict and the ECOWAS-UN Partnership', *Third World Quarterly*, 18, 3.

Afrifa, A. A., 1966, *The Ghana Coup, February 1966*, London: Frank Cass.

Ager, A., 1999, Perspectives on the Refugees Experience: in A. Ager (ed.) *Perspectives on the Experience of Forced Migration*, Guildford and King's Lynn U.K: Bibbles Limited.

Ake, C., 1980, *A Political Economy of Africa*, London: Longman.

Ake, C., 1992, *The Feasibility of Democracy in Africa*, Occasional Publication No. 1, Centre for Research, Documentation and University Exchange, Ibadan: University of Ibadan.

Ake, C., 1994, *The Democratisation of Disempowerment*, CASS Occasional Monograph.

Ake, C., 1995, 'Democracy and Africa: The Residual Option', Reprinted in Adetula, Victor (ed.) (1997), *Claude Ake and Democracy in Africa: A Tribute*, AFRIGOV Monograph Series No.4, Jos: African Centre for Democratic Governance.

Ake, C., 1996, 'The Political Question', in Oyeleye Oyediran (ed.) *Governance and Development in Nigeria: Essays in Honour of Professor Billy J. Dudley*, Ibadan: Agbo Areo Publishers.

Alao, A., Mackinlay, J. and Olonisakin, F., 1999, *Peacekeepers, Politicians, and Warlords: The Liberian Peace Process*, Tokyo, New York, and Paris: UN University Press.

Ali, T. and Mathews, R., eds., 1999, *Civil Wars in Africa: Roots and Resolution*, Montreal: McGill-Queen's University Press.

Amuwo, K. & Herault, G., 1998, 'On the Notion of Political Restructuring in a Federal System', in K. Amuwo, A. Agbaje, R. Suberu & G. Herault (eds.) *Federalism and Political Restructuring in Nigeria*, Ibadan: Spectrum Books.

Amuwo, K., 1998, 'Beyond the Orthodoxy of Political Restructuring: The Abacha Junta and the Political Economy of Force', in K. Amuwo, A. Agbaje, R. Suberu & G. Herault (eds.) *Federalism and Political Restructuring in Nigeria*, Ibadan: Spectrum Books.

Annan, K., 1998, 'The Causes of Conflict and the Promotion of Durable Peace and Sustainable Development in Africa', Report of the Secretary General on Africa to the Security Council. Mimeograph, April.

Aristotle, 1958, *The Politics*, Edited and Translated by Ernest Baker, London: Oxford University Press.

Asiwaju, A., 1976, *Western Yorubaland Under European Rule (1889-1945)*, London: Longman.

Atkinson, R. R., 1999, 'The (Re) construction of Ethnicity in Africa: Extending the Chronology, Conceptualization Discourse', in Paris Yeros (ed.) *Ethnicity and Nationalism in Africa: Constructivist Reflections and Contemporary Politics*, Houndsmill: Macmillan.

Avruch, K. and Vejarano, B., 2000, 'Truth and Reconciliation Commissions: A Review Essay and Annotated Bibliography', *The Online Journal of Peace and Conflict Resolution* 4.2: 37-79.

Awa, E., 1996, 'Democracy in Nigeria: A Political Scientist's View', in O. Oyediran, (ed.) *Governance and Development in Nigeria*, Ibadan: Oyediran Consult Int., pp. 1-21.

Bach, D.C., 1997, 'Identity, Ethnicity and Federalism', in Larry Diamond, A. Kirk Greene and Oyeleye Oyediran (eds.) *Transition Without End: Nigerian Politics and Civil Society Under Babangida*, Ibadan: Vantage Press.

Baker, B., 1999, 'African Anarchy: Is it the States, Regimes or Societies that are Collapsing?', *Politics* 19(3).

Beck, E.M., 1980, 'Labour Unionism and Racial Income Inequality: A Time-Series analysis of Post-World War period', *America Journal of Sociology*, .85.

Betts, T., 1980, *Spontaneous Settlement of Rural Refugees in Africa*, London: Euro Action.

Bloomfield, D. et al., 2003, *Reconciliation After Violent Conflict: A Handbook*, International Institute for Democracy and Electoral Assistance (IDEA).

Boafo-Arthur, K., 1998, 'Structural Adjustment Programs (SAPS) in Ghana: Interrogating PNDC's Implementation', *Journal of African Policy Studies*, 4, 2 & 3: 1-23.

Boafo-Arthur, K., 2000, 'The Political Economy of Ghana's Foreign Policy: Past, Present and the Future', *Ghana Social Science Journal* (New Series), 1, 1: 17.

Booths, J., 1981, *Writers and Politics in Nigeria*, London: Hodder and Stoughton.

Boudin, J., 1945, *Method for Easy Comprehension of History*, Translated by Beatrice Reynolds, New York.

Brubakar, R., 1992, *Citizenship and Nationhood in France and Germany*, Cambridge: Harvard University Press.

Brume, F., 2000, 'Oil Pipelines Vandalization: The Way out', Paper delivered at the Annual Dinner of the National Association of Niger Delta Professionals, Bauchi, December, 2000.

Bulcha, M., 1988, *Flight and Integration*, Uppsala: Scandinavian Institute of African Studies.

Calinescu, M., 1982, 'Literature and Politics', in J. Barricelli and J. Gibaldi, (eds.,) *Interrelations of Literature*, New York: MLA, pp. 123-49.

Cato, A., 1967, 'Refugee Problem in Southern Africa', in S. Hamell (ed.), *Refugee Problems in Africa*, Uppsala: Scandinavian Institute of African Studies.

Chambers S. R., 1979, 'Rural Refugees in Africa: What the Eye does not See' *Disasters* 3:4.

Chambers, R. and Conway, G., 1992, 'Sustainable Rural Livelihoods: Practical Concepts for the 21st Century', *IDS Discussion Paper 296*, Brighton.

Chambers, R., 1969, *Settlement Schemes in Tropical Africa: A Study of Organisation and Development*, London: Routledge and Began Paul.

Citizens Forum for Constitutional Reform, 2002, *Memoranda Submitted to the Presidential Committee on the Provisions for and Practice of Citizenship and Rights in Nigeria and the Presidential Committee on National Security in Nigeria*, Lagos: CFCR.

Clark, E., 1979, *Hubert Ogunde: The Making of Nigerian Theatre*, Oxford: Oxford University Press.

Clark, H., et al., 1999, 'Oil for Nothing: Multinational Corporations, Environmental Destruction, Death and Impunity in the Niger Delta'. A US Non-Governmental Delegation Trip Report, 6-20, September.

Cockburn, C., 1999, 'Gender, Armed Conflicts and Political Violence', Workshop Paper on Gender and Peace Support Operations of the World Bank.

Cohen, R. and Deng, M. F., 1998, *Mass in Flight. The Global Crisis Internal Displacement*, Washington D.C.: Brookings International Press.

Copson, R., 1994, *Africa's Wars and Prospects for Peace*, New York: M.E. Sharpe.

Crowder, M. and Ikime, O., 1970, 'Introduction', in Michael Crowder and Obaro Ikime (eds.) *West African Chiefs: Their Changing Status Under Colonial Rule and Independence*, New York and Ile-Ife: African Publishing Corporation and University of Ife Press.

Da Costa, 2001, 'Oil Pollution in Nigeria'. www.greennature.com/articles/266.htm; accessed 01/25/03.

Davidson, B., 1992, *The Black Man's Burden: Africa and the Curse of the Nation-State*, New York: Times Books, p. 208.

Diamond, L., 1988, *Class, Ethnicity and Democracy in Nigeria: The Failure of the First Republic*, Syracuse, New York: Syracuse University Press.

Diamond, L., 1995, 'Preventive Diplomacy for Nigeria: Imperative for US and International Policy', Paper presented to the House International Relations Committee, US Congress, Washington D.C. 28 November.

Diamond, L., 1999, *Developing Democracy: Toward Consolidation*, Baltimore: The John Hopkins University. Press.

Duncan S. A. Bell, 2003, 'History and Globalisation: Reflections on Temporality', Review Article in *International Affairs* 79, 4: 801-814.

ECOWAS, 2001, Protocol on Democracy and Good Governance Supplementary to the Protocol Relating to the Mechanisms for Conflict Prevention, Management.

ECOWAS, Revised Treaty of the Economic Community of West African States, Abuja: ECOWAS Secretariat.

Egwu, S.G., 2001, 'Ethnic and Religious Violence in Nigeria', Abuja: The African Centre for Democratic Governance.

Ekeh, P., 1972, 'Citizenship and Political Conflict: A Sociological Interpretation of the Nigerian Crisis', in J. Okpaku (ed.) *Nigeria: Dilemma of Nationhood*, New York: The Third World Press.

Ekeh, P., 1975, 'Colonialism and the Two Publics in Africa: A Theoretical Statement', *Comparative Studies in Society and History*, (17) 1.

Ekeh, P., 1980, 'Colonialism and Social Structure', Inaugural Lecture, University of Ibadan, Nigeria.

Ekekwe, E., 1986, *Class and State in Nigeria*, Lagos: Longman.

Ekwuasi, H., 2002, 'Towards a Sustainable Motion Picture Industry', Lagos: *The Guardian*, Thursday, May 2, p. 64.

Eliot, T.S., 1968, 'The Literature of Politics', in *To Criticize the Critic*, London: Faber and Faber, pp. 136-144.

Enloe, C., 1980, *Ethnic Soldiers*, Athens, GA: University of Georgia Press.

ERA/FOEN, 2000, 'The Emperor Has No Clothes', Report of the Proceedings of the Conference on the Peoples of the Niger Delta and the 1999 Constitution, held in Port Harcourt , November 1999.

Esman, J.M., 1994, *Ethnic Politics*, Ithaca, NY: Cornell University Press.

Eteng, I., 1998, 'The National Question and Federal Restructuring in Nigeria' in *The Challenges of African Development: Tributes and Essays in Honour of Claude Ake*, Port Harcourt: CASS.

Etherton, M., 1982, *The Development of African Drama*, London: Hutchinson University Library.

Farah, N., 2005, 'Peace and Disarmament in the New Somalia' *Taflastse* Vol. 1 No. 1 p. 2 February 14-23.

Fawole, A. W., 2001, 'The Nigeria Military and Prospects for Democratic Rule', in W. Alade Fawole (ed.), *Beyond the Transition to Civil Rule: Consolidating Democracy in Post-Military Nigeria*, Lagos: Amkra Books, pp. 57-76.

Fawole, A. W., 2002, *Military Power and Third-Party Conflict Mediation in West Africa: The Liberian and Sierra Leone Case Studies*, Ile-Ife: Obafemi Awolowo University Press.

Ford Foundation, 1983, *Refugees and Migrants. Problems and Program Responses: Working Paper*, New York: Ford Foundation

Forrest, T., 1995, *Politics and Economic Development in Nigeria*, Colorado, : Westview Press.

Fukuyama, F., 1992, *The End of History and the Last Man*, London: Hamish Hamilton.

Gabriel, A. O., 1993, 'Women and Nigeria/Equatorial Guinea Transborder Cooperation: Challenges for the Nineties', *Nigerian Journal of Interdisciplinary Studies* Vol. 3.

Garkawe, S., 2003, '"Amnesty for Truth"- A Violation of Human Rights by South Africa's Truth and Reconciliation Commission?', Paper presented at the Activating Human Rights and Diversity Conference July 1-4, 2003, Byron Bay, Australia.

Gbilekaa, S., 1997, *Radical Theatre in Nigeria*, Ibadan: Caltop Publishers.

Gilbert, H. and Tompkins, J., 1996, *Post-Colonial Drama: Theory, Practice, Politics*, London: Routledge.

Gorman, R. F., 1987, Taking Stock of the Second International Conference on Assistance to Refugees in Africa (ICARA II), *Journal of African Studies*,14: 1

Gould, W. T. S., 1974, 'Refugee in Tropical Africa', *International Migration Review* 8.3.

Government of Ghana, 1992, *The Constitution of the Republic of Ghana*, State Publishing Corp.

Graf, W.D., 1986, 'African Elite Theories and the Nigerian Elite Consolidation: A Political Economy Analysis', in Yolamu Barongo (ed.) *Political Science in Africa: A Critical Review*, London: Zed Press.

Grodzin, M., 1966, *The Loyal and the Disloyal: Social Boundaries of Patriotism and Treason*, Cleveland: World Publishing Co.

Grown, C. and Sebstad, J., 1989, 'Introduction: Towards a Wider Perspective on Women's employment', *World Development*,Vol.17 No.17.

Gurr, T. and Hart, B., 1994, *Ethnic Conflict in World Politics*, Boulder, Colorado: Westview Press.

Gurr, T., 1994, *Minority at Risk: A Global View of Ethno-Political Conflicts*, Washington: United States Institute for Peace.

Gyimah-Boadi, E., 1990, 'Economic Recovery and Politics in PNDC's Ghana', *The Journal of Commonwealth and Comparative Politics* XXVIII, No. 3.

Hansen, A., 1990, Refugee Self-Settlement Versus Settlement on Government Schemes. The Long-term Consequences for Security, Integration Economic Development of Angolan Refugees (1966-1989) in Zambia, A United Nations Research Institute for Social Development, *Discussion Paper No 17*.

Harmon, Z., 1997, 'World Bank, Big Oil and the Niger Delta' (http.www.waado.org/Environment/Oil Companies/World Bank-Bigoil.html (accessed 3/11/03).

Harrell-Bond, B. E., 1990, Breaking the Vicious Circle: Refugees and Other Persons in Africa, in *The African Social Situation. Crucial Factors of Development and Transformation*, Oxford: Hans Zell Publishers.

Harsh, E., 1992, 'More African States as Least Developed' *Africa Recovery*, 6 April, p. 11.

Hayner, P. B., 1994, 'Fifteen Truth Commissions-1974 to 1994: A Comparative Study', *Human Rights Quarterly*, 16: 597-655

Hodgkin, T., 1957, 'Letter to Biobaku', *Odu* 4

Hoogvelt, A., 2002, 'Globalisation, Imperialism and Exclusion: The Case of Sub-Saharan Africa', in Tunde Zack-Williams, Diane Frost and Alex Thomson, (eds.), *Africa in Crisis: New Challenges and Possibilities*, London: Pluto Press, pp. 23-24.

Horowitz, L.D., 1985, *Ethnic Groups in Conflict*, Berkeley: University of California Press.

Human Rights Watch, 1999, *The Price of Oil: Corporate Responsibility and Human Rights Violations in Nigeria's Oil Producing Communities*, New York.: Human Rights Watch.

Huntington, S., 1996, *The Clash of Civilizations and the Remaking of the World Order*, New York: Touchstone.

Hutchful, E., 1997, 'Military Policy and Reform in Ghana', *The Journal of Modern African Studies* 35, 2.

Ibeanu, O., 1997, 'Oil, Conflict and Security in Rural Nigeria: Issues in the Ogoni Crisis', Harare, African Association of Political Science, *Occasional Paper Series* 1 (2).

Ibeanu, O., 2002, 'Democracy, Environment and Security in Nigeria: Reflections on Environment and Governance in the Post-military era', Paper presented at a Conference on Assessment of Nigeria's Democratic Journey So Far', Organised by the Centre for Advanced Social Science with the support of the Open Society Initiative for West Africa, Abuja, February 18-21, 2002.

Idowu W.O.O., 1999, 'Citizenship, Alienation and Conflict in Nigeria', *Africa Development*, XXIV (1&2).

Ifidon, E.A., 1996, 'Citizenship, Statehood and the Problem of Democratization in Nigeria', *Africa Development*, Vol. 21 (4).

Ignatief, M., 1999, *The Warrior's Honour: Ethnic War and the Modern Conscience*, London: Vintage.

Ihonvbere, J. O., 1999, 'Federalism, Power Sharing, and the Politics of Redistribution in Nigeria', Paper presented at the International Conference on Consolidating Democracy: Nigeria in Comparative Perspective, Lisbon, September 21-25.

Ihonvbere, J.O., 1988, 'The "Irrelevant" State: Ethnicity and the Subversion of the Goals of Nationhood in Africa', Paper prepared for the International Conference on Ethnicity and Nationhood in Africa, University of Sokoto, Sokoto, Nigeria.

Ijediogor, G., 2000, 'Militant Groups Only Let off Tension', *The Guardian*, Saturday, July 22.

Ikelegbe, A.O., 2003, 'Civil Society and Alternative Approaches to Conflict Management', in T.A Imobighe (ed.) *Civil Society and Ethnic Conflict Management in Nigeria*, Ibadan: Spectrum Books.

Ikhariale, M., 2002, *The Oputa Reports: An Unfinished Job*. Available on the internet on http://www.nigerdeltacongress.com/oarticles/oputa_reports.htm

Ikime, O., ed., 1980, *Groundwork on Nigerian History*, Ibadan: Heinemann.

ILO/WEM/JASPA, 1990, *African Employment Report*, Addis Ababa: ILO/JASPA, 155.

Institute for Democracy and Electoral Assistance (IDEA), 2000, 'Democracy in Nigeria: Continuing Dialogue(s) for Nation Building (Capacity Building', Series 10).

International IDEA, 2000, *Democracy in Nigeria*.Capacity Building Series 10, Continuing Dialogue(s) for Nation-Building: Stockholm.

Iweze, C.Y., 1993, 'Nigeria in Liberia: The Military Operations of ECOMOG', in M.A. Vogt and E.E. Ekoko (eds.), *Nigeria in International Peacekeeping, 1960-1992*, Lagos: Malthouse Press Limited.

Jackson, R. H., 1982, 'Why Africa's Weak States Persist. The Empirical and the Juridical in Statehood', *World Politics* 27 (1-24).

Jega, A., 2000, 'The State and Identity Transformation under Structural Adjustment in Nigeria', in Attahiru Jega (ed.) *Identity Transformation and Identity Politics under Structural Adjustment in Nigeria*, Uppsala: Nordiska Afrikainstitutet and CRD: Kano.

Jelin, E., 1996, 'Citizenship Revisited: Solidarity, Responsibility and Rights', in Elizabeth Jelin and Eric Herhberg (eds.) *Constructing Democracy: Human Rights, Citizenship, and Society in Latin America*, Boulder: Westview.

Jemibewon, D. M., 2001, *The Nigeria Police in Transition: Issues, Problems and Prospects*, Ibadan: Spectrum Books, (preface), p. xx.

Jinadu, L.A., 2003, 'Democratization, Development and the Identity Crisis in Nigeria', Second Annual Lecture, Department of Sociology, University of Lagos, Lagos July, 30.

Joseph, R., 1991, *Democracy and Prebendal Politics in Nigeria: The Rise and Fall of the Second Republic*, Ibadan: Spectrum Books.

Joseph, R., 1999, 'Nigerian: Inside the Dismal Tunnel', *Current History* 95, 601:193-200.

Kagan, M. and Doctor, S., 2002, 'Assessment of Refugee Status Determination; Procedure of UNHCR; Cairo Office 2001-2002' A Working Paper for Forced Migration and Refugee Studies, American University, Cairo.

Kalyango, R., 2003, 'Challenges of Integration Faced by Urban Refugees: A Case Review of Cairo and Kampala', Paper Presented at the International Association for the Study of Forced Migration Conference in Changmai Thailand.

Kamara-Taylor, A., 1975, Vice President of Sierra Leone, to the *Second Session of the Mano River Union Ministerial Council, (MRU/MC/2)* Annex 11. Freetown, Sierra Leone, December, p.99.

Kassim, S. T., 1999, Knowledge, Attitude and Practice of Contraceptives Among Refugees in Nigeria: A Case Study of Refugee Camp Oru, Ogun State, Nigeria. Unpublished M.Sc. Thesis.

Katepe-Kalala, J., 1997, *Sustainable Livelihood Approaches in Operation: A Gender Perspective*, New York: United Nations Publications.

Kelman, C., 1998, 'The Place of Ethnic Identity in the Development of Personal Identity: A Challenge for the Jewish Family', in Peter Meddling (ed.) *Coping with Life and Death: Jewish Families in the 20th Century*, Oxford: Oxford University Press.

Kerber, L., 1997, 'The Meaning of Citizenship', *The Journal of American History*, December.

Kerr, D., 1995, *African Popular Theatre: From Precolonial Times to the Present Day*, London: James Currey.

Kieh, G.K., 2001, 'Reconstituting a Collapsed State. The Liberian case', in Segun Jegede, Ayodele Ale and Eni Akinsola (eds.) *State Reconstruction in West Africa*, Lagos: Committee for the Defence of Human Rights.

Kofi, O. K., 1993, 'The Legality of the Intervention in the Liberian Civil War by the Economic Community of West African States', *African Journal of International and Comparative Law*, 5, 3: 525-560.

Konings, P., 2000, 'Institutionalising Democracy in Ghana', Text of seminar paper delivered at the African Studies Centre, Leiden, The Netherlands, 16 November.

Kornfield, P., 1990, 'ECOWAS, the First Decade: Towards Collective Self-Reliance, or Maintenance of the Status Quo?', in Okolo, Julius Emeka and Steven Wright (eds.), *West African Regional Cooperation and Development*, Boulder, Co.: Westview Press: 87-114.

Kukah, M., 1998, 'The Fractured Microcosm: The African Condition and the Search for Moral Balance in the New World Order', Lagos State University, Faculty of Social Sciences Guest Lecture Series 1, June.

Kwesi, A. E., 1999, 'From Eco-pessimism to Eco-Optimism: ECOMOG and West African Integration Process', *African Journal of Political Science*, 4, 1.

Lake, D. and Rothchild, D., 1996, 'Ethnic Fears and Global Engagement: The International Spread and Management of Global Conflict', Report of the International Global Conflict and Cooperation Working Group on the Spread and Management of Ethnic Conflict, Mimeograph.

Lerche, Charles O., 'Truth Commissions and National Reconciliation: Some Reflections on Theory and Practice' http://www.gmu.edu/academic/pcs/LERCHE71PCS.html

Lihamba, A., 1994, 'Theatre and Political Struggle in East Africa', in E. Osaghae, (ed.) *Between State and Civil Society in Africa: Perspectives on Development*, Dakar: CODESRIA, 196-216.

Lobe, J., 2002, 'People Versus Big Oil. Rights of Nigerian Indigenous People Recognized', www.africaaction.org/docs02/nig0207 a.htm (accessed 03/01/03).

Longva, A., 1995, 'Citizenship, Identity and the Question of Supreme Loyalty: The Case of Kuwait', *Forum for Development Studies*, No.2.

Luckman, R., 1971, *The Nigerian Military: A Sociological Analysis of Authority and Revolt, 1966–67*, London: Cambridge University Press.

Mackintosh, J.P., 1966, *Nigerian Government and Politics*, London: Allen and Unwin.

Mafeje, A., 1999, 'State and Civil Society in Independent Africa', in Henrich Boll Foundation (ed.) *Networking With a View to Promoting Peace: Conflicts in the Horn of Africa*, Addis Ababa: Henrich Boll.

Magbagbeola, H., 2003, 'The Quest for a West African Monetary Union: Implementation Issues, Progress and Prospects', Paper delivered at the 30th Anniversary Sub-Regional Conference of CODESRIA, Cotonou, September 6-7.

Maier, K., 2000, *This House Has Fallen: Midnight in Nigeria*, New York: Public Affairs.

Maiz, R., 2003, 'Politics and the Nation: Nationalist Mobilization of Ethnic Differences', *Nation and Nationalism*, 9 (2). p. 197.

Malomo, J. and Gbilekaa, S., eds., 1993, *Theatre and Politics in Nigeria*, Ibadan: Caltop Publishers.

Mamdani, M., 1982, 'Karamoja: Colonial Roots of Famine in North-East Uganda', *Review of African Political Economy*, No. 25.

Mamdani, M., 1996, *Citizen and Subject: Contemporary Africa and the Legacy of Late Colonialism*, Princeton: Princeton University Press.

Mamdani, M., 1998, 'When Does a Settler Become a Native? Reflections on the Colonial Roots of Citizenship in Equatorial and South Africa', Inaugural Lecture, May 13, University of Cape Town, South Africa.

Mamdani, M., 2000, 'Indirect Rule and the Struggle for Democracy: A Response to Bridget O'Laughlin', *African Affairs*, 99.

Mamdani, M., 2001, *When Victims Become Killers: Colonialism, Nativism and Genocide in Rwanda*, Princeton: Princeton University Press.

Marshall, T., 1964, *Class, Citizenship and Social Development*, New York: Doubleday and Company Inc.

Marx, A., 1996, 'Contested Citizenship: The Dynamics of Racial Identity and Social movements', in Charles Tilly (ed.) 'Citizenship, Identity and Social History', *International Review of Social History*, Supplement 3, Cambridge: Cambridge University Press.

Mazrui, A., 1999, 'Identity Politics and the Nation-State Under Siege: Towards a Theory of Reverse Evolution', *Social Dynamics*, Vol. 25, No.2.

Mazur, R. E., 1988, Refugees in Africa: The Role of Sociologist Analysis and Praxis, *Current Sociology, 36: 2.*

McGowan, P. and Johnson, J.H., 1986, 'Sixty Coups in Thirty years: Further Evidence Regarding African Coups d'état', *The Journal of Modern African Studies*, Vol. 24, No. 3: 539-546.

Melson, R. and Wolpe, H., 1971, *Nigeria: Modernisation and the Politics of Communalism*, East Lansing: Michigan State University Press.

Miners, N. J., 1971, *The Nigerian Army, 1956-1966*, London: Methuen and Co.

Momoh, A., 2001, 'Even Birds Have a Home: Explaining the Pathologies of the Citizenship Question in Nigeria', Empowerment and Action Research Centre (EMPARC) Annual Lecture Series, No. 7.

Muazzam, I. and Ibrahim, J., 2000, 'Religious Identity in the Context of Structural Adjustment in Nigeria', in Attahiru Jega (ed.) *Identity Transformation and Identity Politics under Structural Adjustment in Nigeria*, Uppsala: Nordiska Afrikainstitutet, & Kano: CRD.

Nabudere, D., 1999, 'African States and Conflict in Africa', in Henrich Boll Foundation (ed.) *Networking With a View To Promoting Peace: Conflicts in the Horn of Africa*, Addis Ababa: Henrich Boll.

National Agenda, Lagos July/August 1995.

National Film and Video Censor's Board, 2003, Lagos, April.

Ndikumana, L., 1998, 'International Failure and Ethnic Conflicts in Burundi', *African Studies Review* 1998 (4)(1).

New Patriotic Party, Agenda for Positive Change, Manifesto 2000 of the New Patriotic Party, p. 37 (n.d.).

Newman, S., 1991, 'Does Modernization Breed Ethnic Political Violence?', *World Politics* 43.

Ngugi wa Thiong'o, 1981, *Writers In Politics: Essays*, London: Heinemann.

Nigeria, Federal Republic, 1987, *The Report of the Political Bureau*, Lagos.

Ninsin, K. A., 1998, 'Civic Associations and the Transition to Democracy', in Ninsin, Kwame A (ed.), *Ghana: Transition to Democracy*, Accra: Freedom Publications.

Nkrumah, K., 1963, *Africa Must Unite*, London: Panaf Books, p. 16.

Nnoli, O., 1978, *Ethnic Politics in Nigeria*, Enugu: Fourth Dimension Publishers.

Nnoli, O., 1989, *Ethnic Politics in Africa*, Ibadan: AAPS.

Nnoma, V., 1999, 'The Civil War and the Refugee Crisis in Liberia', *Journal of Conflict Studies*, XVII, 1: 101-125.

Nwosu, H., 1977, *Political Authority and the Nigerian Civil Service*, Enugu: Fourth Dimension.

Nzongola-Ntalaja, G., 2001, 'Political Reforms and Conflict Management in the African Democratic Transition', in Raymond Suttner (ed.) *Africa in the New Millennium*, Nordiska Afrikainstitutet, Uppsala, p.13.

Nzongola-Ntalaja, G., 2002, 'Democracy and Development in Africa: A Tribute to Claude Ake', in Claude Ake Memorial Lecture Series 4, Abuja: Centre for Democratic Governance.

O'Connell, J., 1967, 'The Inevitability of Instability', *Journal of Modern African Studies*, Vol. 5, No. 2, , pp. 181-191.

O'Connell, J., 1971, 'Authority and Community in Nigeria', in Melson, Robert and Howard Wolpe (eds.) *Nigeria Modernisation and the Politics of Communalism*, East Lansing: Michigan State University Press.

O'Laughlin, B., 2000, 'Class and the Customary: The Ambiguous Legacy of the Indigenato in Mozambique', *African Affairs*, 99.

Obadan, M., 1996. *The Nigerian Economy and the External Sector*, CASS Occasional Monograph No. 8, Lagos: Malthouse Press.

Obi, C.I., 1997, 'Oil, Environmental Conflict and National Security in Nigeria: Ramifications of the Ecology-Security Nexus for Sub-Regional Peace', University of Illinois at Urbana Champaign.

Odion, L., 2002, Reconciliation: Between Substance and Symbolism: The Bottomline, THISDAY online, http://www.thisdayonline.com/archive/2002/05/31/

Ogachi, O., 1999, 'Economic Reform, Political Liberation and Ethnic Conflicts in Kenya', *Africa Development* XXIV, (1&2).

Ogunbiyi, Y., ed., 1981, *Drama and Theatre in Nigeria: A Critical Source Book*, Lagos: Nigeria Magazine.

Okolo, J. E., 2002, 'The Babangida Regime and ECOWAS', in Muhammad, Baba Yunus and Amuta, Chidi (eds.) *IBB - A Heritage of Reform Vol 1: Perspectives and Interpretations*, Zaria: Open Press Ltd.

Olzak, S., 1983, 'The Economic Construction of Ethnicity', Paper Presented at Annual Meetings of the *American Sociological Association*, Detroit.

Onimode, B., 1988, *A Political Economy of the African Crisis*, London: Zed Books.

Onwuka, R. and Sesay, A., 1985, *The Future of Regionalism in Africa*, London: Macmillan Publishers.

Onwuka, R. I., 1981, *Development and Integration in West Africa: The Case of the Economic Community of West African States*, Ile-Ife: University of Ife Press.

Oomen, T., 1997, *Citizenship, Nationality and Ethnicity: Reconciling Competing Identities*, Cambridge: Polity Press.

Osaghae, E., 2001, 'From Accommodation to Self Determination: Minority Nationalism and Restructuring of the Nigeria State', *Nationalism and Ethnic Politics*, 7 (1).

Osaghae, E., 1990, 'The Problems of Citizenship in Nigeria', *AFRICA: Revista Trimestrale di Studi e documentazione* (Roma), Vol. XLV, No. 4, December.

Osaghae, E., 1994, *Ethnicity and its Management in Africa: The Democratization Link*, CASS Occasional Monograph No. 2.

Osofisan, F., 1997, 'Playing Dangerously: Drama at the Frontiers of Terror in a Post-colonial State', Inaugural Lecture, University of Ibadan, July 31.

Otite, O., 1990, *Ethnic Pluralism and Ethnicity in Nigeria*, Ibadan: Shaneson.

Ottaway, M., 1999, 'Ethnic Politics in Africa: Change and Continuity', in Richard Joseph (ed.) *State, Conflict and Democracy in Africa*, Boulder: Lynne Rienner.

Owugah, L., 2000, 'The Political Economy of Resistance in the Niger Delta', in ERA/FOEN 'The Emperor Has No Clothes', Report of the Proceedings of the Conference on the Peoples of the Niger Delta and the 1999 Constitution, held in Port Harcourt, November 1999.

Pitts, M., 1999, 'Sub-Regional Solutions for African Conflicts: The ECOMOG Experience', *Journal of Conflict Studies*, XIX: 1.

Post, K. and Vickers, M., 1973, *The Structure of Conflict in Nigeria 1960-1966*, London: Heinemann.

Prunier, G., 1995, *The Rwandan Crisis, 1959-1994: History of a Genocide*, London: Hurst.

Ravenhill, J., 1985, 'The Future of Regionalism in Africa', in R.I. Onwuka and A. Sesay (eds.), *The Future of Regionalism in Africa*, London and Basingstoke: Macmillan Publishers Ltd: 205-224.

Reno, W., 'The Business of War in Liberia', *Current History*, May 1996.

Richardson, Jr J.M. and Sen, S., 1997, 'Ethnic Conflict and Economic Development: A Policy Oriented Analysis', *Ethnic Studies Report* XV, (1) January.

Riley, S. P., 'Democratic Transition in Africa', *Conflict Studies*, No. 245

Roger, J. R., 1981, Africa's Resettlement Strategies, *International Migration Review*, 15: 53-54.

Rugumamu, S. M., 2001, Globalization and Africa's Future: Towards Structural Stability, Integration and Sustainable Development, *AAPS Occasional Paper* No. 5

Sanberg, K. and Smith, D., 1994, 'Conflicts in Africa', *Afrika Mellon Konfleter Og Utrkling*, Inormasjonshefte, No.2.

Sankore, R., 2001, 'Politics of Ethnic and Religious Conflict', Lagos, *Thisday on Sunday*, October 28.

Saro-Wiwa, K., 1995, *A Month and a Day*, London: Penguin Books.

Sesay, A. and Odebiyi, A., eds., 1998, *Nigerian Women in Society and Development*, Ibadan: Dokun Publishing House.

Sesay, A., 1980, 'Conflict and Collaboration: Sierra Leone and her West African Neighbours, 1961–1980', *Afrika Spectrum*, 80/2, January 12.

Sesay, A., 1985, 'The Mano River Union: Politics of Survival or Dependence?' in R.I. Onwuka and A. Sesay (eds.), *The Future of Regionalism in Africa*, London and Basingstoke: Macmillan Publishers Ltd.

Sesay, A., 1992, 'Historical Background to the Liberian Crisis.' in Margaret Vogt (ed.), *The Liberian Crisis and ECOMOG*, Lagos: Gabumo Press.

Sesay, A., 1999, 'Between the Olive Branch and the AK-47: Paradoxes of Recent Military Intervention in West Africa', University of Pretoria, *ISSUP Bulletin*, 6/99: 1-21.

Sesay, A., 1999, 'Paradise Lost and Regained? The Travails of Democracy in Sierra Leone', in Dele Olowu, Adebayo Williams and Kayode Soremekun (eds.), *Governance and Democratisation in West Africa*, Dakar: CODESRIA, pp. 287-288.

Siobhian, H., 2001, 'The Institutional Foundations of Sub-State National Movements', *Comparative Politics*, 33 (2) January.

Sklar, R. and Whitaker, C.S., 1995, 'Nigeria: Rivers of Oil, Trails of Blood, Prospects for Unity and Democracy', *CSIS Africa Notes*, 179: 1-9.

Sklar, R.L., 1963, *Nigerian Political Parties*, New Jersey: Princeton University Press.

Sparl, S., 2001, Evaluation of UNHCR Policy on Refugee in Urban Areas: A Case Review of Cairo Evaluation Policy Analysis Unit (EPAU).

Stain, B., 1980, Refugee Resettlement Programs and Techniques, Research Report Submitted to the Select Commission on Immigration and Refugee Policy.

Stevens, S., *Republican Sierra Leone*, Freetown: Government Printer, no date, p.8.

Stomberg, P., 1998, The Year of Return in Liberia, *Refugee Magazines*, 112.

Sundberg, A., 1999, 'Class and Ethnicity in the Struggle for Power - The Failure of Democratization in Congo-Brazzaville', *Africa Development* XXIV, (1&2).

Taiwo, F., 1996, 'Of Citizens and Citizenship', Lagos, *The Tempo*, September-October.

Tamuno, T., 1999, 'The Niger Delta Question', A Public Lecture organised by the Rivers State College of Arts and Science and the Rivers State University of Science and Technology, Port Harcourt, September 30.

The National Commission for Refugees Decree No 52 of 1989.

Thomson, A., 2000, *An Introduction to African Politics*, London: Routledge.

Tilly, C., 1996, 'Citizenship, Identity and Social History', in Charles Tilly (ed.) 'Citizenship, Identity and Social History', *International Review of Social History*, Supplement 3, Cambridge: Cambridge University Press.

Timbiah, S.J., 1990, 'Reflections on Communal Violence in South Asia', *Journal of Asian Studies* 49(4).

Torpey, J., Railton, P., Cameron M., and Burns, P., 'Panel Discussion on the Concepts: Truth, Justice, Accountability and Reconciliation', (http://www.ais.ubc.ca/programs/descothe/papers/marchalk/panel.pdf)

Transition Monitoring Group (TMG) and United Nations Electoral Assistance Division 2002. Communiqué: Mechanisms for the Civil Society and the State in Cconflict Management, Abuja, March 6-7.

Uche, C.U, 2002, 'The Idea of a Regional Currency for Anglophone West Africa', Paper delivered at the 10th General Assembly of CODESRIA, Kampala, Uganda, 8-12 December.

Ukeje, C., 2001a, Youth, Violence and the Collapse of Public Order in the Niger Delta of Nigeria, *Africa Development*, XXVI: 1-2, 337-366.

Ukeje, C., 2001b, 'Oil Communities and Political Violence: The Case of Ijaws in Nigeria's Delta Region, *Journal of Terrorism and Political Violence*, 13: 4, Winter 15-36.

UNDP, 1997, *Human Development Report*, New York: Oxford Univ. Press, p.2.

UNHCR, 2003, *Global Refugee Trend*, January 31–March.

UNHCR, 2002, Refugees, Asylum Seekers and Other Person of Concern. Trend in Displacement, Protection and Solution, *Statistical Yearbook 2001*.

UNHCR, 2003, Refugees, Asylum Seekers and Other Persons of Concern-Trend in Displacement, Protection and Solution, *Statistical Yearbook 2002*.

United Nations Institute for Social Development (UNRISD), 2001, *Invisible Hands: Taking Responsibility for Social Development*, Geneva: UNRISD.

United Nations, 1981, The Refugee Situation in Africa: Assistance Measures Proposed; International Conference on Assistance to Refugees in Africa (ICARA) (Geneva 9–10 April).

US Committee for Refugees, 1991, 'Exile From Rwanda: Background to an Invasion', *Issue Paper USCR*, February.

Uya, O.E., 1992, 'Nigeria: The Land and the People', in Okon Edet Uya (ed.) *Contemplated Nigeria*, Buenos Aires: EDIPUBLI S.A.

Vogt, M. A. and Ekoko, A. E., 1993, *Nigeria in International Peace ekeeping 1960-1992*, Lagos: Malthouse Press

Vogt, M. A., 1993, 'Nigeria in Liberia: Historical and Political Analysis of ECOMOG' in *Nigeria and International Peace-keeping*, Lagos: Macmillan

Vogt, M. A., ed., 1992, *The Liberian Crisis and ECOMOG*, Lagos: Gabumo Publishing House.

Walker, G. A., 1978, Refugee in Southern Africa, A Report To The Congress on Development Needs and Opportunities for Co-operation in Southern Africa, Annex B: Refugees, United States Agency for International Development, Washington D. C.

Wallerstein, P., and Sollenberg, M., 1999, 'Armed Conflict', *Journal of Peace Research*, 39 (5).

Walraven, Klaus van., 1999, *The Pretense of Peacekeeping: ECOMOG, West Africa and Liberia (1990–1998)*, Netherlands Institute of International Relations, November.

Walshe, P., 1971, *The Rise of African Nationalism in South Africa*, Berkeley: University of California Press.

Walzer, M., 1970, *Obligations: Essays on Disobedience, War and Citizenship*, Cambridge: MIT Press.

Warren, K.B., 1993, 'Introduction: Revealing Conflicts Across Cultures and Disciplines', in K. B. Warren (ed.) *The Violence Within: Cultural and Political Opposition in Divided Nations*, Boulder: Westview Press Inc.

Williams, A., 1996, 'Literature in the Time of Tyranny: African Writers and the Crisis of Governance', *Third World Quarterly*, Vol. XVII, No 2, pp. 349-62.

Williams, A., 1999, 'Democracy in Nigeria: Retrospect and Prospect', Text of a seminar paper delivered at the African Studies Centre, Leiden, The Netherlands, 11 February.

Williams, A., 1999, 'Nigeria: A Restoration Drama', *African Affairs*, Vol. 98, No. 391, July.

Wilson, R., 2001, 'The Politics of Contemporary Ethno-nationalist Conflicts', *Nations and Nationalism* 7 (3).

Winker, R., 1984, 'Refugee Protection in Africa Current Trends', Paper presented at the Washington Institute for Value in Public Policy Conference on U. S. Policy Toward Africa. Washington D. C.

World Bank, 1993, *World Development Report*, New York: Oxford University Press.

World Bank, 1995, *Defining an Environmental Strategy for the Niger Delta*, Vol. 1. Washington D.C: The World Bank.

World Bank, 1999, *African Development Indicators: 1999/2000*, Washington: World Bank.

Zalaquett, J., 1996, 'The Relevance of Truth Commissions to Different Types of Conflicts'. Harvard Law School, http:www.law.Harvard.edu/programs.

www.ingramcontent.com/pod-product-compliance
Lightning Source LLC
Chambersburg PA
CBHW021900020426
42334CB00013B/421